Open Mind

Intermediate Student's Book

Mickey Rogers

Joanne Taylore-Knowles

Steve Taylore-Knowles

Concept development:
Mariela Gil Vierma

MACMILLAN

Level 3

Contents

PRONUNCIATION	GRAMMAR	VOCABULARY	LIFESKILLS
SOUNDS: /j/ vs /dʒ/	PRESENT PERFECT + *YET/ALREADY/ JUST* FUNCTION talking about goals PRESENT PERFECT CONTINUOUS FUNCTION talking about recent events in your life	*TAKE, MAKE, DO* FUNCTION talking about life experiences THE LEARNING PROCESS FUNCTION talking about the learning process	SELF AND SOCIETY: setting goals FUNCTION discussing personal action plans
	LANGUAGE WRAP-UP		
SOUNDS: emphatic stress	*USED TO* FUNCTION talking about past habits PAST PERFECT FUNCTION talking about memories	PERSONALITY TYPES FUNCTION using qualifying phrases MEMORY FUNCTION talking about memories	STUDY AND LEARNING: preparing and giving a short presentation FUNCTION giving feedback
	LANGUAGE WRAP-UP		
SOUNDS: /ɪ/ vs /iː/	DEFINITE ARTICLE *THE* / ZERO ARTICLE FUNCTION expressing ideas for an advert INDIRECT QUESTIONS FUNCTION asking for help / information in a shop	PROBLEMS WITH PRODUCTS FUNCTION saying what's wrong with a product SOLUTIONS TO PROBLEMS WITH PRODUCTS FUNCTION asking for solutions to problems with products	WORK AND CAREER: persuading others FUNCTION raising objections and making suggestions
	LANGUAGE WRAP-UP		
WORDS: compound nouns vs compound adjectives	CAUSATIVE *HAVE* AND *GET* FUNCTION talking about getting things done ADJECTIVES ENDING IN *-ED/-ING* FUNCTION talking about feelings	BUSINESS FUNCTION talking about things to do when setting up a business DESCRIBING PRODUCTS AND SERVICES FUNCTIONS • describing services • agreeing/disagreeing	WORK AND CAREER: turning problems into opportunities FUNCTION presenting a business idea
	LANGUAGE WRAP-UP		
WORDS: say/says/said	REPORTED SPEECH REPORTED QUESTIONS FUNCTION reporting what people said	ORAL COMMUNICATION FUNCTION talking about oral communication *ASK, SAY, TELL* FUNCTION using collocations on oral communication	STUDY AND LEARNING: reporting information FUNCTION reporting information about media
	LANGUAGE WRAP-UP		
WORDS: past modals	THIRD CONDITIONAL FUNCTION talking about unreal situations *HOPE* AND *WISH* FUNCTION talking about hopes and wishes	DEALING WITH PROBLEMS FUNCTION discussing problems and solutions DECISIONS FUNCTION talking about making decisions	SELF AND SOCIETY: becoming more self-aware FUNCTION responding to feedback
	LANGUAGE WRAP-UP		

PRONUNCIATION	GRAMMAR	VOCABULARY	LIFESKILLS
WORDS: question tags	**MODALS OF DEDUCTION:** *MUST, CAN'T, MIGHT/MAY/COULD* **FUNCTION** making deductions **QUESTION TAGS** **FUNCTION** double-checking information	**ADJECTIVE SUFFIXES** *-FUL, -LESS* **FUNCTION** using adjectives with suffixes to describe things **IMPROVING YOUR BRAIN** **FUNCTION** discussing how to improve your learning using collocations	**STUDY AND LEARNING:** thinking logically **FUNCTION** discussing logical thinking
		LANGUAGE WRAP-UP	
WORDS: /ə/ in multisyllable words	**RELATIVE CLAUSES** **FUNCTION** giving information about people, places and things **VERB + GERUND/INFINITIVE** **FUNCTION** reading a book blurb	**EMBARRASSING EVENTS** **FUNCTION** talking about embarrassing events **ADJECTIVES FOR DESCRIBING STORIES** **FUNCTION** talking about how stories make you feel	**SELF AND SOCIETY:** learning from experience **FUNCTION** discussing a past experience
		LANGUAGE WRAP-UP	
SOUNDS: /ɜː/	**INFINITIVE CLAUSES WITH IMPERSONAL** *IT* **FUNCTION** giving advice on medical problems *WISH* **AND** *IF ONLY* **FOR REGRETS** **FUNCTION** describing regrets	**INJURIES** **FUNCTION** talking about injuries **HEALTH PROBLEMS AND SYMPTOMS** **FUNCTION** describing health problems and symptoms	**STUDY AND LEARNING:** developing your memory **FUNCTION** using memory tools
		LANGUAGE WRAP-UP	
SOUNDS: /æ/ vs /ʌ/	**NON-DEFINING RELATIVE CLAUSES** **DEFINING RELATIVE CLAUSES** **FUNCTION** giving information about people, places and things	**AT A LIVE PERFORMANCE** **FUNCTION** talking about live performances **AT THE OSCARS** **FUNCTION** talking about films	**SELF AND SOCIETY:** working as part of a team **FUNCTION** reflecting on teamwork
		LANGUAGE WRAP-UP	
SOUNDS: /tʃ/ vs /ʃ/	*SHOULD/SHOULDN'T HAVE* **FUNCTION** reflecting on past situations *WAS/WERE GOING TO* **AND** *WAS/WERE SUPPOSED TO* **FUNCTION** talking about unfulfilled plans and intentions	**BREAKING THE RULES** **FUNCTION** talking about breaking the rules **GOOD AND BAD BEHAVIOUR** **FUNCTION** talking about good and bad behaviour	**WORK AND CAREER:** understanding graphs **FUNCTION** talking about charts
		LANGUAGE WRAP-UP	
WORDS: stress patterns with phrasal verbs	*SO, SUCH, TOO, ENOUGH* **FUNCTION** describing a degree or quality **SEPARABLE AND INSEPARABLE PHRASAL VERBS** **FUNCTION** talking about setting up a business	**THE WORLD OF WORK** **FUNCTION** talking about jobs and career goals **PHRASAL VERBS FOR TALKING ABOUT WORK** **FUNCTION** talking about work and jobs	**WORK AND CAREER:** preparing for a job interview **FUNCTION** describing work experience
		LANGUAGE WRAP-UP	

Grammar review

1 Complete the sentences with the past simple or past continuous of the verbs in brackets.

1 While Becky _____ (type) an email, a message from Ed _____ (appear) in her inbox.
2 What _____ (do) when you _____ (hear) the terrible news?
3 We _____ (not pay attention) so we _____ (not see) the sign. Where was it?
4 Jack _____ (run) for the bus when he _____ (drop) his wallet.
5 Gemma's mobile phone suddenly _____ (ring) while she _____ (sit) in a meeting.

2 Choose the correct option to complete the sentences.

1 Would you like having / to have some vegetables with the chicken?
2 Liz and I would like / like to watch an action film instead of a comedy.
3 Would you rather eat out / to eat out tonight?
4 They would prefer not to buy / not buying it online.
5 They'd rather work / to work late tonight and not have to arrive early tomorrow.

3 Choose the correct word to complete the sentence.

1 Kate, you have to do your homework by yourself / yourselves.
2 She burnt himself / herself when she was cooking.
3 They wanted to start a business by themselves / them.
4 We raised all the money by ourselves / itself.
5 I hurt itself / myself when I was at the gym.

4 Complete the questions with the words from the box. Then match them to the answers a–e.

Will	Should	Would	Could	Where

1 _____ were you sitting at the concert? ☐
2 _____ you open the window, please? ☐
3 _____ you rather send me a text or call? ☐
4 _____ we bring anything with us to the picnic? ☐
5 _____ the next Euro Football Championship be held in France? ☐

a) Yes please, maybe some bread and cheese.
b) Yes, I think so.
c) What's best for you?
d) Certainly.
e) Near the stage.

5 There is one mistake in each sentence. Rewrite the sentences correctly.

1 The broadband at my office is more faster than at home.
   _____
2 The New Year celebration is most important event in the Chinese calendar.
   _____
3 Spain is as popular France for British tourists.
   _____
4 That was the baddest film I've ever seen.
   _____
5 Hull isn't as beautiful than York.
   _____
6 You must listen most carefully next time.
   _____

6 Rewrite these sentences using the passive.

1 People download millions of songs every day.
   Millions of songs _____.
2 The French celebrate Bastille Day on the 14th July.
   Bastille Day _____.
3 Scientists didn't take the first X-ray until 1895.
   The first X-ray _____.
4 People speak German, Italian and French in Switzerland.
   German, Italian and French _____.
5 Jane Austen wrote Emma and Sense and Sensibility.
   Emma and Sense and Sensibility _____.

7 Complete the sentences with one word.

1 Has Olivia _____ been to India?
2 How _____ have you known your husband?
3 I think they've lived there _____ 2010.
4 Rita and Nick have _____ visited their friends in Brazil. Nick doesn't like flying.
5 Where have you _____? I was looking for you.

8 Choose the correct option to complete the sentences.

1 You have / should try to learn five new English words a day.
2 Customers don't have to / have to pay for all items before they leave the shop.
3 Passengers must / have wear a seat belt during take-off.
4 You mustn't / don't have to pay to enter. We ask for a voluntary contribution.
5 Mum ought / should to see a doctor about her sore throat.

9 Complete the sentences with *too*, *enough* or *not enough* and the adjective in brackets.

1 Hey! Can you turn the music down? It's _____ in here. (*loud*)
2 Is there chilli in this? I can't taste it. It's _____. (*spicy*)
3 I don't think I can eat all those chips. They're _____. (*greasy*)
4 This house is _____ for the three of us. We don't need to move. (*big*)
5 We should go to the beach tomorrow instead. The weather is _____ today. (*warm*)

10 Choose the correct option to complete the sentences.

1 That's enough, thanks. I don't want too much / many cream.
2 I'll put a bit / few more salt in the soup next time.
3 The Christmas tree would look better with fewer / less decorations.
4 There isn't / aren't enough space on my computer for all these songs.
5 There'll be too many / much people at the shopping centre today.

11 Choose the correct option to complete the sentences.

1 The exam starts / is starting at 10am on Monday.
2 My horoscope says I will meet / I'm meeting a tall, handsome stranger this week.
3 A: Would you like to go to the cinema tonight?
   B: Yes, I'll / I'm going to meet you there.
4 We're travelling / We will travel to Brazil this summer. We've booked the tickets.
5 What time does the bus leave / is the bus leaving?

12 Tick the correct sentences. Rewrite the incorrect sentences.

1 Would you change jobs if you won £20,000? ☐
   _____
2 If dad had more time, he'll decorate the house. ☐
   _____
3 When you go to Barcelona, you should visit the Picasso museum. ☐
   _____
4 They'd buy a bigger house if they don't live in the city. ☐
   _____
5 I'll go to Oslo next month if I find a cheap flight. ☐
   _____

13 Complete the sentences with gerunds formed from the verbs in the box.

shop   make   do   eat   speak

1 I don't like cooking, I much prefer _____ out in restaurants.
2 Janice is really good at _____ Spanish.
3 What are you thinking of _____ tonight – shall we go to the cinema?
4 _____ for clothes is one of my favourite things to do at weekends.
5 He's worried about _____ the wrong decision.

14 Choose the correct option to complete the sentences.

1 I might / will go to see the show, I'm not sure yet.
2 She probably might / won't be able to come because she has too much work.
3 Don't worry, the letter will / won't probably arrive tomorrow.
4 Jack told me that he might / will definitely help.
5 We will / might go for a walk, it depends on the weather.

UNIT 1 LIVE AND LEARN

IN THIS UNIT YOU

- ⚙ learn language to talk about recent events in your life
- ⚙ read about the stages of learning something new
- ⚙ talk about recent events in your life
- ⚙ listen to advice about learning
- ⚙ write a diary entry
- ⚙ learn how to set goals
- ▶ watch a video about studying at university

SPEAKING
encouraging the speaker
What kinds of words or phrases do people use to indicate that they are interested in what another person is saying?

READING
for the main idea
Do a class survey. How many people think they are making faster progress with their English now than when they were beginners?

LIFE SKILLS

SELF & SOCIETY

Setting goals
Some people like to set specific goals in their lives. Others prefer to see where life leads them. Which type of person are you?

A Life is often referred to as a road or a journey. Look at the photos and decide which road best represents your life and why. Explain your ideas to your class or group.

A: *I think my life is like photo 2. There are sunny parts and cloudy parts, and maybe the future is a bit scary and unpredictable, like going towards all those clouds.*

B: *My life is definitely like photo 1! It is exciting and full of changes. I do off-road biking, and it's a little dangerous, but I love it.*

'Two roads diverged in a wood, and I –
I took the one less travelled by,
And that has made all the difference.'

Robert Frost, poet

'The road of life twists and turns and no two directions are ever the same. Yet our lessons come from the journey, not the destination.'

Don Williams, Jr, novelist

'Map out your future – but do it in pencil. The road ahead is as long as you make it. Make it worth the trip.'

Jon Bon Jovi, musician

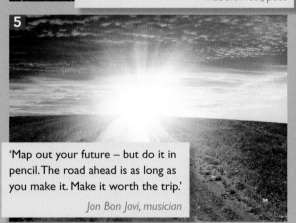

HOW TO SAY IT

Using descriptive words

The road is scary/ boring/hazardous/ dangerous/safe/ relaxing/winding/nice.

I think my life is (a bit) scary/exciting/ (un)predictable/full of changes/confusing/nice.

B Read the three quotes about life above. Which one do you like the best? Why?

A: *I like the Bon Jovi quote the best because it means that we control what happens in our lives. We can make our lives go in any direction we want.*

B: *I like the Robert Frost quote because he is talking about making life interesting and not just doing the same things everyone does.*

VOCABULARY: *take, make, do*

A Write each phrase in the correct column of the table.

> a big mistake   a donation to a charity   a very important exam
> an extreme sport   time off school or work   volunteer work

take	make	do
an important step in your life	*a video*	*something artistic*

B 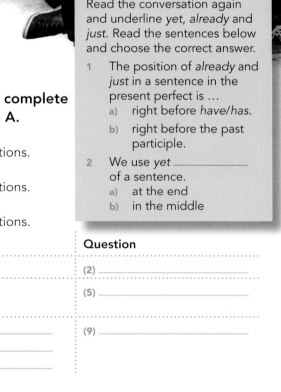 Work in pairs. Find out which things in Exercise A your partner has done. Ask for details.

A: *Have you ever taken a very important step in your life?*
B: *Yes, I have. I got married.*
A: *Wow! How long have you been married?*

GRAMMAR: present perfect + *yet/already/just*

A 🎧 **1.01** **LANGUAGE IN CONTEXT** Listen to the conversation. What are Olly and Sean talking about?

Olly: I've just finished my last exam and in one week I'm going to leave university!

Sean: Lucky you. I haven't finished my exams yet. I've got two more. I've already taken the most difficult ones though, so that's good.

Olly: What are you going to do after university? Have you decided yet?

Sean: Not yet. But I think I want to travel for a couple of months.

Olly: Yeah, I'm not sure, either. I'm considering a couple of jobs, but I'd really like to take the summer off and do some volunteer work.

Sean: So have you already received some job offers?

Olly: Well, I've had interviews with two companies, but I haven't had any job offers yet.

Sean: Wow. You're lucky to have had interviews. Hey, have you just texted me? There's a message from you.

Olly: Well, I texted you about an hour ago, but it seems you've only just received it for some reason.

B **ANALYSE** Read the conversation in Exercise A again.

Form **Choose the two correct options for each rule. Then complete the table where appropriate with examples from Exercise A.**

1 We use *already* in …
   a) affirmative statements.   b) negative statements.   c) questions.
2 We use *just* in …
   a) affirmative statements.   b) negative statements.   c) questions.
3 We use *yet* in …
   a) affirmative statements.   b) negative statements.   c) questions.

> **NOTICE!**
>
> Read the conversation again and underline *yet*, *already* and *just*. Read the sentences below and choose the correct answer.
>
> 1 The position of *already* and *just* in a sentence in the present perfect is …
>   a) right before *have/has*.
>   b) right before the past participle.
>
> 2 We use *yet* _____ of a sentence.
>   a) at the end
>   b) in the middle

	Affirmative	Negative	Question
already	(1) _____		(2) _____
just	(3) _____ (4) _____		(5) _____
yet		(6) _____ (7) _____ (8) _____	(9) _____

Function **Complete the rules with *yet, already* and *just*.**

1 We use ________ to say that something hasn't happened, but it will soon.
2 We use ________ to say that something has happened in the immediate or very recent past.
3 We use ________ to say that something happened sooner than expected, or to emphasise that it has happened.

WHAT'S RIGHT?

- ◯ I have already done volunteer work.
- ◯ I already have done volunteer work.
- ◯ He just has sent me an email.
- ◯ He has just sent me an email.

C PRACTISE Complete these conversations with *already*, *just* and *yet*.

1 A: So, have you found a job ________?
B: Yes, I've ________ been offered a job in a bookshop. They phoned me this morning.
2 A: You need to live on the beach once in your life.
B: I've ________ done that. I lived on the beach last summer.
3 A: Have you taken any important exams ________?
B: No. I've ________ taken a few small exams, but I haven't taken an important one ________.
4 A: Have you ________ made a donation to charity this year?
B: Yes, I gave some money last week.
5 A: You haven't filled out that job application ________!
B: Yes, I have. I didn't have time earlier, but I've ________ finished it, and I'm sending it now.
6 A: Look! The university has ________ sent me an email saying that I'm accepted!
B: That was fast! You only sent in your application a month ago!

D NOW YOU DO IT Work in groups. First, think about how you would complete these statements about events in your life. Then discuss the statements with your group.

I've just … (My … has just …)
Two of my goals are to … and to …
I've already …, but I haven't … yet.

HOW TO SAY IT

Talking about goals
When/Where/Why/How did you …?
Why haven't you … yet?
When are you planning to …?

PRONUNCIATION: /j/ vs /ʤ/

A 1.02 Listen to these sounds and words. Can you hear the difference between the sounds /j/ and /ʤ/? Now listen again and repeat.

/j/ yet /ʤ/ jet

B 1.03 Listen and write these words in the correct column.

yes yak joke Jess yolk Jack

/j/	/ʤ/

C Work in pairs. Practise saying these sentences.

1 Have you flown on a jet yet?
2 I don't like egg yolk.
3 Is your friend's name Jess or Jack?
4 Have you talked to Jess yet?
5 Do you know a good joke?

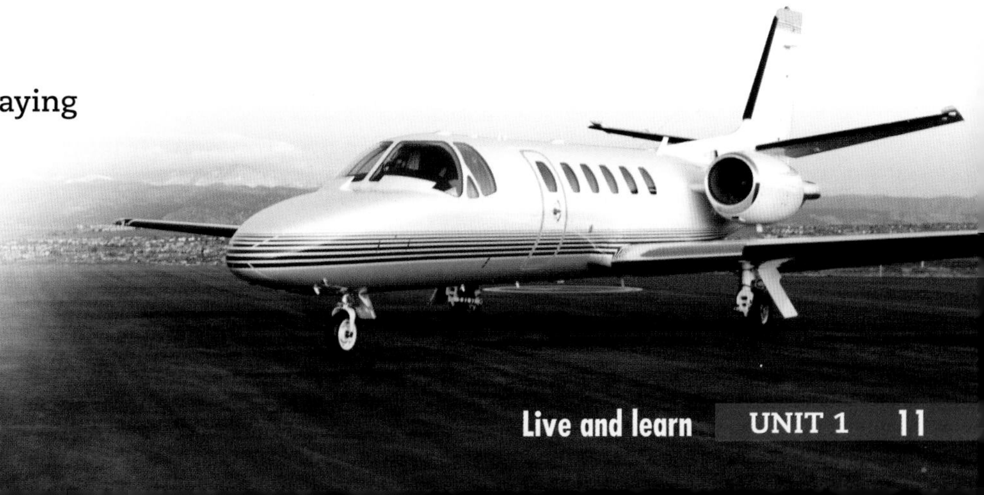

Remember that the topic sentence of a paragraph states the main idea. The topic sentence is often, but not always, the first sentence of the paragraph.

A **Work in pairs. Discuss these questions.**

1 Apart from English, what other things are you learning right now?

2 What do you like about learning new things? What don't you like about it?

B **Read the article. Underline the topic sentence in each of the two paragraphs.**

THE INTERMEDIATE PLATEAU

When we learn something new, there are times when we advance quickly and times when we advance more slowly. Typically, the intermediate level is a period when we make less progress than we did at earlier levels. This is true for learning anything – a language, a sport or a new job. At intermediate level, progress is usually slower because we are focusing on more complex details than we did at earlier levels. Because progress slows down, the learner often feels that they are staying at the same level, and not increasing their skills or knowledge. We often refer to this stage as the 'intermediate plateau', and it is a time when many learners become frustrated and give up.

The model shown in Diagram 1 shows the stages of learning. The theory behind the model is that, in order to learn something new, we first have to be conscious of what we know and what we do not know. Then we can develop competence, or the abilities we need to do something. In the first stage on the ladder, 'unconscious incompetence', we do not know how much we need to learn. Everything is new and we are excited about learning, so we advance quickly. In the second stage, 'conscious incompetence', we know how much we don't know! This can be a very frustrating period because we are aware of how much there is to learn. In the

third stage, 'conscious competence', we are more competent, but we still have to work hard to maintain our competence. Sometimes this stage can seem like too much work! However, if we don't give up, we will finally reach the last stage, 'unconscious competence'. At this stage, our new skills have become automatic. We don't have to think about everything before we do it.

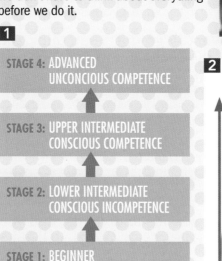

1

| STAGE 4: ADVANCED UNCONCIOUS COMPETENCE |
| STAGE 3: UPPER INTERMEDIATE CONSCIOUS COMPETENCE |
| STAGE 2: LOWER INTERMEDIATE CONSCIOUS INCOMPETENCE |
| STAGE 1: BEGINNER UNCONSCIOUS INCOMPETENCE |

2 LEARNING CURVE

Ability

Time

C **Choose the correct option to complete the sentences. Then go back and look at the sentences you underlined in the text. Did you choose the correct topic sentences?**

1 Paragraph 1 is about …
   a) learning in general.
   b) the intermediate stage of learning.

2 The main idea of paragraph 1 is that …
   a) we usually learn more slowly at intermediate level.
   b) we learn some things quickly and other things more slowly.

3 Paragraph 2 is about …
   a) a diagram that explains how learning happens.
   b) how we learn at intermediate level.

4 The main idea of paragraph 2 is that …
   a) there are clear stages in the learning process.
   b) almost everyone learns slowly at intermediate level.

D **Read the statements and choose T (true) or F (false).**

1 Some stages of learning are more difficult than others. T / F

2 Many people do not progress to an advanced level when they are learning something new. T / F

3 At beginner level, learners know exactly how much they need to learn. T / F

4 Progress is usually very slow at beginner level. T / F

5 Conscious incompetence means that you know how much you haven't learnt yet. T / F

6 In the case of English learners, by stage 3, students are fluent enough to think in English. T / F

VOCABULARY: the learning process

A Read the paragraph. Then match the phrases in bold with the correct definitions below.

People who reach an advanced level in a sport, a language or any other skill have several characteristics in common. First, they **(a) push** themselves beyond their **(b) comfort zone**. In other words, they **(c) take risks** and try things a little beyond their abilities. Second, they don't **(d) give up** during periods when they don't **(e) progress**. Third and finally, they **(f) measure** their **(g) progress** often by competing or taking exams, and they learn from their mistakes.

1 b : a situation or state that you feel relaxed in
2 ☐ your ☐ : to check development or improvement
3 ☐ yourself: to make a determined effort to do something

4 ☐ : to stop trying to do something
5 ☐ : to develop or improve
6 ☐ : to do something, although you know that something bad could happen

B Complete the sentences with the correct form of the phrases in Exercise A.

1 I was trying to learn to paint, but I was terrible at it and I finally _____.
2 I want to run a 10 km race, so I _____ myself to run further every day.
3 You can run short practice races with friends to _____ your progress.
4 Successful people are usually not afraid to _____ and try new things.
5 You will not _____ in anything if you do not move beyond your _____.

LISTENING: to advice

A 🔊 Work in pairs. Read the list below. With your partner, tick the things that you think a person has to do to progress from an intermediate to an advanced level in a sport.

To become an advanced-level athlete, you have to …

☐ get a professional trainer.
☐ win a lot of competitions.
☐ really want to get to an advanced level.
☐ lose a lot of competitions.

☐ feel very secure at intermediate level.
☐ practise every day.
☐ take risks and try new things.

☐ practise as much as you can.
☐ make a lot of mistakes.
☐ take some time off.

B 🎧 **1.04** Listen to the conversation and check your answers to Exercise A. Did you guess correctly?

C 🔊 Work in pairs. Discuss these questions.

1 When you are learning something new, do you usually push yourself, or do you prefer to stay in your comfort zone?
2 Have you or has someone you know ever taken any risks? Was the result positive or negative?
3 When you are learning something, do you prefer to measure your progress rarely or often?
4 Have you ever given up something you were trying to learn? If so, why?

GRAMMAR: present perfect continuous

A LANGUAGE IN CONTEXT Read the email. What big change has just happened in Melissa's life?

Hi Sean,
I'm sorry I haven't written for a while but I've been really busy. I was promoted at work last month, and since then I've been working really hard to learn all the new things I have to do! I'm really happy, though. Since I started my new job I've made a lot of suggestions that my manager likes, and we've been developing a new marketing strategy together. It's a lot of work but we hope to finish next week. What have you been doing? My mum told me you have moved to Manchester. When did you move? How long have you been living there?
Love, Melissa

NOTICE!
Read the underlined verb form in the text. Underline any other similar verb forms that you can find.

B ANALYSE Read the email in Exercise A again.

Form Complete the table with examples from Exercise A.

Affirmative	Negative	Questions	Short answers
have/has + been + -ing form of the verb	I haven't been working really hard.	Have you been working really hard?	Yes, I have. No, I haven't.
I (1) _____ _____ _____ really hard.		How long (2) _____ you _____ there?	

Function Choose the correct option to complete the rules.

1 We use the present perfect continuous to talk about …
   a) an experience or event that happened at an unspecified time in the past.
   b) an activity that started in the past and is still in progress now.
2 We use the present perfect continuous to talk about …
   a) the result of a recent continuing activity.
   b) the result of a complete action in the past.
3 We use the present perfect continuous with questions starting with …
   a) How long. b) When.
4 We use the present perfect simple to talk about something that happened …
   a) at an unspecified time in the past.
   b) at a specific moment in the past.

WHAT'S RIGHT?
- ○ I've been working here since July.
- ○ I'm working here since July.
- ○ I've been knowing her for two years.
- ○ I've known her for two years.

C PRACTISE Complete Sean's reply to Melissa's email with the present perfect simple or present perfect continuous form of the verbs in brackets.

Hi Melissa,
Great to hear from you! Congratulations on your promotion! I (1) _____ (be) really busy, too. My cousin opened a shop three weeks ago and I (2) _____ (make) promotional videos for him. I (3) _____ already _____ (make) two, and I'm finishing one more at the moment. At the same time, I (4) _____ (study) a lot for my university exams. They're next month. And, yes, I (5) _____ (move) to Manchester for the summer! I (6) _____ (live) here for two weeks, and I'll be here until the end of the month. Also, I (7) _____ (meet) someone I really like. Her name's Helena, and we (8) _____ (go) out together for about two months. Actually, we (9) _____ (not see) each other for about three weeks now because she's in Germany for the summer. Oh, and I've got a car! I (10) _____ (have) it for four months now. Anyway, let's get together for lunch soon. I can drive down to London to meet you in my new car!
Love, Sean

D NOW YOU DO IT Work in pairs. Talk about things you have been doing recently.

A: *So what have you been doing recently?*

B: *Well, I haven't been doing anything interesting because I've been studying a lot. I'm studying for my university exams. I've already taken one exam, but there are two more next week. What about you? What have you been doing?*

SPEAKING: encouraging the speaker

⚙ When we are having a conversation, we often use short questions to show interest and encourage the speaker to give more information.

A 🎧 **1.05** Listen to the conversation. Who works as a designer?

B Listen to the conversation in Exercise A again and underline the short questions the speakers use to show interest and encourage the speaker to give more information.

Jody: Amy? Hi, I thought it was you! I haven't seen you for ages!

Amy: Jody! Hi! It's been years! What have you been doing?

Jody: Well, I've been studying a lot recently. I'm doing an MA.

Amy: Are you? Excellent!

Jody: Yes, in chemistry.

Amy: Wow! I'm not at uni anymore. I finished last summer, and I've been working as a designer since then.

Jody: Have you? That sounds interesting!

Amy: Yes, but the job isn't that great, actually.

Jody: Oh, isn't it?

Amy: No. The company's really small, and the work's a bit boring.

Jody: Is it?

Amy: Yes, the boss doesn't give us much freedom to take risks with our designs.

Jody: Oh, doesn't he? What a shame.

Amy: Listen, I have to go, but let's keep in touch, OK?

Jody: Yes, definitely.

> **HOW TO SAY IT** 🗣
>
> **Encouraging the speaker**
> *What have you been doing?*
> *Are you? / Have you? / Do you?*
> *Excellent!*
> *Wow!*
> *What a shame.*

C 🗣 **Work in pairs. Roleplay a conversation like the one in Exercise A. Then swap roles and roleplay the conversation again.**

- Student A, tell Student B your news and what you have been doing recently.
- Student B, respond to Student A and keep the conversation flowing. Use questions to show interest and encourage Student A to give more information.

WRITING: a diary entry

A **Read the diary entry and choose the correct option to complete the sentences.**

1 The journal entry is about a specific event / a period in the writer's life.
2 The writer feels confident / worried about getting a job.
3 The writer has / hasn't been learning new things.
4 The writer feels satisfied / dissatisfied with their life.

B **You are going to write your own diary entry. Make notes to plan your writing. Think about:**

- what you'll write about.
- your feelings and thoughts.
- other things you've been doing recently.
- general feelings about your life.

C **Write your diary entry on a sheet of paper.**

D 🗣 **Work in groups. Mix up the diary entries and take one. Make sure it isn't your own. Read the entry and try to guess who wrote it.**

Tuesday, August 10

Recently, I've been reflecting on my life over the past year or so. What have I been doing? What have I accomplished? Sometimes I think I haven't achieved any of my goals yet, but really that isn't true. I've almost finished my university degree – just one more term! I've started contacting potential employers, and I've already heard from a couple of them, so I'm feeling quite good about that. For a long time, I've wanted to learn to do something artistic, and I finally decided to do it. I've been doing a course in photography and I really like it! I've taken about a million photos, and I've made a gazillion mistakes, but I've really learnt a lot. I haven't reached a really good level yet, but maybe I will one day. I've just enrolled for a special effects class, and that's going to be great. Let's see, what else? Well, that marathon I've always wanted to do? I don't know about that. The next one is in March, and I really haven't been training enough. I'm a bit sad about that. But overall assessment? Life is good.

LifeSkills

SETTING GOALS

- Identify a personal goal.
- Think of steps to help you achieve your goal.
- Make a realistic plan.

A Read the information about setting personal goals. Then tick the areas that are most important to you.

Setting Personal Goals

⌂ Home   ❓ Advice   ✉ Contact

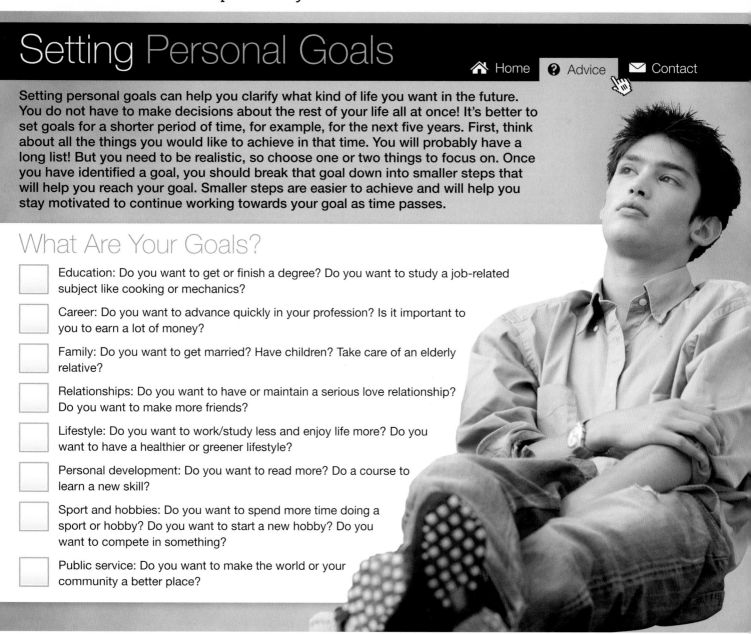

Setting personal goals can help you clarify what kind of life you want in the future. You do not have to make decisions about the rest of your life all at once! It's better to set goals for a shorter period of time, for example, for the next five years. First, think about all the things you would like to achieve in that time. You will probably have a long list! But you need to be realistic, so choose one or two things to focus on. Once you have identified a goal, you should break that goal down into smaller steps that will help you reach your goal. Smaller steps are easier to achieve and will help you stay motivated to continue working towards your goal as time passes.

What Are Your Goals?

☐ Education: Do you want to get or finish a degree? Do you want to study a job-related subject like cooking or mechanics?

☐ Career: Do you want to advance quickly in your profession? Is it important to you to earn a lot of money?

☐ Family: Do you want to get married? Have children? Take care of an elderly relative?

☐ Relationships: Do you want to have or maintain a serious love relationship? Do you want to make more friends?

☐ Lifestyle: Do you want to work/study less and enjoy life more? Do you want to have a healthier or greener lifestyle?

☐ Personal development: Do you want to read more? Do a course to learn a new skill?

☐ Sport and hobbies: Do you want to spend more time doing a sport or hobby? Do you want to start a new hobby? Do you want to compete in something?

☐ Public service: Do you want to make the world or your community a better place?

B Now choose the area that is the most important to you. Think of a goal to achieve in that area. Write a short personal goal statement.

> *Personal goal statement:*
> I will focus on education: I want to do a degree in IT.

C Work in pairs. Read your goal statements to each other. Then brainstorm a list of intermediate steps to help you reach your goal.

> ## Main goal: Do a degree in IT
> Steps:
> - Do an online IT course, or evening course
> - Look for a job in an IT company for the summer
> - Study hard to get really good grades at school
> - Find out about different IT courses at universities
> - Apply to several universities

D Write down when you will do each step and organise them in chronological order to make an action plan. Make notes about what you need to do to complete each step.

Main goal: Do a degree in IT

Step	Time	To do
Study hard to get really good grades at school	Now and for the next 14 months!	Get organised Do extra work
Look for a job in an IT company for the summer	Now	Find local companies and email/call them
Do an online IT course, or evening course	September	Call the local college Look online
Find out about different IT courses at universities	After the summer holiday	Talk to a careers advisor Look at university websites
Apply to several universities	Next year	Get application form online

E Explain your plan to your partner. Make further suggestions about each other's plans.

HOW TO SAY IT

Discussing personal action plans

I'm going to …

Have you … yet?

Maybe you could also …

Another thing you could do is …

REFLECT … How can the skill of setting goals be useful to you in **Work and Career** and **Study and Learning**?

Language wrap-up

1 VOCABULARY

A Complete the conversation with the correct form of *take*, *make* and *do*. (9 points)

Maria: I'm so bored with work. I'm going to ask my boss if I can (1) _____ some time off and learn to (2) _____ something artistic, or (3) _____ some volunteer work. Yesterday I (4) _____ a donation to a charity that builds houses for homeless people. Maybe I'll volunteer there. I studied film, so maybe I could (5) _____ promotional videos for them or something.

Lisa: I wish I could do something like that, but I don't have any time because I'm going to (6) _____ my final teacher training exam next month. And I'm (7) _____ lots of sport at the moment, too. I hope I'm not (8) _____ a big mistake by becoming a teacher.

Maria: Well, it's an important step to (9) _____, but I'm sure you're going to love teaching.

Lisa: I hope so!

B Complete the text with the phrases in the box. (6 points)

comfort zone   give up   measure our progress   progress (*v*)   push yourself   take risks

Keys to professional advancement

Many of us (1) _____ in our careers by how many promotions we get. Are you tired of seeing other people get promoted before you? Do you want to (2) _____ faster in your job or career? To get promoted, you really have to make an effort and (3) _____ to do more. You can't stay in your (4) _____. You have to (5) _____ and try new things. If you haven't advanced in your job as quickly as you would like, don't (6) _____! Sign up for our two-day seminar and get the keys to success!

> **11 – 15 correct:** I can use phrases with *take*, *make* and *do* and phrases related to the learning process.
> **0 – 10 correct:** Look again at the vocabulary sections on pages 10 and 13.   **SCORE:**   /15

2 GRAMMAR

A Write sentences with the present perfect and *yet*, *already* or *just*. (6 points)

1   you / see / this film / already / ?
2   they / move / to a new house / just
3   he / not eat / his dinner / yet
4   my friends / leave / just
5   you / arrive / just / ?
6   she / find / a new job / already

B Complete the email with the correct present perfect simple or present perfect continuous form of the verbs in brackets. (9 points)

Hi Mum and Dad!

Well, I (1) _____ (*be*) at university for two whole weeks now, and I really like it! I (2) _____ (*meet*) some new people. I went out with them last weekend. Of course, I (3) _____ (*study*) too, so don't worry! I (4) _____ (*not have*) any exams, but there's a chemistry test next week. But I'm afraid that I (5) _____ (*spend*) most of the money you gave me, so maybe you could send some more? I (6) _____ (*look*) for a part-time job, but I (7) _____ (*not find*) one. I (8) _____ (*apply*) for a job in a bookshop here, but I (9) _____ (*not hear*) if I've got it or not. They said they would phone me today.

Love Pete

> **11 – 15 correct:** I can use the present perfect with *yet*, *already* and *just*. I can use the present perfect simple and present perfect continuous.
> **0 – 10 correct:** Look again at the grammar sections on pages 10–11 and 14.   **SCORE:**   /15

WRITING WORKSHOP

a diary entry

I've been looking for a job for two months now, but I haven't had any luck. I'm starting to feel really discouraged! I've already contacted most of the big companies in my area, and I've had several interviews, but no offers. So what have I been doing wrong? Why can't I get a job? My dad thinks I don't seem very self-confident in my interviews. I've got good qualifications, so maybe he's right. Maybe my interview skills aren't very good. I've got an idea – I'm going to ask my dad to roleplay some interviews with me and give me some tips. First tip to myself – be positive!

A Read the diary entry and answer the questions.

1 How long has the writer been looking for a job?
2 How many job interviews has she had?
3 How many job offers has she had?
4 What does she think she's doing wrong?
5 Who is she going to ask to help her?

B Read the diary entry again and answer the questions.

1 What feelings and emotions does the writer express?
2 Are the writer's questions addressed to herself or someone else?
3 Does the writer use a formal or informal style of writing?

C Choose one of these topics or think of another topic to write a diary entry about. Make notes about what you want to include.

- a recent event or experience
- a problem that you have solved or need to solve
- a current event that you have a strong opinion about
- a family member or other person who is important to you

D Write your diary entry in your notebook. Use your notes from Exercise C to help you.

HOW ARE YOU DOING?

Look back at your writing and tick the statements that are true.

◯ I have described my feelings and emotions about the event or experience.

◯ I have used rhetorical questions.

◯ I have used a chatty, informal style of writing.

Now ask a partner to look at your writing and tick:

Does the diary entry clearly describe an event, a situation or a person?

⬤   ◯   ⬤

Well done!   Nearly!   Think again!
             Look at the   Ask your teacher
             unit again.   for help.

UNIT 2 THEN AND NOW

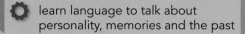

IN THIS UNIT YOU

- ⚙ learn language to talk about personality, memories and the past
- ⚙ listen to how people express emotions and attitudes
- ⚙ read a magazine article about smell and memory
- ⚙ talk about memories
- ⚙ write about a favourite memory
- ⚙ learn steps for preparing and giving a short presentation
- ▶ watch a video about memory

LISTENING
identifying emotion and attitude
In what ways do speakers let their listeners know how they feel about something?

WRITING
organising a paragraph
What are some reasons why you might want to write down your childhood memories?

LIFE SKILLS
STUDY & LEARNING

preparing and giving a short presentation
What was the last presentation you had to give, in English or in your own language? Did it go well? Why or why not?

A Look at the photos and tick the photo that shows the child (or children) that seem(s) the most like you when you were young. It doesn't matter if he or she is a different gender from you.

A ☐

B ☐

C ☐

D ☐

E ☐

F ☐

B 🔊 Tell your classmates which child (or children) in the photos you were similar to, and why.

A: *I was similar to the little boy in photo C because I liked doing dangerous things. I always terrified my mother.*

B: *I was like the girl in photo A. I was shy and quiet.*

HOW TO SAY IT 🔊

Talking about yourself
This boy/girl reminds me of me at that age.
I was exactly like him/her.
I think I was like this boy/girl because I liked …
I think I was …

A Match the words for stereotypical personality types with the people in the pictures.

a joker   a rebel   academic   geeky   a party animal   a troublemaker   popular   sporty

B 🎧 Work in groups. Talk about what you and your friends were like at school.

A: Sarah, did you fit any of these stereotypes when you were at school?

B: I was a bit of a rebel, I suppose. You know, black clothes, loud music. I always questioned authority, like teachers and my parents. I never did anything really bad though. What about you, Holly?

A: I was quite academic and I enjoyed school. I generally didn't get into trouble, so the teachers liked me. Well, except the P.E. teacher. I wasn't very sporty!

HOW TO SAY IT 🎧

Qualifying phrases
a bit of a …
sort of a …
quite / fairly / a bit …
very / not very …

GRAMMAR: *used to*

A 🎧 **1.06 LANGUAGE IN CONTEXT** Listen to the conversation below. Is Kevin the same now as he was at school?

James: Is this a picture of you at school?

Kevin: Yes, that was in the Sixth Form.

James: That's you? I don't believe it! <u>You used to have really long hair! Now your hair is really short!</u>

Kevin: Yeah, I used to be a bit of a rebel. You know, long hair, weird clothes. I used to play in a band, so I wanted to look cool. But those were the old days. I don't do that anymore.

James: Did your band use to play at parties?

Kevin: Yeah, parties, and sometimes school events.

James: That's great!

Kevin: Well, we weren't very good. I mean, we didn't do concerts or anything. Anyway, that's all in the past. Now that I work in IT, I'm totally boring!

James: I didn't use to do any of the things you did. Well, I still don't. I am boring now, and I was boring then!

NOTICE!

Look at the underlined sentences. Do we use *used to* to refer to the present or the past?

B ANALYSE Read the conversation in Exercise A again.

Form Choose the correct options. Then complete the table with examples from Exercise A.

1 The verb after *used to* is in the …
   a) base form.
   b) *-ing* form.

2 In affirmative statements, we use …
   a) *used to.*
   b) *use to.*

3 In questions and negative statements, we use …
   a) *used to.*
   b) *use to.*

Affirmative	Negative	Questions	Short answers
You _____ _____ _____ really long hair.	I _____ _____ any of the things you did.	_____ your band _____ _____ _____ at parties?	Yes, it did. No, it didn't.

Function Choose the correct option to complete the rule.

We use *used to* to talk about

a) things that were true in the past and are still true in the present.

b) things that were true in the past, but are not true in the present.

You can use *never* and *always* with *used to*:
e.g. *My brother always used to get up really early.*
I never used to get up before 11am at weekends.

WHAT'S RIGHT?
○ I didn't use to run.
○ I didn't used to run.
○ Did you use to play in a band?
○ Did you used to play in a band?

C PRACTISE Complete the conversation with the correct form of *used to.*

A: Do you think you've changed a lot in the last five or ten years?

B: Yeah, a lot. I didn't (1) _____ work full time, so I had a lot more time to go out.

A: Yeah, me too. Also, I (2) _____ go out with a lot of different girls, but now I have a girlfriend.

B: Well, that's nice.

A: Yeah, we'll probably get married. Anyway, I remember I never (3) _____ get home before 4am at weekends. I was definitely a party animal!

B: Yeah, I always (4) _____ stay out late, too. Where did you (5) _____ go?

A: To live music clubs, mostly. I (6) _____ go to hear music a lot. They always had great bands. We (7) _____ dance all night!

B: I liked going out to hear live music, too, but I didn't (8) _____ like dancing. I actually dance more now because my wife loves dancing.

D NOW YOU DO IT Work in pairs. Talk about what you used to be like and things you used to do when you were younger. Use the conversation in Exercise C and the ideas below to help you.

- appearance
- personality
- routines
- leisure activities

PRONUNCIATION: emphatic stress

A 1.07 Listen to these sentences. Underline the words the speaker stresses in the answers.

1 A: Did your brother use to have long hair?
   B: No, my sister used to have long hair.

2 A: Did your brother use to have long hair?
   B: No, my brother used to have short hair.

B Read these questions and answers. Underline the words in the answers that you think will be stressed.

1 A: Did you use to have a blue car?
   B: No, we used to have a red car.

2 A: Did you use to like dogs?
   B: No, we used to like cats.

3 A: Did your brother use to play football?
   B: No, I used to play football.

4 A: Do you live in a flat?
   B: No, we used to live in a flat.

C 1.08 Listen to the sentences and check. Practise saying the questions and answers in pairs.

LISTENING: identifying emotion and attitude

⚙ When you listen to someone, pay attention to a person's tone of voice.
It will help you understand their emotions and attitude.

A 🎧 **1.09** Listen to the speakers.
Match each speaker to these emotions.

Speaker 1 ☐
Speaker 2 ☐
Speaker 3 ☐
Speaker 4 ☐
Speaker 5 ☐
Speaker 6 ☐

A excited

B angry

C sad

B 🎧 **1.10** Listen to four conversations.
Choose the correct option.

1 The man feels sad / nervous.
2 The woman feels angry / excited.
3 The woman feels bored / uncertain.
4 The woman feels bored / sad.

D bored   **E uncertain**   **F nervous**

VOCABULARY: memory

A Read the webpage. Circle the sense which is NOT mentioned.

a) sight   b) smell   c) taste   d) touch   e) hearing

 www.askandanswer.com

Home   About   *Questions*

QUESTION: WHAT MEMORIES DO YOU ASSOCIATE WITH SPECIFIC THINGS?

I haven't got a very good memory, but it's funny how certain sights, smells, tastes or even sounds can bring back vivid memories of your childhood. For example, the smell and taste of fresh chocolate-chip cookies always remind me of my mum because she used to make them a lot when I was young. And hearing the song *Call Me Maybe* makes me think of school and the friends I had there. We had all memorised that song, and we used to sing it to remind each other to phone! And let's see … when I see a beagle puppy, I think back to when I got my first dog. She was a beagle named Lucky. I can clearly remember the day I got her. I was really excited. It was my eighth birthday. She was SO sweet!

Fiona, Glasgow

B Match the sentence halves.

1 I memorised
2 It reminds me
3 Please remind me
4 It brings back
5 I think back
6 That makes me
7 I can clearly/definitely/vaguely
8 I have an excellent / a good / a really bad

a) think of my grandma.
b) memory.
c) to when we met.
d) remember when I started school.
e) poems and my times tables at school.
f) to phone them.
g) vivid memories.
h) of the time when we went skiing.

C Complete the sentences with your own ideas. Then work in pairs and compare your sentences.

1 The smell of _____ reminds me of _____

2 The song _____ brings back memories of _____

3 The taste of _____ makes me think of _____

4 As a young child, I can clearly remember when _____

5 When I see _____, I think back to when _____

READING: a magazine article

A Read these statements about the sense of smell and choose *T* (true) or *F* (false). Then scan the article quickly to check your answers.

1 Smells can cause us to remember things very clearly.   T / F
2 Humans have about 220 million smell receptors.   T / F
3 Smells do not help us remember things from our early childhood.   T / F
4 Smells can help older people remember things from their past.   T / F

B Now read the text carefully and answer the questions below.

1 What is one important characteristic of smell memories?
2 Why do humans have a weaker sense of smell than animals?
3 Why do smells cause strong emotional responses?
4 Why do smells often help us remember things from a very early age?
5 What medical implications does research in smell and memory have?

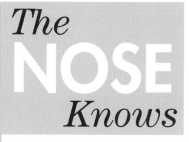

The NOSE Knows

Almost everyone has experienced vivid memories associated with smells. Smell memories are so strong that they can transport us immediately to the past. You smell a certain perfume or cologne, and you are with an old love again. You smell popcorn, and you are a child at a fair. We often forget an experience until we smell something associated with it; then we can suddenly see and hear the whole experience and feel the emotions that we felt. It's as if we are having the experience again.

The sense of smell is very important for animals, as it helps them find food, recognise danger and recognise other members of the same species. However, when humans developed higher cognitive abilities, such as language, the sense of smell became less important for survival. This is why humans only have about 20 million smell receptors, while a bloodhound has 220 million. So why are our smell memories so strong? The answer is in our physiology. The reason that we usually have strong emotional responses to smell memories is that the olfactory cortex, where our sense of smell is located, is close to the amygdala, which is the centre of emotions and memories.

Researchers have done experiments to compare smell stimuli with other stimuli as memory cues. With visual cues and word cues, people tended to remember things that happened after the age of 10. With smell cues, they remembered more things from early childhood. This makes sense, because the sense of smell develops in babies before the senses of vision and later, words.

These findings have positive implications for helping people who suffer from dementia. If they can't remember things from their past, the memories can often be stimulated with smells. Researchers have found that when people with memory loss smell something associated with their youth, they are often able to describe a memory in great detail.

C Work in groups. Talk about your own 'smell memories'.

The smell of flowers makes me think of my grandma. She had a beautiful flower garden.

A 🎧 **1.11 LANGUAGE IN CONTEXT** Listen to the conversation below. What made Lauren remember something from her childhood?

Lauren: It's so great to be at the beach! The smell of the sea brings back memories of one of the best times of my life.

Danielle: Really? When was that?

Lauren: The summer when I was eight years old. **We went to visit my grandparents for two weeks. They had just bought a little house by the beach,** and we swam and played on the beach every day.

Danielle: That sounds really nice.

Lauren: Yeah, even the drive to get there from London was fun. My mum had just bought a new car. When we started the journey, we hadn't been in the new car yet, so we were really excited.

Danielle: Had you and your brother been to the beach before?

Lauren: No, we hadn't, so you can imagine how exciting it was! We had never tasted salt water or seen waves! I can clearly remember my little brother's face when he accidentally swallowed some water! He was so surprised!

B ANALYSE Read the conversation in Exercise A again.

Form Choose the correct option to complete the rules. Complete the table with examples from Exercise A.

We form the past perfect with …

a) *have/has* + the past participle of the verb.

b) *had* + the past participle of the verb.

NOTICE!

Look at the sentences in bold in the conversation. Which of the two actions happened first?

Affirmative	Negative	Questions	Short answers
They _____	*We* _____	_____ *you and your brother*	*Yes, we had.*
_____ *a little house by the beach.*	_____ *in the car yet.*	_____ *to the beach before?*	*No, we* _____.

Function

We use the past perfect to talk about

a) something that happened before a specific time in the past.

b) something that happened a very long time ago.

C PRACTISE Complete the sentences with the correct past simple or past perfect form of the verbs in brackets.

1 When we _____ (*arrive*), our parents _____ already _____ (*eat*).

2 I _____ already _____ (*have*) two jobs by the time I _____ (*be*) 18.

3 I _____ just _____ (*finish*) my work when you _____ (*phone*).

4 By the age of five, my brother _____ already _____ (*learn*) how to use a computer.

5 We _____ (*not finish*) our exam when the bell _____ (*ring*).

6 I _____ (*go*) to New York last summer. I _____ never _____ (*go*) there before.

7 Why _____ we _____ (*not see*) this movie before last night?

8 _____ you already _____ (*meet*) Sally when you _____ (*start*) university?

D 🎤 **NOW YOU DO IT** Work in groups. Complete the sentences about your experiences. Then tell your group.

WHAT'S RIGHT?

○ They already left when we had arrived.

○ They had already left when we arrived.

○ I saw this play at the theatre in 2000.

○ I had seen this play at the theatre in 2000.

HOW TO SAY IT

Talking about memories

By the time I was …, I had already …

When I … for the first time, I had never …

When …, I hadn't … yet.

When …, I had just …

SPEAKING: talking about memories

A 🎧 **1.12** **Listen to the conversation. Then choose T (true) or F (false) for the statements.**

1	Michael is telling Tom about a recent event in his life.	T / F
2	Both men like the car they are looking at.	T / F
3	Michael used to have a Jaguar.	T / F
4	Michael's grandfather had had several sports cars before he got the Jaguar.	T / F
5	Michael hadn't ridden in a soft-top before.	T / F

B **Think of a memory of a childhood event or experience to share. Use these questions as a guide to help you plan what to say.**

1 What was the event or experience, and what reminds you of it?
2 When did it happen?
3 What was the background? (something you used to do/had never done/had always wanted, etc.)
4 What happened?

C 🗣 **Work in pairs. Tell your partner about your memory. When you listen to your partner's story, ask questions to find out more about the event or experience.**

One of my best memories was when …

WRITING: organising a paragraph

⚙ A formal paragraph usually has three main elements: a topic sentence, supporting details and a concluding sentence. The topic sentence gives the main idea of the paragraph. This is often, but not always, the first sentence. Then there are usually several sentences that explain the main idea or give examples. Finally, the concluding sentence summarises or restates the main idea.

A Read the paragraph and underline the topic sentence and the concluding sentence.

B You are going to write a paragraph about a favourite memory. First, make some notes to help you organise your paragraph.

• Choose a topic. Write a topic sentence in your notebook.
• Under the topic sentence, write four or five details that you want to include in your paragraph. You do not have to write complete sentences.
• Write a concluding sentence. Remember that this sentence summarises the main idea or restates your topic sentence in a different way.

C Write your paragraph. Make sure the supporting details are in a logical order. Use linking words and time expressions as necessary.

> One of my favourite memories from my teenage years is my first concert. It was in 2008, and I was 15. I really loved music, but I had never been to a concert before. There was an American band called Fall Out Boy, and they were my favourite band at that time. They were touring Europe that year, and one of the venues was London. My brother was going to the concert with some friends, and I convinced my parents to let me go with them. The concert was amazing! Maybe it's because it was my first concert, but I have more memories of that concert than of any of the other concerts I saw in those years.

HOW TO SAY IT

Linking words
and, but, also, so, because

Time expressions
*at that time, that year, my first …
in those years*

Adverbs
already, just, never, yet, before

LifeSkills

PREPARING AND GIVING A SHORT PRESENTATION

- Choose a topic for a presentation and brainstorm ideas about it.
- Decide which ideas you want to include and organise them.
- Practise your presentation and make any necessary changes.

A You are going to prepare a three-minute presentation. First, choose a topic. You can choose from the table below, or think of your own topic. Brainstorm your ideas on the word web.

Society	The world	Education
• How technology has changed society • Changes in male and female roles • How entertainment has changed in my lifetime	• Has the world become better or worse in recent years? • A very positive or negative change in my country • An event that had international importance	• How I have changed since I started/left school/university • How technology has changed education • Education now and in my parents' generation

TOPIC

B Decide which ideas from your word web you want to talk about in your presentation. Write notes about them on a piece of paper or on small cards in the order you want to talk about them. Add details, if necessary, but you don't have to use complete sentences.

> Topic: How technology has changed education
> * The past: boring – teacher, book and blackboard only
> * Now: more interesting because of variety in the classroom: DVDs, presentations with video or slide shows, the internet
> * Result: better learning – more interesting, more access to information

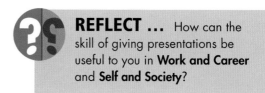

C Practise your presentation on your own. Follow the steps below.

* Practise the whole presentation and time yourself. You have three minutes!
* If your presentation is too long, cut some information and time yourself again.
* Practise one part of your presentation at a time to help you learn it. Remember, you want to sound as natural as possible.

I remember when education was very different from how it is now. Teachers and students didn't use to have all the resources they have now, so learning was more boring. I mean, good teachers made it interesting, but they had only books and the blackboard, and maybe a CD player. Education has really changed since then. Now, …

D Work in pairs, Student A and Student B.

Student A, give your presentation.
Student B, listen carefully and complete the evaluation form.
Then swap roles.

Presentation evaluation	
Was the talk three minutes or less?	Yes / No
Was the talk interesting?	Yes / No
Did the speaker speak slowly and clearly?	Yes / No
Did everything in the talk relate to the topic?	Yes / No
Should the speaker add more information?	Yes / No
Does the speaker need to cut any information?	Yes / No

HOW TO SAY IT

Giving feedback
I thought your presentation was …
I think you need to …
I didn't understand the part about …
Maybe you should give more information about …
I think you should cut the part about …

E Look at each other's evaluation forms. Then help your partner revise their presentation notes.

F Give your revised presentation to the class.

REFLECT … How can the skill of giving presentations be useful to you in **Work and Career** and **Self and Society**?

Language wrap-up

1 VOCABULARY

A Complete the definitions with the personality types in the box. (8 points)

| geeky | joker | party animal | popular | rebel | sporty | academic | troublemaker |

1 A/An _____ person is liked by a lot of people.
2 A/An _____ does bad things and causes problems.
3 A/An _____ constantly questions authority.
4 A/An _____ tells jokes and does silly things.
5 A/An _____ person is fascinated with technology.
6 A/An _____ person gets good grades and likes learning.
7 A/An _____ person spends most of his/her time doing exercise.
8 A/An _____ loves socialising and going out at night.

B Complete the sentences with the correct form of a verb connected with memory. (7 points)

1 Whenever I smell roses, it _____ me think of my mum.
2 I can clearly _____ the first time I went on a plane.
3 If I smell freshly cut grass, I _____ of my dad.
4 The taste of popcorn _____ me of the circus.
5 The smell of pine trees _____ _____ wonderful memories of my grandma's house.
6 Do you try to _____ a story before you tell it?
7 Please _____ me to give you back your jacket.

11 – 15 correct: I can describe people's personality types and use phrases to talk about memories.
0 – 10 correct: Look again at the vocabulary sections on pages 22 and 24–25.　　　　**SCORE:**　　　**/15**

2 GRAMMAR

Complete the conversation with the correct form of *used to* or the past simple or past perfect form of the verbs in brackets. (15 points)

Jenny: Did you (1) _____ have a pet when you were a child, Sofia?

Sofia: No. I got my first pet when I (2) _____ (be) a teenager. I (3) _____ (want) one for years, and my dream finally (4) _____ (come) true on my 14th birthday when my parents (5) _____ (give) me a kitten.

Jenny: (6) _____ your parents _____ (have) pets before?

Sofia: No, they (7) _____. Well, I think my dad (8) _____ have a fish or something, but nothing like a dog or a cat, and my mum didn't even (9) _____ like animals.

Jenny: Wow. I (10) _____ (grow) up with loads of animals. My parents (11) _____ _____ (have) pets all their lives. I remember that when I (12) _____ (be) very small, our two cats (13) _____ sleep downstairs in a basket in the kitchen. My parents (14) _____ just _____ (got) a puppy when I was born, and that dog (15) _____ (become) my best friend!

11 – 15 correct: I can use *used to*, the past simple and the past perfect to talk about the past.
0 – 10 correct: Look again at the grammar sections on pages 22–23 and 26.　　　　**SCORE:**　　　**/15**

A **Read the conversation and answer the questions below.**

1 Where did Lauren use to live when she was younger?
2 Why did the family move?
3 What did Lauren eat for the first time on the pier?

Lauren: When I come to Brighton beach, it always brings back great memories of my childhood.

Mike: Did you use to live near here or something?

Lauren: Yes, we moved to Brighton from Leeds, and we were living in a flat, so we didn't have a garden to play in. We used to have a big garden in Leeds, so being in a flat was difficult.

Mike: Why did you move here?

Lauren: My dad had lost his job in Leeds, and he got a job offer here, so …

Mike: And the beach became your garden?

Lauren: Yeah, we had a lot of fun here. I can clearly remember the first time we bought candy floss on the pier. I had seen people eating candy floss, but I'd never eaten it myself.

Mike: Really? You'd never eaten candy floss? How old were you?

Lauren: I was about ten, but we never used to eat things like candy floss.

Mike: Wow! Well, so how was your first seaside candy floss?

Lauren: It was amazing! I remember that by the time my mum started to eat hers, I'd already finished mine!

B **Read the conversation again and find these things.**

1 two phrases to talk about memories
2 four questions asking for more information
3 two expressions of surprise
4 three adjectives to describe the experience

C **Think of a memory of a childhood event or experience. Answer these questions about the event or experience.**

1 Where did it take place?
2 What details do you remember about it?
3 How did you feel?

D **Work in pairs. Tell your partner about your memory. Include words related to memory and adjectives to describe the experience. When you listen to your partner, ask questions to get more information.**

E **Find a new partner and tell them about your memory again.**

HOW ARE YOU DOING?

Think about your speaking and tick the statements that are true.

I feel confident using …

○ phrases to talk about memories.
○ the past simple, the past perfect and *used to* to talk about the past.
○ adjectives to describe experiences.

How do you feel about your speaking generally?

● Very confident   ○ Not sure …   ● Need to practise

UNIT 3 BUYING POWER

IN THIS UNIT YOU

- ⚙ learn language to talk about advertising, products and customer service
- ⚙ read about how much money people spend on proms
- ⚙ write about shopping online and in real shops
- ⚙ listen to complaints about products
- ⚙ talk about problems with products
- ⚙ learn techniques for persuading people
- ▶ watch a video about advertising

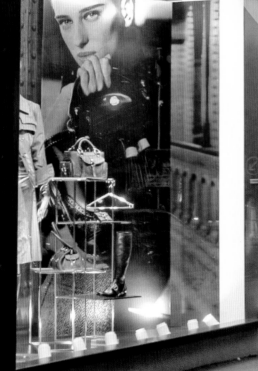

SPEAKING
politely insisting
In what situations do people need to be able to politely insist on something?

READING
reading for the main idea
Advertisements seem to be getting better. They are more interesting and entertaining than in the past. Do you agree?

LIFE SKILLS

WORK & CAREER

Persuading others
Do you think you are good at persuading people? Why or why not?

A Look at these photos of two famous cities. Do the photos give you positive or negative impressions of these two places? Why?

Piccadilly Circus, London

Times Square, New York

HOW TO SAY IT

Talking about advertising

Types of signs: *billboards, (electronic) signs, posters*

Signs are distracting/ unattractive/effective.

Cities should/shouldn't allow/ban/limit public advertising.

Ads stimulate the economy/ trick people/make the city unattractive.

B Think about your own town or city. Are there lots of advertisements, or very few? How do you feel about the amount of advertising around you?

A: *There are lots of ads in my city. They're everywhere.*

B: *Yeah. I think there are too many, especially big billboards. I don't think the city should allow them.*

A LANGUAGE IN CONTEXT Read this article.
How does Joel Moss Levinson make money?

Joel Moss Levinson is a highly successful creator and producer of adverts. He stars in them himself, and they are filmed on a small video camera. Apart from the cost of the camera, he has spent almost no money on them. So how does Joel make money from the adverts? Creativity and innovation are the keys.

The advertising industry today realises that it needs to use new media, such as online videos, to advertise. The videos have to be funny and appeal to young people, so many companies run competitions to get them. What are the organisers looking for? The competitions are for homemade videos that they can use as adverts. That's where Joel Moss Levinson comes in: his crazy sense of humour is perfect for the internet. He's won over $200,000 in money and other prizes, including trips abroad. Joel lives in the USA, but because his adverts are online, people in the UK, Canada and many other countries watch them, so the companies can advertise their products all over the world.

> **NOTICE!**
> Find three countries mentioned in the text. Which countries take *the* before their name?

B ANALYSE Read the article in Exercise A again.

Function Complete the table with examples from Exercise A.

We use the definite article *the* ...	Examples
when something has been mentioned before.	*the adverts,* _____, _____, _____
when there is only one of something or the reference is to a whole group.	*the universe, the car industry, the BBC,* _____, _____,
with some country names that have plural nouns or the words *States*, *Kingdom* or *Republic* in the name.	*the Netherlands,* _____, _____
with geographical features.	*the Atlantic Ocean, the Amazon, the Greek Islands*
when the noun answers the question *which?* or *what?*	*the cost of the camera (The cost of what?),* _____

We use no article ...	Examples
with plural countable nouns when talking about them generally.	*adverts,* _____, _____, _____, _____, _____, _____,
with uncountable nouns when talking about them generally.	*money,* _____, _____, _____
with names of people, months, cities, most countries, products, etc.	*Joel Moss Levinson,* _____

C PRACTISE Complete the advert with *the* or put X for no article.

We believe that (1) _____ young people have (2) _____ types of ideas we're looking for, and we're having a competition for a new advert for (3) _____ Jupiter Chocolate! (4) _____ advert will run on (5) _____ internet, and (6) _____ people all over (7) _____ world will see it. We have lots of (8) _____ prizes to give away. (9) _____ top prize is a cruise on (10) _____ River Nile! So send your videos to (11) _____ email address below. We'll announce (12) _____ winners here on this website!

> **WHAT'S RIGHT?**
> ○ She makes videos. The videos are brilliant.
> ○ She makes videos. Videos are brilliant.
> ○ I think adverts in the UK are better than adverts in France.
> ○ I think adverts in the UK are better than adverts in the France.

D NOW YOU DO IT Work in pairs. Talk about what would make a good advert for the competition in Exercise C.

> **HOW TO SAY IT**
>
> **Expressing ideas for an advert**
> *Young people like adverts that are …, so the advert should have …*
> *The advert will be on the internet, so it should …*
> *I like the idea of using children / a handheld camera / music …*
> *The children / the camera / the music could …*

In a text with more than one paragraph, there is a main idea for the whole text. Each paragraph relates to the main idea of the whole text, but also has its own idea and supporting details.

A Read this article. Then choose the title, 1 or 2 below, that best expresses the main idea of the whole article.

1   Boys are now spending almost as much as girls on their prom outfits
2   Prom night is more important for boys than for girls

1   American-style prom nights are sending sales of tuxedos rocketing as boys get a glam makeover to keep up with the girls. Image-conscious teenage lads are ditching trainers and T-shirts for a slick, groomed look, spending 24% more on their outfit than a year ago. And they are tidying up monobrows and facial hair as they head to beauty salons for head-to-toe treatments from eyebrow threading and face masks to spray tans.

2   According to a study by department store Debenhams, the influence of top US programmes like *Beverley Hills 90210* and fashion icons including David Beckham and screen hero James Bond are smartening up male school leavers with sales of tuxedos rocketing 60% and formal shirts, shoes and bow ties soaring by 20%. Boys are kitting themselves out with cufflinks, cummerbunds and silk hankies, spending an average £385 on the school prom, compared with girls who blow £467.25.

3   Debenhams spokesman Ed Watson said: 'The amount a guy will spend on getting prom-ready is now close to rivalling a girl. Prom fever has hit and guys are going all out to look their best and it doesn't stop at the suit. Budding prom kings want to achieve a polished, groomed look and are looking to celebrities such as David Beckham and Daniel Craig for their inspiration.'

4   The big party to mark the end of school has snowballed in recent years, taking over from the traditional disco in the school hall to themed events in posh locations. British teenagers have made *High School Musical*-style prom nights big business as they follow the American trend for stretch limos, designer frocks, suits and expensive accessories.

5   And they have given rise to the 'Promzilla' – prom-obsessed teenage girls who book their outfits up to a year in advance and plan the night with the precision of a would-be bride. Mr Watson said: 'The ladies seem to be better prepared – we have seen an increase in occasionwear sales since January whereas guys have been rushing in last minute to get ready for the big night.'

Cost of prom night

Boys

Suit	£110
Shirt	£28
Bow tie	£12
Shoes	£65
Accessories	£60
Beauty treatments	£69
Haircut	£41
TOTAL:	**£385**

Girls

Dress	£160
Shoes	£30
Bag	£25
Hair styling	£30.50
Beauty treatments	£159
Jewellery	£33
TOTAL:	**£437.50**

B Read the text again. Match each paragraph 1–5 to the sentence a–e which best expresses the main idea of the paragraph.

a)   Proms have become big events in recent years.

b)   Boys now spend almost as much as girls on their prom.

c)   British boys are dressing up for prom night more than they used to.

d)   Girls start getting ready for their prom earlier than boys do.

e)   A study shows that boys are spending a lot of money to look like celebrities.

C Read each paragraph in Exercise A again. Underline key words and phrases which helped you identify the main idea of the paragraph.

D 🗣 Work in pairs. Answer the questions.

1   What specific things do British boys now do to look their best for prom night?

2   What is causing boys to change the way they dress for their proms?

3   How have British end-of-school celebrations changed in recent years?

4   What is a 'Promzilla'?

5   Look at the list of prom night costs. Which things are similar for boys and girls? Do any of the things on the list surprise you?

GRAMMAR: indirect questions

A 🎧 **1.13 LANGUAGE IN CONTEXT** Listen to the conversation below. What is the customer asking the shop assistant about?

Assistant:	Good morning. How can I help you?
Customer:	Hi. I'm looking for a CD by Paul Oaks. I think it's called *Forward*. Do you know if you have it in stock?
Assistant:	Hmm, I'm afraid we've sold out. I could order it for you.
Customer:	Oh thanks, that's a good idea. <u>Do you know</u> how long it takes to arrive?
Assistant:	It takes about four days.
Customer:	Oh, that's quite long. I wonder whether it's easier to get it online?
Assistant:	Well, you could download the MP3 from our website.
Customer:	Ah I see. Do you have any idea how much that costs?
Assistant:	Yes, it's cheaper – only £6.99. So could you tell me if you still need me to order the CD?
Customer:	I think I'll just download it. Thanks for your help. Can you tell me what the website address is?
Assistant:	It's yourmegamusic.com.
Customer:	Thanks!
Assistant:	You're welcome!

> **NOTICE!**
> Look at the underlined phrase in the conversation which introduces an indirect question. Find and underline other similar phrases that introduce indirect questions.

B ANALYSE Read the conversation in Exercise A again.

Form Complete the table with examples from Exercise A.

	Direct question **Use normal question order**	Indirect question **Use affirmative word order**
Information question	How long does it take to arrive?	*Do you know how long* **(1)** _____?
	How much does that cost?	*Do you have any idea* **(2)** _____?
	What's the website address?	*Can you tell me* **(3)** _____?
Yes/No question	Do you have it in stock?	*Do you* **(4)** _____ *have it in stock?*
	Is it easier to get it online?	*I* **(5)** _____ *it's easier to get it online?*
	Do you still need me to order the CD?	**(6)** _____ *me if you still need me to order the CD?*

Function Choose the correct option to complete the statement.

Using indirect questions is more / less polite.

C PRACTISE Write indirect questions starting with the phrases given.

1 Do you have this in a bigger size?
Do you know *if you have this in a bigger size?*

2 Do you accept credit cards?
Could you tell me _____?

3 When can you send it to me?
I wonder _____?

4 How much is this?
Can you tell me _____?

5 What's her email address?
Do you know _____?

6 What was the total cost?
Could you tell me _____?

7 Did Sally get a new phone?
I wonder _____?

8 Who is the manager?
Can you tell me _____?

> **WHAT'S RIGHT?**
> ○ Could you tell me what time the shop closes?
> ○ Could you tell me what time does the shop close?
> ○ I wonder where did he buy his tablet?
> ○ I wonder where he bought his tablet?
> ○ Do you know if it is expensive?
> ○ Do you know if is it expensive?

D 🗣 **NOW YOU DO IT** Work in pairs. Think of five questions to ask your partner. Ask and answer each other's questions politely.

A: *Could you tell me what the last CD you bought was?*
B: *Of course. The last CD I bought was …*

VOCABULARY: problems with products

A Match these sentences to the correct picture.

1 It doesn't fit. It's too big.
2 It doesn't work. It doesn't turn on.
3 They're broken. I hope I can fix them.
4 It's the wrong colour. I want a lighter blue.
5 It's the wrong one. The holes don't match.
6 There's something missing. I can't complete it.

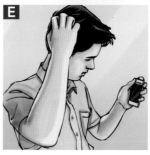

B Work in pairs. Read what these customers say. Use phrases from Exercise A to describe the problem.

> 1 When I try to turn the camera on, nothing happens.

> 2 I wanted a pink mobile phone, but they sent me a blue one.

> 3 There should be a DVD of extras too, but there's only one disc in the case.

> 4 I was trying to put a new game into the console when part of the plastic fell off!

> 5 I asked for the latest model, but this one is at least 18 months old.

> 6 I'll take it back to the shop and see if they have an extra large.

C Work in groups. Talk about problems you have had with products.

A: *I bought paint to paint my bedroom, but it was the wrong colour. I wanted pale yellow, but it was really bright when I put it on the wall, and I didn't like it.*
B: *What did you do?*
A: *I took it back to the paint shop and they re-mixed it for me. Now it's perfect.*

WRITING: an opinion paragraph

A Read this paragraph from an article. What four advantages of shopping online does it mention? What disadvantage does it mention?

> Whether it's CDs, DVDs, books, clothes or even food, many people these days do their shopping online. And why not? Shopping online is great! The main advantage is that it's so convenient. You can shop whenever you want and not only when the shops are open. Another advantage is that you don't have to wait in a long queue to pay for things. Also, it's much easier to shop around for the lowest prices. Finally, you don't have to carry all your purchases home because everything is delivered straight to your door. However, some people feel nervous about using their credit cards online. It's true that not all websites are safe, but you just need to be careful. All in all, I love shopping online, and I sometimes wonder why people don't buy everything online!

B 1.14 Listen to this advert. Make notes on the three advantages of shopping in a real shop that it mentions. Why doesn't it mention a disadvantage?

C Write a paragraph about the advantages of shopping in a real shop. Use ideas from Exercise B, and your own ideas. Present three or four advantages and one disadvantage.

HOW TO SAY IT

Sequencing words and phrases

The main advantage/reason/thing is that …

Another advantage/reason/thing is that …

First, … Second, … Third, … Also, … Finally, …

Introducing a contrasting opinion/disadvantage

However, … …, but …

Summarising an opinion

All in all, … In general, …

A 🎧 **1.15** Listen to these sounds and words. Can you hear the difference between the /ɪ/ and /iː/ sounds? Now listen again and repeat.

/ɪ/ fill   /iː/ feel

B 🎧 **1.16** 📝 Listen and write /i/ or /iː/ next to each word. Practise saying the words.

grin ___	green ___	eat ___	it ___	sit ___	seat ___	slip ___	sleep ___	steal ___	still ___

C 🎧 **1.17** 📝 Work in pairs. Practise saying these sentences. Pay special attention to the /ɪ/ and /iː/ sounds. Listen and check.

1 Please drink this green tea.   2 I feel like sitting on this seat.   3 The thin sheep will eat the big cheese.

VOCABULARY: solutions to problems with products

A Match the problems 1–6 with the solutions a–f.

1 It doesn't fit. ☐
2 It doesn't work. ☐
3 It's the wrong colour. ☐
4 There's something missing. ☐
5 It's broken. ☐
6 It's the wrong one. ☐

a) Can I **order the missing piece**?
b) Can you **replace it**, please?
c) Could I **exchange it for the right one**?
d) I'd like to **exchange it for a white one**.
e) Can I **get it repaired**, or **exchange it for a new one**?
f) Can I **exchange it for a larger size**, please?

B Complete each conversation with an appropriate phrase in bold from Exercise A.

1

Customer: Someone gave me this T-shirt as a gift, but it's too small for me.

Assistant: We'll be very happy to _____.

2

Customer: When I opened the box of my new phone, I realised that the charger wasn't there.

Assistant: I'm sorry to hear that. Of course we'll _____ immediately.

3

Customer: I ordered a tablet online. I ticked white for the colour choice, but the one I got was black.

Assistant: Just send us the one you have, and we'll be happy to _____.

4

Customer: I bought this DVD for my brother's birthday, but when I got home, I realised that he'd asked for a different one.

Assistant: Don't worry. We can just _____.

5

Customer: The keyboard on this laptop seems to be broken. Could you tell me if you can _____?

Assistant: I'm not sure, but leave it with me and we'll try.

6

Customer: I bought this DVD player here yesterday, but it won't turn on.

Assistant: Oh, I'm sorry. Let me _____ for you.

SPEAKING: politely insisting

⚙ When you want someone to do something for you, you may need to insist. Start with an appropriate phrase and explain what you want them to do politely but firmly. If necessary, repeat what you want to happen.

A 🎧 **1.18** Listen to the conversation below. What solutions does the salesperson propose?

Customer:	Hi. I bought a tablet here recently, and I'm not happy with it. I'd like to get a refund.
Salesperson:	Oh, I'm sorry about that. What's the problem?
Customer:	I don't like it. The data download is really slow, and the camera isn't good.
Salesperson:	OK. Have you got the receipt?
Customer:	No. I lost it.
Salesperson:	I'm sorry, but I'm afraid we don't usually give refunds without a receipt.
Customer:	I definitely bought it here.
Salesperson:	Yes, madam, but the problem is that we need the receipt.
Customer:	I understand that, but maybe you can check your records. I paid by credit card. My last name is Jackson.
Salesperson:	OK, let me check. Yes, here it is. You bought the Lasertab. Well, we could exchange it for another model. You'd just have to pay the difference in cost.
Customer:	I'm sorry to insist, but I don't really want to exchange it. I want a refund.
Salesperson:	The other thing we could do is install a memory upgrade. That's £60.
Customer:	No, thanks. I would really prefer a refund.
Salesperson:	OK, madam. Just a moment. I'll need to get the manager.

B Read the conversation in Exercise A again. What phrases does the customer use to politely insist? Underline them.

C 🗣 Work in pairs. Roleplay a situation like the one in Exercise A. When you finish, swap roles.

- Student A, you are the customer. You bought something (decide what), but there is a problem (decide what). Explain the problem and say you want a refund. You have lost the receipt. Insist politely!
- Student B, you are the sales assistant. Ask for the receipt. Explain that you can't give the customer their money without a receipt. Propose some solutions.

LISTENING: to a complaint

A Have you ever had a problem with an electronic product? If so, what? What other possible problems with these products can you think of?

B 🎧 **1.19** Listen to the conversations. Complete the employee evaluation forms.

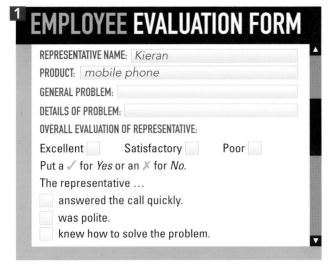

1 EMPLOYEE EVALUATION FORM

REPRESENTATIVE NAME: *Kieran*
PRODUCT: *mobile phone*
GENERAL PROBLEM:
DETAILS OF PROBLEM:
OVERALL EVALUATION OF REPRESENTATIVE:

Excellent ☐   Satisfactory ☐   Poor ☐
Put a ✓ for *Yes* or an ✗ for *No*.
The representative …
☐ answered the call quickly.
☐ was polite.
☐ knew how to solve the problem.

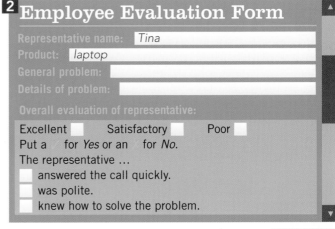

2 Employee Evaluation Form

Representative name: *Tina*
Product: *laptop*
General problem:
Details of problem:
Overall evaluation of representative:

Excellent ☐   Satisfactory ☐   Poor ☐
Put a   for *Yes* or an   for *No*.
The representative …
☐ answered the call quickly.
☐ was polite.
☐ knew how to solve the problem.

LifeSkills

PERSUADING OTHERS

- Consider your audience (age, preferences, habits, etc).
- Think of arguments and then adjust them to your audience and the context (business, social, etc).
- Present your ideas. Be prepared to respond to objections!

A You are going to design a new credit card to be marketed to young adults. First, read these adverts for different credit cards. What are the key features of each card? Which card do you think will be your main competitor? Why?

ECO-CARD

The new credit card from Multibank helps you protect the environment as you spend!

Every time you use it, we give 2% to EnviroAid, a charity organisation that invests in projects around the world. Not only that, but every Eco-Card holder is entered into a monthly draw to win an eco-holiday to one of EnviroAid's projects around the world!

ECO-CARD

9658 5554 4520 7845

VALID FROM ▼ 02/13 UNTIL END ▼ 09/17

MR A.N. OTHER

GOLD PLUS

Your Gold Plus card is your ticket to freedom. It has a low interest rate (14%) and is accepted everywhere you see the Gold sign. That includes thousands of travel agents across the country – and when you buy tickets for any bus, train or plane, we'll give you a massive 10% discount! So what are you waiting for? Hit the road with Gold Plus!

GOLD PLUS

4869 4903 2045 2394

VALID FROM ▼ 02/13 UNTIL END ▼ 09/17

MR A.N. OTHER

B Work in pairs. You are going to design your credit card and then persuade your classmates to apply for it. To get started, answer these questions about your target audience.

1 What things do they buy? Brainstorm a list.
2 What things do they like and dislike? Brainstorm a list.
3 What issues are important to them? Brainstorm a list.
4 Which of the things on your lists do you think are most important to your audience? Put a star (*) next to them.

C 🗣 With the same partner, complete the new product profile below for your credit card. Use the information about your audience from Exercise B to help you decide on the key features. Make your ideas interesting, but realistic. Think of possible objections so that you can be ready to respond to them!

NEW PRODUCT PROFILE

Name of card: _____

_____

Types of people who will use the card: _____

_____

Key features:

_____

_____

_____

_____

Possible objections:

_____

_____

_____

D Now create an advert for your credit card to appear in a magazine. Describe the image that will appear in your advert and write a short text like the adverts in Exercise A. Remember who your audience is.

E 🗣 With your partner, present your ideas to the class. Follow the instructions below. Remember: your aim is to persuade as many people in the class as you can to sign up for your credit card!

- Describe the image and read the text from your advert. Remember that your body language and tone of voice are very important.
- Explain your ideas clearly, using what you know about your audience's needs and interests.
- Answer any questions.
- Respond to any objections and try to persuade your classmates by explaining your ideas further and appealing to their emotions.

While you are listening to presentations:
- Listen carefully to the description of each credit card.
- Make notes of the things you like and don't like about each card.
- Ask questions and raise any objections you have.

After you have listened to all of the descriptions, decide whether you will apply for one of the credit cards, and if so, which one.

F 🗣 Take a class vote. Which credit card is the most popular?

HOW TO SAY IT 🗣

Raising objections and making suggestions
Yes, but you have to remember that …
That's a good point, but …
You're interested in … so I think you should …
Wouldn't you like to …?

 REFLECT … How can the skill of persuading others be useful to you in **Study and Learning** and **Self and Society**?

Language wrap-up

1 VOCABULARY

Complete the sentences with the words in the box. (15 points)

a larger size   broken   exchange   fit   fix it   get it repaired   match   missing   order
replace   the wrong colour   the wrong one   too small   turn on   work

1   I bought these jeans, but when I got home I realised they were _____ . I wanted dark blue, not black. Can I _____ them for the blue ones?
2   If your new MP3 player doesn't _____ , take it back to the shop. It has a guarantee, so they'll have to _____ it with another one.
3   Mum got me a great new shirt. It's small, and I'm medium. It doesn't _____ . I'm going to try and exchange it for _____ .
4   Liz sent me a porcelain vase for my birthday, but when I opened the parcel, it was _____ ! Unfortunately, I don't think I can _____ .
5   When I opened the box, I realised the instructions were _____ . Can I _____ some new ones?
6   I bought _____ . The holes don't _____ the ones on my laptop.
7   These shoes are _____ . My feet hurt!
8   My computer stopped working. It doesn't _____ . I'm going to _____ at the shop if I can.

11 – 15 correct: I can talk about problems with products and solutions to those problems.
0 – 10 correct: Look again at the vocabulary sections on pages 37 and 38.   SCORE: /15

2 GRAMMAR

A   Complete these sentences with *the* or *X* (no article). (9 points)

1   I think that _____ sports companies should advertise on _____ internet.
2   Do you like _____ adverts for cars that are on TV now?
3   I prefer _____ advert from _____ Japan.
4   I think _____ UK has very interesting adverts.
5   Almost all _____ people who saw _____ adverts in the competition liked them.
6   People all over _____ world see the same adverts for certain products.

B   Complete each question so that it means the same as the first one. (6 points)

1   How much is this?
    Can you tell me _____ ?
2   Does the price include delivery?
    Do you know _____ ?
3   Do adverts affect how you shop?
    I wonder _____ ?
4   Which adverts do you find interesting?
    Could you tell me _____ ?
5   How do adverts persuade people?
    Do you know _____ ?
6   Is this advert right for our audience?
    I wonder _____ ?

11 – 15 correct: I can use the definite article accurately and I can use indirect questions.
0 – 10 correct: Look again at the grammar sections on pages 34 and 36.   SCORE: /15

WRITING WORKSHOP
an opinion paragraph

A Read this paragraph from a blog. What is the writer's opinion of film cameras? How many reasons does the writer give for his opinion?

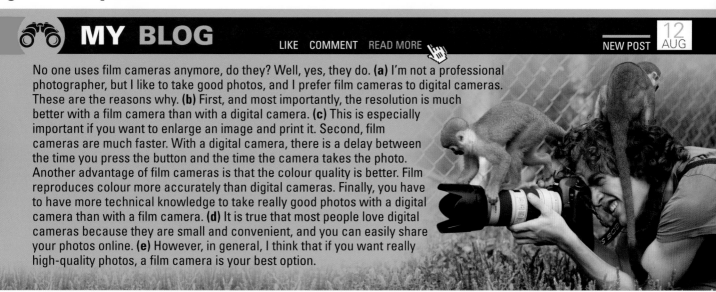

MY BLOG

LIKE   COMMENT   READ MORE

NEW POST   12 AUG

No one uses film cameras anymore, do they? Well, yes, they do. **(a)** I'm not a professional photographer, but I like to take good photos, and I prefer film cameras to digital cameras. These are the reasons why. **(b)** First, and most importantly, the resolution is much better with a film camera than with a digital camera. **(c)** This is especially important if you want to enlarge an image and print it. Second, film cameras are much faster. With a digital camera, there is a delay between the time you press the button and the time the camera takes the photo. Another advantage of film cameras is that the colour quality is better. Film reproduces colour more accurately than digital cameras. Finally, you have to have more technical knowledge to take really good photos with a digital camera than with a film camera. **(d)** It is true that most people love digital cameras because they are small and convenient, and you can easily share your photos online. **(e)** However, in general, I think that if you want really high-quality photos, a film camera is your best option.

B Read the blog again. Match sentences a–e in the blog with their functions 1–5 below.

1 the main reason for the writer's opinion ___
2 a summary or restatement of the opinion ___
3 another reason for the writer's opinion ___
4 the topic sentence, stating the writer's opinion ___
5 a contrasting opinion ___

C You are going to write an opinion paragraph in favour of digital cameras. First, make notes about the advantages of digital cameras.

1 the main reason in favour of digital cameras _____
2 other reasons to support your opinion _____ _____ _____
3 a contrasting opinion _____
4 a summary or restatement of your opinion _____

D Write a paragraph in favour of digital cameras in your notebook. Use your notes from Exercise C to help you.

HOW TO SAY IT

Sequencing words
First,/Second,/Third, …
Another reason is …
Also, …
Introducing a contrasting opinion
However, …
but …
Summarising or restating an opinion
All in all, …
In general, …

HOW ARE YOU DOING?

Look back at your writing and tick the statements that are true.
○ I have clearly stated my opinion in my topic sentence.
○ I have included at least three reasons for my opinion.
○ I have given a contrasting opinion.
○ I have used sequencing words.
Now ask a partner to look at your writing and tick.
Does the paragraph clearly explain the reasons for the writer's opinion?
● Well done!
○ Nearly!
   Look at the unit again.
● Think again!
   Ask your teacher for help.

UNIT 4 TAKING CARE OF BUSINESS

IN THIS UNIT YOU

- learn language to talk about business, products and services
- write a paragraph explaining a point of view
- read an online guide to setting up a business
- listen to customers' emotions and attitudes
- talk about an unusual service
- learn strategies for converting problems into opportunities
- ▶ watch a video about setting up a business

WRITING
organising a paragraph

Why is it a good idea to write a concluding sentence in a paragraph explaining a point of view?

LISTENING
identifying emotion and attitude

Is it a good idea to show anger when you are making a complaint about a product or a service? Why or why not?

LIFE SKILLS

WORK & CAREER

Turning problems into opportunities
What does the phrase 'There are no problems, only opportunities' mean? Do you think it's true?

A Look at the list of businesses. Tick the ones that would be interesting to you and that you think you have the right skills for.

Ten businesses that you can start for less than £5,000!

1	eCommerce	☐	6	A market stall	☐
2	Wedding planning	☐	7	Sports coaching	☐
3	Childcare and babysitting	☐	8	Home maintenance services	☐
4	Tutoring	☐	9	Cleaning services	☐
5	Editing and proofreading	☐	10	IT support and repairs	☐

HOW TO SAY IT

Talking about preferences and abilities

I would be a good editor/wedding planner/IT person/coach.

I'm good at planning/writing/selling things/sports/IT.

I would like to have a market stall/ IT business/ebusiness.

I have good writing/computer/language/ planning skills.

I like children/weddings/mending things/ organising.

B Work in groups. Talk about what types of businesses you would be interested in starting up and why. You can talk about the businesses on this page and any other business ideas that you have.

A: *I think I would be good at home maintenance. I do all the repairs around my house.*

B: *Really? I would hire you. I don't know how to do anything like that! I would be a good proofreader. I like to write, and I have good grammar and spelling.*

WRITING: organising a paragraph page 27 ⚙

In a paragraph where you argue for or against something and explain your point of view, you can organise the main points by listing them from the most to the least important, or vice versa.

A Read the paragraph and answer the questions.

1 Does the writer argue for or against lots of planning?
2 Which is the topic sentence? Which is the concluding sentence?
3 Are the points organised from the most to the least important, or from the least to the most important?
4 How many main points does the writer include?
5 What additional information does the writer include to support or explain each point?

Many people like to plan every detail of their lives, but in fact, too much planning is just as bad as too little planning. First, planners are often inflexible. They get nervous or angry if they have to do something that isn't in their plan. Another problem is that they spend too much time making a list of things to do. They don't have any time left to do the things on their list! Another problem is that many people make very long and ambitious lists. When they can't do everything on their list, they feel frustrated. Finally, in my opinion, the biggest problem with planning too much is that people get stuck in the planning stage. They think they have to resolve every detail before they start something, so they never start. Of course, it's good to plan, but don't spend all your time planning instead of doing things!

B 🗣 Work in pairs. You are going to write a paragraph arguing the opposite point of view. First, make notes to help you decide what to say.

Topic sentence: _____
Point 1: _____   Additional information: _____
Point 2 (etc.): _____   Additional information: _____
Concluding sentence: _____

C 🗣 With your partner, decide whether you want to list your points in order of the most to the least important or vice versa. Then write your paragraph.

D 🗣 Work with another pair. Is the argument clear? Are the points organised clearly? Is there additional information to support each point?

VOCABULARY: business

A Complete the phrases with the correct verb, a or b.

1 _____ a business plan
   a) create   b) advertise
2 _____ a website
   a) research   b) set up
3 _____ the target market and the competition
   a) register   b) research
4 _____ a product or service online, in print publications, with signs or on radio or TV
   a) plan   b) advertise

5 _____ a logo and promotional material
   a) launch   b) design
6 _____ a business
   a) design   b) launch
7 _____ a marketing strategy
   a) plan   b) advertise
8 _____ a business with the proper authorities
   a) set up   b) register

B 🗣 Work in pairs. Number the phrases in Exercise A in the order you think you would do them when starting a business.

C 🗣 Work in pairs and discuss these questions.

1 What do you have to do to set up your own business?
2 What do you think is the best way to advertise a new product or service?

GRAMMAR: causative *have* and *get*

A LANGUAGE IN CONTEXT Read the website information. Would you use this service? Why or why not?

GET IT DONE!

HOME | ABOUT US | SERVICES BY AREA | PLACE AN ORDER

The all-in-one solution for busy people
Too busy to get your hair cut? To take the dog to the vet? To shop for your mum's birthday present? Too busy even to look for people to do these things for you? Get us to do it!
- Get your hair cut in your own home when it's convenient for you.
- Have dinner cooked and served in your own home. Have us cook you a fabulous dinner while you spend time with your family.
- Have your home computer system checked by an IT professional.
- Need to wash the dog? Get our professionals to do it at your home.

These are just a few of the many services we offer!
Click on *Services by area* and enter your postcode to find a complete list of services available in your area.
What are you waiting for? Get it done!

NOTICE!
Underline the phrases with *have* and *get*. Which phrases use the past participle? Which phrase uses the base form of the verb? Which uses the *to-* infinitive?

B ANALYSE Read the text in Exercise A again.

Form Complete the table with examples from Exercise A.

get/have + direct object + past participle	have + indirect object + base form	get + indirect object + infinitive form
Get your hair cut.	4 _____	5 _____
1 _____		6 _____
2 _____		
3 _____		

Function Choose the correct option to complete the rules.
1 To *have/get something done* means that …
  a) you do something you need to do.
  b) another person does something for you.
2 *Have someone do something* and *get someone to do something* mean …
  a) the same thing: to ask/hire someone to do something for you
  b) different things.

WHAT'S RIGHT?
- ○ I'm having my bicycle fixed.
- ○ I'm having fixed my bicycle.
- ○ I'm getting my hair to be cut.
- ○ I'm getting my hair cut.

C PRACTISE Complete the questions with the correct form of the verbs in brackets.

1 Where can I get my car _____? (*fix*)
2 Where can I have my hair _____? (*cut*)
3 Who can I get _____ my phone line? (*repair*)
4 Who can I call to have my house _____? (*paint*)
5 I want to have someone _____ my car seats. (*clean*)
6 Where can I get someone _____ a stereo in my car? (*install*)
7 Is there a quiet place where I can get my homework _____? (*do*)
8 Is there an online service where I can have someone _____ a website for me? (*create*)

D ▱ NOW YOU DO IT Work in groups. Ask and answer the questions from Exercise C.

A: *Where can I get my car fixed?*
B: *There's a good car service centre on …*

PRONUNCIATION: compound nouns vs compound adjectives

A 🎧 **1.20** Listen to the phrases in the table. For each group, tick the word that is stressed.

Compound nouns
* noun ☐ + noun ☐

Compound adjectives
* adjective ☐ + noun ☐
* adverb ☐ + past participle ☐

	Compound nouns		Compound adjectives
1	You have to make a **business plan**.	1	These chairs are very **high quality**.
2	We need a **marketing strategy**.	2	This jacket isn't very **well made**.
3	Our office has a good **cleaning service**.	3	Their salespeople are very **well informed**.
4	My sister is a **wedding planner**.	4	Cars are very **poorly made** these days.

B 🎧 **1.21** Read these sentences and underline the stressed words. Listen and check.

1 I've never played this **computer game** before. Is it good?
2 This change was very **last minute**. Apologies for any inconvenience.
3 Your business idea is really **high risk**.
4 I had my **phone line** repaired yesterday.
5 We bought a nice TV at that big **department store**.
6 He's very **low profile** in the office but he's excellent at his job.

C 🗣 Work in pairs. Practise saying the sentences in Exercise B with the stress in the correct places.

VOCABULARY: describing products and services

A Write the words in the box in the correct columns in the table.

helpful   high quality   polite   poorly made   poor quality   professional   rude
unhelpful   well informed   uninformed   unprofessional   well made

People		Products	
Positive	Negative	Positive	Negative

B Complete the sentences with words from the table and any other necessary words to express your opinions.

1 I think most shop assistants are _____.
2 Products made in my country are usually _____.
3 I think the food at _____ [name of a restaurant] is
   really _____, and the staff are
   _____.
4 Imported products from _____ [country] are usually
   _____.
5 To work in a shop, you need to be _____ and
   _____.

C 🗣 Work in pairs. Compare opinions. Say whether you agree or disagree with your partner.

A: *I think most shop assistants are …*
B: *So do I. And they're often very …*

HOW TO SAY IT 🗣

Agreeing and disagreeing
I think so, too. / I agree with you.
I don't really agree because …
Well, actually, I think …

A Discuss these questions as a class.

1 Why do you think more people don't start their own businesses?
2 What are some things you have to think about and do if you want to start a business?

B Choose T (true) or F (false) for the statements. Then read the article to check your answers.

1 Most people who want their own business start one.   T / F
2 Starting a business is always expensive.   T / F
3 It is very difficult to start a business to sell things online.   T / F
4 Selling a service is a good business option.   T / F
5 You have to get professionals to help you create your business plan.   T / F
6 Running a business is as much work as working for someone else.   T / F

DIY BUSINESS START-UPS

Many people would like to have their own business, but most never do it. Starting a business isn't easy, but with passion, hard work and a little creative thinking, you can do it!

Maybe you think starting a business is too expensive and complicated. Think again! You don't have to be a millionaire to start a business like these:

eCommerce: You simply join an eCommerce site and start selling things! Of course, you need to think about what you want to sell and you need to do research to find out what people are already selling, but this is one of the easiest businesses to launch on a low budget.

A service business: You offer a service like babysitting, lawn care, basic home repairs, shopping for people, etc. Busy people often need to have other people do things for them. The key is to set up a website and project a professional image.

Once you decide to start a business, you need to do the work to make it a success:

First, research the business. What's the competition? Which businesses of this type are successful, and why? What kinds of goods or services does the market want?

The next thing you have to do is plan. There are online sites to show you how to create a business plan or a marketing strategy, or design a website. If you can pay to have professionals create a logo and set up a website for you, that's great. If not, use one of the many good online sites.

Finally, once you launch your business, you have to be prepared to work, work, work. Many people think that having a business is easier than working for a company. It isn't! Running a business is very hard work, but it can also be very satisfying, both financially and personally.

C Work in groups. Answer these questions.

1 What small local businesses and online businesses do you, your family and your friends use?
2 What does each business do or sell? Make a list.
3 What new businesses could you start in your area? Brainstorm ideas.

How about a combined hair salon and internet café? You can check your email while your friend has her hair cut.

D Tell the class your ideas. Say which of the ideas you heard you think would really work.

A 🎧 **1.22 LANGUAGE IN CONTEXT Listen to the conversation. What are Patty and Anna complaining about?**

Patty: Oh, I am so <u>frustrated</u> with all of these huge electronics shops! The salespeople are completely uninterested in helping customers!

Anna: I agree. These shops are really <u>frustrating</u> and annoying. You can never get anyone to help you, and if you do find someone, they don't seem to know very much. That man you talked to looked surprised when you started asking questions!

Patty: I know. I think he was as confused as I was! It's a shame that there aren't many shops with good service anymore.

Anna: Yeah, it's a depressing feature of 21st century life! OK, I'm exhausted. Let's go and have lunch.

Patty: Good idea. Let's go to Jenny's Café. I really like their frozen yoghurt.

NOTICE!

Look at the underlined words in the conversation. Which is a past participle? Which is a present participle? Underline other present and past participles in the text.

B **ANALYSE Read the conversation in Exercise A again.**

Function Choose the correct word, *present* or *past*, to complete the rules. Then give examples from Exercise A.

1 _____ participles used as adjectives describe an effect on a person or thing.

a _____   c _____   e _____
b _____   d _____   f _____

2 _____ participles used as adjectives describe the person or thing that causes an effect.

a _____   b _____   c _____

Form Complete the pairs of adjectives.

frustrated – *frustrating*   confused – _____
uninterested – _____   _____ – depressing
_____ – annoying   exhausted – _____
surprised – _____

WHAT'S RIGHT?
○ My new phone is amazed!
○ My new phone is amazing!
○ Were you surprised when you got a tablet for your birthday?
○ Were you surprising when you got a tablet for your birthday?

C **PRACTISE Choose the correct adjective form to complete the sentences.**

1 I like interesting / interested, unusual furniture.
2 I thought that was a very entertaining / entertained film!
3 Our business goal is to have 100% satisfying / satisfied customers.
4 Sofia is very exciting / excited about her new tablet.
5 I want to relax before we go out because I had a really tiring / tired day.
6 I don't like that colour blue. It makes me feel depressing / depressed.
7 Almost all children's toys are importing / imported from China these days.
8 I think this product manual is confusing / confused. I don't understand it.

D 🗣 **NOW YOU DO IT Work in groups. Talk about the following things and how they make you feel. Use as many participle adjectives as possible.**

• shopping at big shopping centres
• shopping in open-air markets
• talking to technical support people on the phone
• shopping at your favourite store

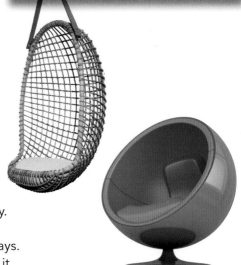

LISTENING: identifying emotion and attitude page 24 ⚙

When you listen to someone, notice how the words they use and their tone of voice can express their emotions and attitude.

A Match the phrases 1–5 to the attitudes a–e they express.

1 Perfect! ☐   a) satisfied
2 Let me check. ☐   b) dissatisfied
3 I'm not happy with this. ☐   c) without an opinion
4 Really? How annoying. ☐   d) sympathetic
5 It's up to you. ☐   e) helpful

B »)) 1.23 Listen to five short conversations. Circle the attitude of each speaker.

1 Customer: a) sympathetic b) satisfied
  Assistant: a) helpful b) without an opinion
2 Customer: a) dissatisfied b) satisfied
  Assistant: a) helpful b) unhelpful
3 Woman 1: a) dissatisfied b) unhelpful
  Woman 2: a) helpful b) without an opinion
4 Woman: a) dissatisfied b) without an opinion
  Man: a) helpful b) unhelpful
5 Woman 1: a) unhelpful b) dissatisfied
  Woman 2: a) satisfied b) sympathetic

C Listen to the conversations in Exercise B again. After each conversation, say the phrases which helped you identify the attitudes.

SPEAKING: talking about a business

A »)) 1.24 Listen to the conversation. What kind of service does Isabel's business offer?

B Listen to the conversation in Exercise A again and:
- underline the questions Mia asks to find out more information.
- choose the phrases Isabel uses to explain what her business is about.

Mia: I heard you left your job recently!
Isabel: Yes, I left because I wanted to start a home-organising business.
Mia: A home-organising business? What is that, exactly?
Isabel: The main thing we do is de-clutter, that is, throw away old things and reorganise cupboards, wardrobes, even entire rooms.
Mia: Wow. Aren't people worried that you'll throw away things they want to keep?
Isabel: Not really. You see, we consult the family before we make any big changes.
Mia: Right. So throwing away things is all you do?
Isabel: Well, some people really just want to get someone to clean their house, so we offer that service, too.
Mia: So, who uses this kind of service?
Isabel: It's mostly families where both parents work, but anybody can use it.
Mia: It sounds very useful. I would definitely pay someone to reorganise my kitchen!
Isabel: Here's my card! You know, it's very satisfying to see how happy people are with their nice, organised houses.

> **HOW TO SAY IT** 〔{
>
> **Asking for and giving explanations**
> *What is that?*
> *So … (-ing) is all you do?*
> *Who uses this service?*
> *The main thing (we) do is …*
> *… that is …*
> *Well, …*
> *You see/know …*
> *It's mostly …*

C 〔{ Work in pairs. Think of some unusual services that people would pay for. Roleplay a conversation like the one in Exercise A.

LifeSkills

TURNING PROBLEMS INTO OPPORTUNITIES

- Identify problems.
- Brainstorm possible opportunities.
- Identify the advantages and disadvantages of each idea.
- Choose one idea and develop it.

A **Read this text and answer the questions.**

1 What characteristic do many great inventions or ideas share?
2 What is one way to think of an idea for a new business?

There are no problems, only opportunities!

The title of this article is an old saying. You might be tempted to say, 'I don't believe that. My problems are problems, full stop.' But many of the best inventions and business ideas were the result of solving problems. A classic example is the wheel, the earliest example of which was found in Mesopotamia. The ancient Mesopotamians had the problem of moving extremely heavy building materials from place to place. This was a slow process involving many people, until they started to use the wheel. This very simple idea changed civilisation for ever. Another example of a simple, effective solution to a problem is the assembly line. Before 1908, cars were made one by one, and this meant that cars were very, very expensive. In 1908, Henry Ford invented the assembly line. He could produce a large number of cars in a short time, which meant that he could sell his cars to the general public at a much lower price.

Today there are different everyday problems waiting for creative solutions. One way to become a successful entrepreneur is to think of a solution to a problem in your life, become an expert on it, and offer the solution to other people. People are happy to pay for ways to make their lives easier!

B 🗣 Work in pairs. You want to set up a business that will be successful in your local area. Use the table to make a list of big and small problems that affect you or your community.

Problem	Details
Transport	*The university campus is enormous, and students have to walk from one building to another in a short amount of time. People are often late for lectures, and all that walking is tiring and time consuming.*
Food	
Daily chores	
Lifestyle and recreation	
Study and research	
Pets	
Other (specify)	

C With your partner, choose one of the problems from Exercise B. Brainstorm several different business opportunities. Look at the example below. Be creative!

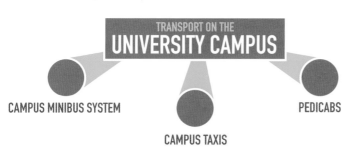

TRANSPORT ON THE
UNIVERSITY CAMPUS

CAMPUS MINIBUS SYSTEM

CAMPUS TAXIS

PEDICABS

D Make a list of advantages and disadvantages of each idea.

Campus minibus system

Advantages: carry lots of people, fast

Disadvantages: expensive investment; legal requirements; requires professional drivers

Campus taxis

Advantages: Fast and comfortable

Disadvantages: Very expensive investment; many legal requirements; too expensive for students

Pedicabs

Advantages: Fairly small investment; few or no legal restrictions; cheap enough for students; drivers can be students

Disadvantages: Slower than buses or taxis; can carry only two people at a time

E Choose your best business idea. Then read the example description below and create a similar table for your idea.

Business idea	Product/Service	Market	Details
A campus minibus system.	To transport students from bus stops to classroom buildings, or from one building to another.	Students and maybe some staff members.	1 Start with about 3 minibuses. 2 Can be used all day. 3 Offer payment options: single journey, multiple journey, termly bus pass.

F Present your business idea to the class. Listen to the other pairs and make a list of all of the different ideas on the board.

G Take a class vote on the best business idea.

HOW TO SAY IT

Presenting a business idea

Our idea is to have a … business.
We're going to offer …
Our main market(s) will be …
The advantages of this idea are …
Here's how it works. We can get people to … / We can charge … / We can have …

? REFLECT … How can the skill of turning problems into opportunities be useful to you in **Study and Learning** and **Self and Society**?

Language wrap-up

1 VOCABULARY

A Complete the sentences with the words in the box. (8 points)

advertise   create   design   launch   plan   register   research   set up

1 My brother will _____ our logo and promotional material. He's an artist.
2 It takes a lot of hard work to _____ your own business.
3 I'm going to have to learn how to _____ a marketing strategy.
4 Will we need to _____ our business with the tax office?
5 To get a loan from the bank, you'll need to _____ a business plan.
6 We are going to _____ a website about the new service we offer.
7 It's a good idea to _____ the target market and the competition.
8 Most businesses these days _____ their products online as well as on radio or TV.

B Choose the correct option to complete the sentences. (7 points)

1 The assistants in the computer shop were very helpful / unhelpful. They showed me the best product for my needs.
2 I'm not going to buy this jacket because it's well made / poorly made.
3 The instructors here are excellent – very uninformed / professional.
4 I don't like this necklace. It looks poor quality / high quality.
5 I'm going to complain to the manager. That assistant was very polite / rude.
6 This shop has a good furniture department. The furniture is inexpensive but high quality / poorly made.
7 I like this shop because the staff are very well informed / high quality.

11 – 15 correct: I can use phrases to talk about business and describe products and services.
0 – 10 correct: Look again at the vocabulary sections on pages 46 and 48.   SCORE: /15

2 GRAMMAR

Complete the conversation with the correct form of the verbs in brackets. (15 points)

Amy: Hi. I've got a problem with my printer – it won't print. Can I get it (1) _____ (check) here?

Salesperson: I'm sorry to hear that. Yes, I can get someone (2) _____ (look) at it. However, I have to tell you that we can't usually repair them.

Amy: Oh! That's really (3) _____ (annoy)! It's only a year old.

Salesperson: I know. It's (4) _____ (frustrate), but they don't have many parts that we can fix or replace.

Amy: Well, it stopped working once before, and I got a friend (5) _____ (fix) it. But I'm really (6) _____ (surprise) that it's stopped working again when it's not even a year old!

Salesperson: Unfortunately we've had a lot of complaints about it.

Amy: Oh, that's (7) _____ (interest). So, I'm not the only person having problems?

Salesperson: No. We've had a lot of (8) _____ (disappoint) customers complaining about this model, and it's always (9) _____ (worry) when we get a lot of complaints about a specific product.

Amy: Are you going to get the manufacturer (10) _____ (do) something about it? Advertisers make all these (11) _____ (amaze) claims about their products, and really, a lot of them are just plastic junk. I'm going to be really (12) _____ (annoy) if I have to buy a new printer.

Salesperson: Well, we'll see what we can do. Now, can I just get you (13) _____ (fill) in this form? It's a bit (14) _____ (confuse), so let me know if you have any questions. Then I'll get one of our engineers (15) _____ (phone) you to let you know when it's ready.

11 – 15 correct: I can use *have* and *get* to talk about services. I can use *-ed* and *-ing* adjectives.
0 – 10 correct: Look again at the grammar sections on pages 47 and 50.   SCORE: /15

A Read the conversation and answer the questions below.

1 Why are these people talking about this topic?
2 Did Jack invent the ideas that he is talking about?
3 Who has positive reactions to the ideas? Who has negative reactions?
4 What does Jack say that people have to do to get ideas for jobs?

James: I don't want to do a boring office job after uni. I want to do something interesting with my life.

Jack: Me too. I've been doing some research on unusual jobs or businesses, and there are some fascinating ideas.

Hayley: Really? Like what?

Jack: Well, for example, James, you love animals, so here's one for you. Dog birthday parties. Guests bring their dogs to the house of the birthday dog, and you go and organise the party. You take lots of dog toys and play games with the dogs, and you give them dog-friendly snacks. The human guests just relax and enjoy the party!

James: Wow, that's an amazing idea!

Imogen: You're joking! People actually have birthday parties for their dogs?

Jack: Believe me, they do. Hayley, you're into fashion, so you'll like this one. You rent out designer accessories, like jewellery, bags and sunglasses. So someone can rent a £600 designer handbag from you for £50.

Hayley: Really? That's a great idea! A lot of people would be interested in that!

Jack: Exactly! And there are lots more great ideas. You just have to do some internet searches and some brainstorming.

B Read the conversation again and find these things.

1 two phrases to encourage the speaker to give more information
2 two phrases to express a positive reaction
3 one phrase to express disbelief
4 two phrases of agreement

C Think of an unusual job that you've heard about, or think of a new idea for a job. Make notes about the job.

D [icon] Work in small groups. Talk about your ideas for unusual jobs. Use some of the phrases from the conversation in Exercise A.

HOW ARE YOU DOING?

Think about your speaking and tick the statements that are true.

I feel confident ...
○ explaining an idea.
○ responding to other people's ideas.
○ using adjectives of opinion.

How do you feel about your speaking generally?

●   ○   ●

Very confident   Not sure ...   Need to practise

UNIT 5 THROUGH THE GRAPEVINE

IN THIS UNIT YOU

- ⚙ learn language to report information
- ⚙ read an article about gossip
- ⚙ talk about things going on in people's lives
- ⚙ listen to phone messages
- ⚙ write a short article about a radio interview
- ⚙ learn how to prepare a report using information from a survey
- ▶ watch a video about social media

READING
distinguishing fact and opinion

What phrases can you think of that indicate that something is an opinion? A fact?

SPEAKING
introducing a new topic

Do you sometimes find it difficult to follow a conversation in English? Why?

LIFE SKILLS
STUDY & LEARNING

reporting information

What kinds of things are surveys useful for? Do you ever have to present information to colleagues or classmates? How?

A Read the headlines. Where do you see or hear stories like these? Do you like reading these types of stories? Why or why not?

SPORTS STAR STRIPPED OF GOLD MEDAL

AUTHORITIES HAVE CONFIRMED THAT HE WAS USING STEROIDS WHEN HE WON THE GOLD.

This week's
FASHION DISASTER

LOCAL COUNCILLOR BUYS SECOND HOME ... AT TAXPAYERS' EXPENSE

BRITAIN'S FAVOURITE COUPLE GET MARRIED IN ITALY

FORMER TOP MODEL
STANDS FOR LOCAL ELECTIONS
TOO MANY SECRETS IN HER PAST?

TOP BUSINESSMAN FOUND GUILTY OF FRAUD

DIETING MADE ME SICK

HOW TO SAY IT

Giving reasons

I don't think stories about ... are real news because those things are not important.

It's news if people want to know about it / if it affects the public.

It's important because it's about a public official / a problem in society.

B  Work in groups. Say which of the stories, if any, you consider to be news. Give reasons.

A: *I don't think articles about fashion are news.*
B: *I don't know. I think anything the public is interested in can be news.*
C: *What about the dieting one?*
A: *I think that's news because the public should know if there's a problem with some kind of diet.*

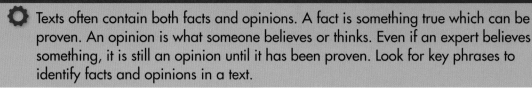

Texts often contain both facts and opinions. A fact is something true which can be proven. An opinion is what someone believes or thinks. Even if an expert believes something, it is still an opinion until it has been proven. Look for key phrases to identify facts and opinions in a text.

A Discuss these questions.

1 Do you think men or women gossip more?
2 In your opinion, is gossiping a positive or negative social activity?

B Read the article. According to the text, is gossip good or bad for us?

What is gossip? We all know about its negative connotations. But, in the opinion of psychologists, gossip is simply informal communication about people, with an evaluative element. People usually state or imply their opinions or feelings about the information, but these don't necessarily have to be negative. In fact, one recent study showed that most gossip is not based on criticism, but is simply socially interesting, and is primarily on topics like relationships, personal experiences and advice.

Most people believe that they don't gossip because they see this kind of information as 'trivial'. They have the idea that they spend most of their time talking about 'important' topics, such as business or politics. According to national surveys, this is particularly true of men, who consider that what they do is 'exchanging information' rather than gossiping. However, research has proven that two-thirds of all human conversation is gossip, for both sexes. Studies also show that, in social situations, men spend 0-5% of the time talking about 'serious' subjects, and that they gossip just as much as women.

People used to spend more time gossiping with their friends and neighbours, but today we have less time for face-to-face social interaction, including gossip. However, in recent years communications technology, especially the smart phone, has given us new ways to gossip. Apart from talking on the phone, people use their phones to get news and gossip through social media platforms like Twitter™ and Facebook™. A survey showed that only 17% of participants use their mobile phones primarily for work purposes. Most people feel that their mobile phones are vital for their social lives.

Whether gossip is in person or via technology, it seems to have social and psychological benefits. Research indicates that gossip can lower stress and can help us establish and maintain relationships, learn social skills, resolve conflicts and reinforce social values. Far from being a negative pastime, gossip can actually be good for you!

IS GOSSIP GOOD?

C Find these phrases in the article. Are they facts or opinions? Underline the words that helped you decide.

1 gossip is simply informal communication about people
2 most gossip is not based on criticism
3 (most people) don't gossip because they see this kind of information as 'trivial'
4 (people) spend most of their time talking about 'important' topics
5 (men) consider that what they do is 'exchanging information'
6 two-thirds of all human conversation is gossip
7 (men) gossip just as much as women
8 only 17% of participants use their mobile phones primarily for work purposes
9 mobile phones are vital for their social lives
10 gossip can lower stress

D Work in pairs. Read the questions in Exercise A again. Have any of your opinions changed after reading the article? Explain your reasons.

I have/haven't changed my opinion about men and women gossiping because …
According to the article, …, so now I think … / but I still think …

GRAMMAR: reported speech

A 1.25 LANGUAGE IN CONTEXT Listen to the conversation below. Why is Eric worried?

Eric: You know, I'm a little worried about Scott.

Steve: Why? What's wrong?

Eric: It's his new job. I think he's really unhappy. A couple of days ago, <u>he</u> told me that he wasn't getting on with his manager and he said that he didn't think his manager liked him. He said he had worked really hard on a report but his manager had asked him to write it all over again because he didn't like it.

Steve: It sounds awful. What else did he say?

Eric: He said <u>he</u> was going to talk to the director the next day, so we should ring him to find out what happened. I told him we would take <u>him</u> out to dinner this week, as well, to cheer him up. What do you think?

Steve: Yeah, that's a good idea. I can do Friday. Are you free then?

> **NOTICE!**
>
> Look at the underlined pronouns. Who do *he* and *him* refer to?
>
> a) Eric b) Steve c) Scott

B ANALYSE Read the conversation in Exercise A again.

Function Choose the correct option to complete the sentence.

We use reported / direct speech to repeat what someone said without using their exact words.

Form Study the table, then choose the correct option to complete the sentences.

	Direct speech	Reported speech
present simple	'I don't think my manager likes me.'	He said that he didn't think his manager liked him.
present continuous	'I'm not getting on with my manager.'	Scott told me that he wasn't getting on with his manager.
past simple	'He asked me to write it all over again.'	He said he had asked him to write it all over again.
present perfect simple	'I've worked really hard on a report.'	He said he had worked really hard on a report.
be going to	'I'm going to talk to the director tomorrow.'	He said he was going to talk to the director the next day.
will	'We will take you out to dinner.'	I told him we would take him out to dinner.
pronouns	I, we, me, us, mine, our	he, she, it, they, him, her, his, hers, theirs, them, their
time expressions	today, tomorrow, yesterday, next week, now, last week	that day, the next day, the day before, the following week, then, the week before
place expressions	here	there

1 Reported / Direct speech doesn't use quotation marks (' ').
2 When we use a verb in the past tense to introduce reported speech, for example, *said* or *told*, we change / don't change the tense in the reported speech.
3 In reported speech, we change / don't change other words the person said, for example, pronouns and time and place expressions.

> **WHAT'S RIGHT?**
>
> ○ He told me he was going to talk to them.
> ○ He said me he was going to talk to them.

C PRACTISE Rewrite these sentences as reported speech.

1 'I don't want to go to the meeting.' (Paula)
 Paula said that she didn't want to go to the meeting.
2 'Sarah and I are going to buy a house.' (Sam)
3 'You won't believe the news!' (Lisa)
4 'I went to a great party last week.' (Gary)
5 'I've promised Rick to help him with his homework today.' (Amanda)
6 'I'm watching a great film on TV now.' (Rita)

D NOW YOU DO IT Make a statement about yourself to your partner. Your partner reports to the class what you said. Correct any errors.

A: *He said that he was going to leave his job.*

B: *No. I said that I was going to start a new job.*

VOCABULARY: oral communication

A Match these verbs and verb phrases with their definitions.

1	argue	a	speak to an audience on an informal occasion _____
2	chat	b	to talk about a specific topic with someone _____
3	discuss	c	to speak to someone in an angry way because you disagree; to try to convince someone that you are right about something _____
4	explain		
5	speak	d	speak to an audience on a formal occasion _____
6	give a speech	e	to talk in a friendly way, or have a short informal conversation; to have a conversation through instant messaging on an electronic device _____
7	give a talk		
8	talk	f	to use words to communicate orally; to have a conversation _____
		g	to talk to someone about something; to use your voice to produce language; to use a particular language (e.g. English) _____
		h	to tell someone something so that they understand it better _____

B Complete the questions with words from Exercise A. Sometimes there is more than one possibility.

1 Do you often _____ online with your friends?
2 Have you ever given a _____ on an important occasion?
3 Do you and your family ever _____ politics?
4 Do you often _____ with your friends about controversial subjects?
5 How many languages do you _____ ?
6 Do you like to _____ to your friends on the phone?
7 Can you _____ the cause of global warming?
8 Have you ever given a _____ to your class or workmates about something?

C Work in pairs. Ask and answer the questions in Exercise B.

SPEAKING: introducing a new topic

It is helpful to listen for phrases that signal a change in the topic in a conversation so that you can follow what people are talking about.

A 1.26 Listen to the conversation below. Circle which of these topics the women talk about.

Andy's party   Danielle's dentist appointment   lecture notes   Megan's party
Megan's phone number   Paul's party   Sarah and Charlie's relationship   Sarah's brother

Danielle:	So are we going to Paul's party on Saturday?
Susie:	Yeah, let's go! Oh, hey, have you heard about Sarah and Charlie?
Danielle:	No, what?
Susie:	They had a big argument and split up! She said he was going out with someone else!
Danielle:	Wow, that's big news … So, who is he going out with?
Susie:	I'm not sure, but Anna told me she thought it was Claire Moore. Oh, and guess what! Your friend Darren invited Laura to Andy's party.
Danielle:	I know. Darren said that Megan wasn't speaking to him because she wanted to go to the party with him.
Susie:	Really?
Danielle:	Yeah. Anyway, I've got to go to the dentist now.
Susie:	All right. Good luck at the dentist! By the way, do you have Megan's phone number?
Danielle:	Yes, I'll text it to you. See you tomorrow. Oh, wait … I nearly forgot. Can you lend me your notes from last week's lecture?
Susie:	OK. I'll email them to you. See you.

B Listen again. Underline the phrases used to introduce a new topic.

C 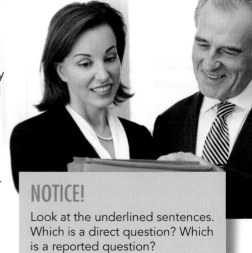 Work in pairs. Have a conversation about something or someone you both know. Include at least three topic changes in the conversation. Practise your conversation several times. Then act it out for the class.

GRAMMAR: reported questions

A 1.27 **LANGUAGE IN CONTEXT** Listen to the conversation below. What kind of gossip were the interviewers interested in?

Candidate:	Hi, Becky. I'm back from the press conference.
Personal assistant:	Hi, Paul. How did it go?
Candidate:	Well, they mostly wanted to talk about silly gossip. They asked if you and I had a 'special relationship'. They wanted to know whether we were going to get married!
Personal assistant:	Oh, right. That is silly gossip. <u>What did you say?</u>
Candidate:	<u>I asked them why the media couldn't focus on real issues.</u> Then I told them that we were friends as well as colleagues, but nothing more.
Personal assistant:	I think they just make up rubbish to entertain the public.
Candidate:	Anyway, when is my next interview?
Personal assistant:	Let's see … You have an interview on *Meet the Candidates* on Thursday evening.

NOTICE!

Look at the underlined sentences. Which is a direct question? Which is a reported question?

B **ANALYSE** Read the conversation in Exercise A again.

Form **Answer the questions. Then complete the table with examples from Exercise A.**

1 What phrases do we often use at the beginning of a reported question?
2 Which two words can we use to report a *yes/no* question?
3 When we use a verb/phrase in the past tense to introduce a reported question, we change / don't change the tense in the reported question.

	Direct question	Reported question
Yes/No questions	Do you and your personal assistant have a 'special relationship'? Are you going to get married?	(4) _____ (5) _____
Information questions	(6) _____ (7) _____ Why can't the media focus on real issues? (9) _____	She asked me how it went. She asked me what I had said. (8) _____ He asked (her) when his next interview was.

C **PRACTISE** Rewrite the direct questions as reported questions.

1 'How did you feel?'
 They asked me _____ .
2 'Do you have any brothers and sisters?'
 She asked him _____ .
3 'Who is Martha working for?'
 He asked them _____ .
4 'Will you run for public office?'
 She asked us _____ .
5 'Is the minister going to resign?'
 We wanted to know _____ .
6 'Can David give us the information?'
 I asked her _____ .

WHAT'S RIGHT?
○ He asked where we were going.
○ He asked where were we going.
○ They wanted to know we liked the candidate.
○ They wanted to know if we liked the candidate.

D 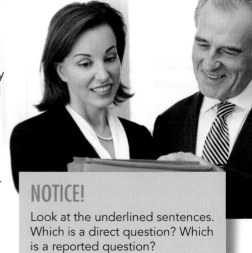 **NOW YOU DO IT** Find out and report information about your partner. Follow these steps.

• Work alone. Write two *yes/no* questions and two information questions for your partner.
• Ask your partner the questions. Listen carefully to their answers.
• Work with another pair. Report the questions you asked and your partner's answers.

I asked Maria if she had a car. She said she didn't. Then I asked her where she lived. She told me …

PRONUNCIATION: *say/says/said*

A))) **1.28** 👂 Listen and repeat these words. Is the vowel sound the same or different in *say*, *says* and *said*?

say   says   said

B))) **1.29** 👂 Practise saying these sentences. Pay attention to the vowel sound in *say*, *says* and *said*. Listen and check.

1   Helena says 'Hello'.
2   I always say what I think.
3   My boss said he wouldn't be here tomorrow.

4   Excuse me. What did you say?
5   He said that Martha didn't say 'Hi'.
6   Don't listen to anything he says!

VOCABULARY: *ask, say, tell*

A Complete the phrases with *ask*, *say* or *tell*.

1	*tell*	a joke	5	_____	hello/goodbye
2	*ask*	permission	6	_____	a story
3	*say*	what you think	7	_____	a question
4	_____	a favour	8	_____	the truth / a lie

B Complete the sentences with the correct form of phrases from Exercise A.

1   My sister is so funny! She _____ a lot of good _____.
2   My brother should be a writer. He _____ great _____!
3   Can I _____ you _____? Could I use your car tomorrow?
4   If you _____ _____, people won't trust you.
5   I think we can use this room for our meeting, but we need to _____ _____ first.
6   Leila is very direct. She always _____ _____ _____, even if other people don't like it.
7   Oh, no! I forgot to _____ _____ to Maria when I left the party.
8   Can I _____ you _____? How do I turn on the printer?

C 👂 Complete the sentences with phrases from Exercise A so they are true for you. Then share them with a partner.

1   I like people who _____.
2   I think children should always _____.

3   I almost never _____.
4   In our class, we always _____.

LISTENING: *to phone messages*

A))) **1.30** Listen to the phone messages. Circle the correct word to describe how each speaker feels.

1   a) angry   b) sad   c) excited
2   a) worried   b) excited   c) indecisive

3   a) sad   b) nervous   c) angry
4   a) excited   b) worried   c) relaxed

B Listen again and complete the notes on the message pads.

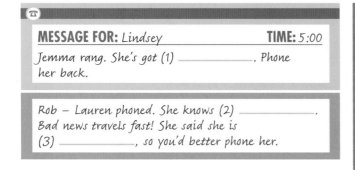

☎
MESSAGE FOR: *Lindsey*   **TIME:** *5:00*
Jemma rang. She's got (1) _____. Phone her back.

Rob – Lauren phoned. She knows (2) _____.
Bad news travels fast! She said she is
(3) _____, so you'd better phone her.

PHONE MESSAGE

Dad – Leo phoned.
He wanted to ask you
(4) _____.
He said he needs
(5) _____.

Mark, John rang to
say that it's OK to
(6) _____. He
wants to (7) _____
Phone him later.

C 🎧 Work in pairs. Compare your notes with your partner. Use reporting language.

A: *Jemma said that …*   B: *Lauren said she …*

D 🎧 With your partner, discuss these questions about the messages.

1 What do you think Jemma is going to tell Lindsey?
2 What do you think Lauren's relationship with Rob is?
3 What favour do you think Leo is going to ask his dad for?
4 What do you think Mark and John's relationship is?

WRITING: a short article

A 🎧 **1.31** Listen to a radio interview with a politician. Then complete the notes for a journalist's article about the interview.

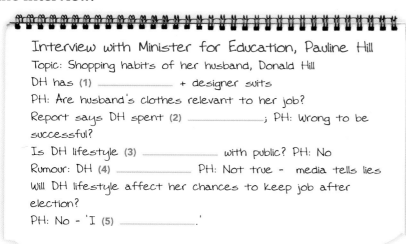

Interview with Minister for Education, Pauline Hill
Topic: Shopping habits of her husband, Donald Hill
DH has (1) _____ + designer suits
PH: Are husband's clothes relevant to her job?
Report says DH spent (2) _____; PH: Wrong to be successful?
Is DH lifestyle (3) _____ with public? PH: No
Rumour: DH (4) _____ PH: Not true - media tells lies
Will DH lifestyle affect her chances to keep job after election?
PH: No - 'I (5) _____.'

B Use the information from the journalist's notes in Exercise A, and reporting language, to complete the journalist's article below.

The topic of Martina Bruce's latest TV interview with Minister for Education, Pauline Hill, was not her opinions on education or exam reforms. The topic was her husband, Donald Hill. Mrs Hill looked rather surprised when Bruce's first question was whether (1) _____ that her husband (2) _____. Mrs Hill asked Bruce if she (3) _____ relevant to her job. When Bruce told her that she had a report that said that (4) _____, Mrs Hill asked her if it (5) _____. Bruce then asked whether (6) _____ a negative public image of her, but Mrs Hill said she didn't think so. Bruce pointed out that there was a rumour that her husband (7) _____, but Mrs Hill said that the rumour (8) _____. Finally, Bruce asked her whether her husband's (9) _____. She said that it definitely would not. She said that she (10) _____. We'll just have to wait until after the election to know if that's true.

C 🎧 Work in pairs. Exchange papers and read your partner's article. Then compare the two articles. Did you and your partner report the information in the same way? If there are differences, who reported the information more accurately?

LifeSkills

REPORTING INFORMATION

- Do a survey to collect data for your report.
- Study your data to identify any unexpected or surprising results.
- Report your findings clearly.

A 🗣 Work in pairs. You are going to write a report for a media studies class. Interview six people about when and how they get news by asking the questions in the survey below. Note down the answers.

	PERSON 1	PERSON 2	PERSON 3	PERSON 4	PERSON 5	PERSON 6
AGE						
GENDER	M/F	M/F	M/F	M/F	M/F	M/F
OCCUPATION						
1 WHAT TYPE OF NEWS ARE YOU MOST INTERESTED IN? a) international news d) entertainment news b) national news e) sports news c) local (city/regional) news						
2 HOW OFTEN DO YOU READ OR LISTEN TO A TYPE OF NEWS? a) every day d) less than once a week b) several times a week e) almost never c) once a week						
3 WHICH NEWS SOURCE DO YOU USE THE MOST? a) newspapers d) radio b) news magazines e) the internet c) TV						
4 WHEN YOU GET NEWS FROM THE INTERNET, WHICH SOURCE DO YOU USE THE MOST? a) online newspapers or magazines b) blogs c) email d) Facebook or a similar social network e) Twitter						
5 IF YOU ACCESS THE NEWS ON THE INTERNET, WHAT DEVICE DO YOU USE MOST OFTEN? a) a desktop computer c) a tablet b) a laptop d) a mobile phone						

B Answer these questions about the results of your survey.

1 Which questions did a majority of the people answer in the same way?
2 Do people of the same age group have similar answers?
3 Are there any areas where men and women gave very different answers?
4 Are there big differences among people in different occupations / areas of study?
5 Were there any unexpected or surprising results? If so, what were they?

C Read this example report and answer the questions.

1 How many sections does the report have?

2 Which section of the report gives information about the people who answered the survey?

3 What useful phrases for reporting information can you identify in the report? Underline them.

Gives the purpose of the study; gives information about the people interviewed; explains the number and type of question in the survey.

BACKGROUND

* Purpose of the study: to identify patterns in news consumption
* Survey group: adults aged 20 to 59 with different occupations
* Survey: five multiple-choice questions

RESULTS

Similarities

* Most people in this age group said that television was their primary news source.
* The majority said that they listened to or read a type of news every day. Most people said that they were most interested in national or international news.
* Most of the people who said that they usually got news from the internet said they read online newspapers or magazines.

Differences

* About 20% of men said that they were most interested in sports news, while about 20% of women said that they followed entertainment news.
* More people in their 20s than in their 50s said that they got most of their news from the internet.
* People in their 40s said they usually used laptops or mobile phones to get news from the internet, while most people in their 50s said they used desktop computers.

Summarises the findings of the survey and describes any surprising results.

CONCLUSIONS

* The men and women I interviewed are interested in news and usually read or listen to some news every day.
* People in the over 50 age group still get most of their news from television.
* Both men and women are interested in national and international news. More men than women are interested in sports news, and more women than men are interested in entertainment news.
* There was one surprising result: Although the main source of news for the over 50 age group is still TV, the number two source of news is the internet. It's surprising that older people are using networking platforms like Facebook and Twitter to get news.

Gives information about the most common answers, and similarities/differences between different groups of people in the survey.

D Work in pairs. Combine and use the results from your surveys in Exercise A to write your own three-section report about news consumption. Use the example report in Exercise C to help you.

E Work with another pair. Read your reports and discuss these questions.

1 Were any of your results similar?

2 Were any of your results different? If so, how can you explain the differences?

3 Were there any surprising results?

REFLECT … How can the skill of reporting information be useful to you in **Work and Career** and **Self and Society**?

Language wrap-up

1 VOCABULARY

Choose the correct words. (15 points)

Toby: Mia, can I **(1)** ask / tell you a favour? I need some advice.

Mia: OK, but be quick! I have to give a **(2)** chat / speech in my English lesson.

Toby: OK, I'm going to **(3)** ask / say you a question. You know that Jade and I split up last month? Well, I told Jade I wasn't interested in anyone else, but I wasn't really **(4)** saying / telling the truth. I want to ask Clare Randall out.

Mia: Do you want me to **(5)** tell / say what I think?

Toby: Of course.

Mia: Then I really think you need to **(6)** explain / argue the situation to Jade. **(7)** Talk / Discuss to her about it. And don't just **(8)** tell / say her some story that isn't true.

Toby: I'm not going to **(9)** tell / say lies! But I'm not **(10)** asking / telling her permission to ask Clare out either.

Mia: No. I'm not **(11)** saying / telling that.

Toby: I know. I'm sorry. I don't want to **(12)** discuss / argue with you. I just feel nervous.

Mia: I understand. Look, I think you really need to **(13)** chat / give a talk to Jade about the situation. Anyway, if you want, we can **(14)** discuss / talk this later after my lesson.

Toby: OK. Hey, Clare is in your lesson, isn't she? **(15)** Say / Tell hello to her from me.

11 – 15 correct: I can use *ask, say, tell* and other words related to oral communication.

0 – 10 correct: Look again at the vocabulary sections on pages 60 and 62.

SCORE: /15

2 GRAMMAR

Read the conversation. Then complete the reported statements and questions. (15 points)

Jenny: **(1)** Are you going to Lisa's party?

David: **(2)** I don't know. **(3)** My cousins are coming to visit this weekend.

Jenny: **(4)** Where do your cousins live?

David: In Brighton. **(5)** They've just come back from Thailand.

Jenny: Wow. **(6)** Did they live in Thailand?

David: Yes. **(7)** Do you want to meet them? **(8)** We'll be at home on Sunday.

Jenny: **(9)** Oh, I can't come on Sunday.

David: **(10)** Well, maybe I can take them to Lisa's party.

Jenny: Good idea! **(11)** I'll ask Lisa if it's OK. **(12)** Do you want me to pick you up?

David: **(13)** That would be perfect! **(14)** I think that's a good plan.

Jenny: OK. **(15)** I'm going to call Lisa tonight.

1   Jenny asked David _____.
2   David said _____.
3   He said _____.
4   Then Jenny asked _____.
5   He told her _____.
6   Jenny asked _____.
7   David asked _____.
8   David said _____.
9   But Jenny said that _____.
10 David said that _____.
11 Jenny said _____.
12 She asked David _____.
13 David said _____.
14 He said he _____.
15 Jenny said _____.

11 – 15 correct: I can use reported speech to report statements and questions.

0 – 10 correct: Look again at the grammar sections on pages 59 and 61.

SCORE: /15

WRITING WORKSHOP

a short article

A Read this news article. What problem does Mr Evans have?

Since MP Paul Evans announced that he would stand as a candidate in elections for the Mayor of London, people seem to be talking about only one thing – his weight! In a press conference yesterday, Mr Evans announced that he was going to have surgery to help him lose weight before the election next spring. He said that he planned to lose a total of about 45 kg by this time next year. The MP said that he was not having the weight loss surgery to help his public image, but because he wanted to improve his health for the physical demands of a political campaign and of being Mayor. He said he would have the surgery in London at the end of this month, and that he would return to work after a few weeks. If the MP's weight loss effort is successful, perhaps the media will stop talking about his weight and start talking about his policies!

B A news article should answer the questions Who? What? When? Where? and if possible, Why? Scan the article and find the answers to these questions.

Who? _____

What? _____

When? _____

Where? _____

Why? *to improve his health*

C Look back at the article. What details does the writer include to give more information about the main points?

D Write a short one-paragraph news article. Include the following things:

- a topic sentence
- answers to the questions Who? What? When? Where? Why?
- supporting details to give more information if necessary
- a concluding sentence

HOW ARE YOU DOING?

Look back at your writing and tick the statements that are true.

◯ I have included a topic sentence and a concluding sentence.

◯ I have included information to answer the questions *Who? What? When? Where? Why?*

Now ask a partner to look at your writing and tick.

The news article clearly answers the questions *Who? What? When? Where? Why?*

●　　　◯　　　●

Well done!　Nearly! Look at　Think again!
　　　　　the unit again.　Ask your teacher
　　　　　　　　　for help.

UNIT 6 DECISIONS, DECISIONS

IN THIS UNIT YOU

- ⚙ learn language to talk about unreal situations, hopes, wishes and decisions
- ⚙ read people's opinions about dilemmas
- ⚙ listen to people talking about big life changes
- ⚙ talk about your hopes and wishes
- ⚙ write about a decision you made recently
- ⚙ learn how to be more aware of the image you project
- ▶ watch a video about decisions

LISTENING
predicting
How can making predictions about what people are going to talk about and what they are going to say help you understand?

WRITING
checking your work
Do you always check your writing before you hand it in? What kinds of things do you check for?

LIFE SKILLS
SELF

becoming more self-aware
Are you almost always aware of things like your body language and tone of voice, or do you think about these things only in certain

A Look at these cartoons. Which do you think is the funniest?

NEW YEAR'S RESOLUTIONS
1. BE MORE DECISIVE.
2.

.NAF.

"Ummmm."

"For goodness sake, just pick one! I'm nearly seventeen!"

.NAF.

© Mike Baldwin / Cornered

"Heads I do, tails I'm outta here."

HOW TO SAY IT

Talking about choices

The last time I had to make a decision was when …

My most difficult decision was when I …

Once I had to decide between a … and a … / going to … and having …

At first I thought …, but then I decided …

B When was the last time you found it difficult to make a decision or had to make a difficult decision? Explain what happened.

The last time I had to make a difficult decision was when I bought a car. I really wanted a hybrid, but the new one I liked was very expensive. I needed to save money, so in the end I bought a small second-hand car, and it was a really good decision.

A Complete the verb phrases with the verbs from the box.

confront	give	keep	promise	tell	trust	wait	warn

1 _____ someone about a problem or something they have done
2 _____ someone some advice
3 _____ and see what happens
4 _____ someone about something that might happen
5 _____ something secret
6 _____ (not) to do something
7 _____ a close friend
8 _____ someone to do something you ask them to

B Match these sentences with the verb phrases in Exercise A.

a) You should try to exercise more often. ☐

d) I'm not happy with what you did. We need to talk about it. ☐

g) Let's not decide now. The situation might change. ☐

b) I haven't told anyone about your problem. ☐

e) Don't worry. I'll talk to Jane for you. I won't forget. ☐

h) You'll be sorry if you decide to drop out, you know. ☐

c) You know me very well, Steve. Can I tell you something? ☐

f) I know that Alice will choose the right hotel. ☐

GRAMMAR: third conditional

A 🎧 **1.32 LANGUAGE IN CONTEXT** Listen to the conversation below. Why is Billy worried?

Dad: What's wrong?

Billy: I'm a bit worried about money.

Dad: Well, if you had studied business, like I said you should, you could have found a good job when you left uni.

Billy: Yeah, but I would've hated studying business.

Dad: You don't know that. You might have liked it.

Billy: In any case, <u>I wouldn't have met Jessica if I hadn't studied philosophy</u>.

Dad: If you hadn't met Jessica, you would have met someone else.

NOTICE!
Look at the underlined sentence. Does it refer to the past, the present or the future?

B ANALYSE Read the conversation in Exercise A again.

Form Choose the correct option to complete the rules.

If-clause	Result clause	Examples
If + **(1)** past simple / past perfect,	**(2)** would, could, might / will, can, may + *have* + past participle	If you had studied business, you could have found a good job.
		If you had studied business, you might have liked it.
We use a comma when the *if*-clause is at **(3)** the beginning / the end of the sentence.		If I hadn't studied philosophy, I wouldn't have met Jessica.
		I wouldn't have met Jessica if I hadn't studied philosophy.

Function Choose the correct option to complete the rules.

1 We use the third conditional to talk about unreal situations in the present / past. e.g. *If I hadn't studied philosophy, I wouldn't have met Jessica.* (The opposite is true: I studied philosophy and so I met Jessica.)

2 We can use *could* or *might* instead of *would* in the result clause to talk about results that were possible / definite in the past.
e.g. *If you had studied business, you could/might have found a good job.* (It's possible that you would have found a good job. But you didn't study business so you didn't find a good job.)

WHAT'S RIGHT?

○ If you had met him, you would have liked him.

○ If you would have met him, you had liked him.

○ We couldn't have finished on time if you hadn't helped us.

○ We couldn't have finished on time if you hadn't help us.

C PRACTISE Complete the sentences with the correct form of the words in brackets.

1 Sally and Mark _____ (*have*) an argument if we _____ (*not be*) there.

2 If I _____ (*explain*) the situation better, you _____ (*not be*) angry.

3 If I _____ (*know*) about the party, I _____ (*could go*) with you.

4 If my friend _____ (*not introduce*) Paula and me, we _____ (*not meet*).

5 Sam _____ (*could not buy*) a car if his brother _____ (*not lend*) him the money.

6 If a friend _____ (*not give*) me some good advice, I _____ (*might lose*) a lot of money.

D NOW YOU DO IT Think of four important events that happened or decisions you made in the past. Write two affirmative sentences and two negative sentences. Then talk about what would, might or could have happened if the opposite had been true.

I passed my exams. If I hadn't passed my exams, I would have retaken them.
I didn't study chemistry, like I planned. If I had studied chemistry, I would have become a chemist.

PRONUNCIATION: past modals

A 1.33 Listen to these sentences. How does the speaker pronounce the phrases *might have*, *could have* and *would have*?

1 If you had told a close friend, you might have felt better.

2 If I had had more money, I could have bought a nicer house.

3 I would have given you some advice if you had asked me.

B Listen again and repeat the sentences. Pay attention to the phrases *might have*, *could have* and *would have*.

A Read the two dilemmas on the webpage below. Don't read the replies. Choose the best summary, a or b, for each dilemma.

1 a) The writer thinks her friend's boyfriend is cheating on her.
   b) The writer isn't sure if her friend's boyfriend is cheating on her or not.
2 a) The writer thinks his friend is going to get into trouble.
   b) The writer thinks his friend was wrong to steal.

THE MORAL DILEMMA

Write about moral and ethical dilemmas you had, and tell us what you did. Find out what other people would have done.

▼ Last week I saw my friend's boyfriend in a café with another woman. I didn't say anything, because if I had told my friend, and it had turned out that the woman was his cousin or something, they both would have thought I was just gossiping! Did I do the right thing? *Milly*

▶ Don't worry, Milly. I wouldn't have said anything to my friend either. I wouldn't have wanted to interfere in their relationship. If he really is cheating on her, she'll find out anyway. *Rachel*

▶ I disagree, Rachel! If I had seen something like that, I would have told my friend right away. She wouldn't have thought you were gossiping, Milly. She would have been happy that you cared about her feelings. *Amandina*

▼ What would you have done if you had seen a friend steal something? That happened to me the other day. My friend and I were in a shop and he took some pens from a display and put them in his pocket. I felt terrible when I saw him do it, but I've been too scared to say anything! *Jake*

▶ If I had seen a friend do that, I would have said something to him immediately. I probably wouldn't have told the shop manager, but I would have confronted my friend about it. Stealing is a serious crime. If a shop assistant had seen him, he could have been arrested. Talk to him about it. Don't let him think that stealing is OK. *Lola*

▶ Do you think he would have been arrested for taking a couple of pens? I wouldn't have said anything about something like that. Now, if he had stolen something more expensive, like a video game or something, that would have been different. Of course stealing is wrong, but I don't think this was that big a deal. *Kevin*

B Read the dilemmas again, and the replies. Choose T (true) or F (false) for each statement.

1 Milly told her friend her boyfriend was cheating on her.   T / F
2 Rachel thinks that Milly did the right thing.   T / F
3 Amandina says that she would have done the same thing.   T / F
4 Jake stole something and now he feels bad about it.   T / F
5 Lola thinks this is a serious problem.   T / F
6 Kevin does not agree with Lola's opinion.   T / F

C 🗣 Work in groups. Discuss the responses to the dilemmas. Which response do you agree with more in each case? What would you have done in these situations?

LISTENING: predicting

⚙ When you listen, you may also have pictures or written information, such as questions, connected to what you are listening to. Look at any information you have before you listen. It can give you important clues about what you are going to hear.

A 🔊 **You are going to hear a family, Michael, Angela and Julia, talking about a big life change they made. Look at the photos which are connected to the life change. Discuss these questions as a class.**

1 What big change do you think the family might have made?
2 Why do you think they might have decided to make this change?
3 What are some of the advantages and disadvantages of making a big life change?

B 🎧 **1.34 Now listen to the family and check your answers to Exercise A.**

C Listen again and choose the correct answers to these questions.

1 Why does Michael think they made a good decision?
   a) Because it was good for his and Angela's careers.
   b) Because their friends and family are all in London.
2 How does he feel about making new friends?
   a) He thinks it's going to be very difficult.
   b) He doesn't think it will be too difficult.
3 How does Angela feel about the move?
   a) She would have been very disappointed if they hadn't done it.
   b) She would have been happy if they hadn't done it.

4 How did she feel about her old job?
   a) She liked it.
   b) She didn't like it.
5 What does Julia say that Angela is worried about?
   a) That Julia will get into trouble.
   b) That Julia won't be able to go to the dancing classes she needs.
6 In general, how does Julia feel about the move?
   a) She's unhappy about it.
   b) She's happy about it.

GRAMMAR: *hope* and *wish*

A LANGUAGE IN CONTEXT Read this online chat between two sisters. Where do you think Abby is?

 Diana1: It's so boring without you at home. I wish you were here.

Abbygirl: Me too! I miss you all so much. If only I lived a bit closer, I could get on a bus and come home for the weekend!

 Diana1: Yeah, I think Mum wishes you lived a bit closer to home, too. How's it going, anyway? I hope you don't study all the time! I hope you're having some fun, too!

Abbygirl: I'm OK, but I do study a lot. I've got exams next week. I hope they won't be too difficult.

Diana1: When does term end? I wish you would come home more often. You only come during the holidays. I really miss you!

NOTICE!

Underline the phrases with *wish*. How many different structures are there?

B **ANALYSE** Read the online chat in Exercise A again.

Form Complete the table with examples from Exercise A.

Present		Past
hope + present simple **(1)** _____		*hope* + past simple
hope + present continuous		*I hope you had a nice time at the party last night.*
(2) _____		
wish + past simple **(3)** _____		**Future**
if only + past simple **(4)** _____		*hope* + will
wish + would **(5)** _____		**(6)** _____

Function Choose the correct option to complete the rules.

1   We use *hope* to refer to things that are possible / impossible in the present and future.
2   We use *wish* and *if only* to refer to things that are possible / impossible in the present.
3   We use *wish* + *would/wouldn't* to express satisfaction / dissatisfaction with a situation in the present.

C **PRACTISE** Rewrite these sentences using the words in brackets. Include *would* or *wouldn't* where necessary.

1   Carol would like to be more self-confident.
     She wishes she were more self-confident. (wish)
2   I would like to live in Canada.
     _____. (if only)
3   Liam would like to have enough money to go on holiday.
     He _____. (wish)
4   Jill left Mark a message yesterday, but she doesn't know if he got it.
     She _____. (hope)
5   Lauren is sad that she can't go to India this summer.
     She _____. (wish)
6   Paul doesn't think his boss gives him enough information.
     He _____. (wish)

> ## WHAT'S RIGHT?
> ○ I wish I had some money.
> ○ I wish I would have some money.
> ○ I hope he arrives soon.
> ○ I hope he would arrive soon.
> ○ If only I have more time.
> ○ If only I had more time.

D **NOW YOU DO IT** Work in pairs. Talk about your hopes and wishes in three or more of the areas below. You can also use your own ideas.

- appearance   • money   • friends   • work   • study   • possessions   • time

I wish I had more money. If I had more money, I would …   *I wish I didn't have to …*
I hope I pass my final exams.   *I wish my best friend wouldn't …*

SPEAKING: talking about hopes and wishes

A Look at these problems of modern life. In your opinion, which of these is the biggest problem? Why? Take a vote to see which problem the class thinks is the most important and which is the least important.

a) dirty cities   b) climate change   c) the economy   d) unsafe drivers

B **1.35** Listen to four people talking about their hopes and wishes. Match each person to the problem in Exercise A they are talking about.

1 ☐   2 ☐   3 ☐   4 ☐

C Work in pairs. Follow the instructions below.

- Choose one of the problems of modern life in Exercise A, or another problem that concerns you.
- Talk about the things you wish were different about it.
- Say what your hopes are for the future.

> ## HOW TO SAY IT
> **Talking about hopes and wishes**
> *I wish there weren't any …*
> *I wish I were / I could …*
> *I wish people would/wouldn't …*
> *I hope that some day, people will …*
> *I hope that in the future …*

VOCABULARY: decisions

A Complete the phrases with the correct verb, a or b.

1 ____ all the options
   a) weigh (up)   b) make up

2 ____ the positive and negative effects
   a) take   b) consider

3 ____ responsibility for a decision
   a) consider   b) take

4 ____ your mind
   a) make up   b) make

5 ____ information
   a) gather   b) think

6 ____ about the consequences
   a) gather   b) think

7 ____ all the factors into account
   a) take
   b) consider

8 ____ a decision
   a) make   b) gather

B Read the definitions and write the numbers of the phrases from Exercise A that mean the same thing.

a) to find out things about the situation ☐
b) to consider all the aspects of a decision ☐
c) to look at all the possible courses of action ☐
d) to think about the results of a decision ☐ ☐
e) to decide something ☐ ☐
f) to accept the consequences of a decision ☐

C 🔊 Now work in pairs. Read the statements below. Which do you agree with? Do you and your partner have the same decision-making style?

1 It's important to be able to make decisions quickly.
2 People should think carefully about the consequences before they decide anything.
3 You can't make a decision without having all the information.
4 Sometimes you have to follow your instincts when making important decisions.

WRITING: checking your work

⚙ It is important to check your written work carefully. Use a checklist to help you remember to check aspects of grammar, vocabulary, spelling and punctuation.

A Read the checklist below. Then read the email and underline one example of each error in the checklist. Rewrite the email without errors.

Checklist
Grammar
1 Does every sentence have a subject and a verb? ☐
2 Are all the verb tenses correct? ☐

Vocabulary and spelling
1 Have you used the correct words? ☐
2 Are all the words spelt correctly? ☐

Punctuation
1 Have you used capital letters correctly? ☐
2 Have you put a punctuation mark at the end of each complete sentence? ☐
3 Have you used commas where necessary? ☐

Hi jerry,
Well, took your advice into account, and I've made up my brain. I'm going to go back to university to finish my degree! I've thought about the advantages and disvantages of leaving my job, and I've realised that if I don't go back to university now I will always regret it. I'm not happy at work anyway, I really wish I were at university. I hope this is the right decision, but I think the only way to get a better job is to finish my degree, so that's what I'm going to do. What did you think?
Anita

B Think of a decision (big or small) that you made recently. Write a short email to a friend telling them about it. Include these points.

- Describe the decision you made.
- Say what you hope the result of the decision will be.
- Explain why you made this decision.

C 🔊 Work in pairs. Read your partner's email and use the checklist in Exercise A to check for errors.

- First, read the whole email.
- Use the checklist in Exercise A to check for errors. Scan the whole email for one type of error. Then scan it again for the next type of error. Circle any errors you find.

D 🔊 Look at your partner's corrections. Ask them or your teacher for clarification. Rewrite your email.

LifeSkills

BECOMING MORE SELF-AWARE

- Find out how others see you.
- Think about how you react in different situations and why.
- Decide how you could change.

A Read this article. Label the sections in the pie chart with these phrases.

Body language   Tone of voice   Words

In any face-to-face communication, there are three basic elements: the words we use, our tone of voice (how we say the words), and our body language (the movements and gestures we make with our arms, hands and face).

We often think that the words we use are the most important factor. In fact, studies have shown that when we are talking about personal feelings, the words only carry 7% of the message. Our tone of voice carries 38% and our body language carries 55%.

Effective communicators are usually people who understand this and are self-aware. Self-awareness is our ability to understand our own reactions and the messages we send out to other people.

38%   **55%**

7%

B Answer these questions by ticking the red boxes.

1 Which word or words best describe the way you usually speak to other people?

| confident | ◯◯ | quiet | ◯◯ | nervous | ◯◯ |
| loud | ◯◯ | friendly | ◯◯ | aggressive | ◯◯ |

2 How much do you use your hands when you talk?

| all the time | ◯◯ | a lot of the time | ◯◯ | sometimes | ◯◯ |
| rarely | ◯◯ | never | ◯◯ | | |

3 How much do you use eye contact when you talk to someone?

| all the time | ◯◯ | a lot of the time | ◯◯ | sometimes | ◯◯ |
| rarely | ◯◯ | never | ◯◯ | | |

4 Which word or words best describe the way you are feeling at the moment?

| comfortable | ◯◯ | defensive | ◯◯ | open | ◯◯ |
| relaxed | ◯◯ | stressed | ◯◯ | nervous | ◯◯ |

C Work with a partner you know well. Ask how they would answer each question about you, and mark your partner's answers about you in the blue boxes.

A: *Which word or words best describe the way I usually speak to other people?*
B: *I think probably …*

D Look back at your answers and your partner's answers about you. In general, does your partner see you in the same way you see yourself? Are there any surprises?

E **You are going to work in groups and give a short talk to your group, and answer their questions. Follow these instructions.**

- Work alone. Complete the sentences so they are true for you.
  I wish I had more time to … because …
  I hope in the future, I …
  If only …
  If I had …, I …
  If I hadn't, I …
- Practise what you are going to say.

F **Work in groups of three, Students A, B and C. Work with students you don't usually work with.**

Student A, stand up and give your talk to your group. Answer any questions.
Student B, listen carefully and ask Student A questions.
Student C, observe Student A carefully, and complete the evaluation form. Don't say anything.

Then swap roles.

Evaluation
Circle all the words that apply.

1 How did Student A appear?
   confident ☐   quiet ☐   nervous ☐
   loud ☐   friendly ☐   aggressive ☐

2 How much did Student A use their hands when they were talking?
   all the time ☐   a lot of the time ☐   sometimes ☐
   rarely ☐   never ☐

3 How much did Student A use eye contact when they were talking?
   all the time ☐   a lot of the time ☐   sometimes ☐
   rarely ☐   never ☐

4 Which word or words best describes Student A's body language?
   comfortable ☐   defensive ☐   open ☐
   relaxed ☐   stressed ☐   nervous ☐

G **Give each other feedback on how you appeared when you were giving your talks. Were you surprised by anything? What would you change about how you appear when you're talking to someone?**

HOW TO SAY IT
Responding to feedback
You said I looked …, but actually I felt …
I don't think I used my hands enough / made enough eye contact.
I think I should … more.
I would like to appear more …, so I'm going to …

REFLECT … How can becoming more self-aware help you in **Work and Career** and **Study and Learning**?

Language wrap-up

Complete the conversation with words from the box. (15 points)

advantages advice close consequences consider gather keep
make make up promise see take trust warn weigh up

Sophie: I just don't know what to do. Should I apply for this new job?

Jessica: Well, maybe it would help you (1) _____ your mind if we thought about the
(2) _____ and disadvantages before you (3) _____ your decision.

Sophie: Good idea. Well, the first thing to (4) _____ into account is the fact that it'll mean more money.

Jessica: That's good! Are there any other (5) _____ that you need to think about?

Sophie: It would mean moving to another city.

Jessica: Why? You could do the job from here. Let me give you some (6) _____ .You could tell
them that you're applying for the job, but you don't want to move.

Sophie: I'm not sure. Do you think I should (7) _____ them that I don't want to move, or should I
get the job first, then tell them?

Jessica: If you just wait and (8) _____ what happens, you might find that you miss your chance to
get what you want.

Sophie: I'll think about it. You have to (9) _____ not to tell anyone about this job, though. I don't
want people to know until I've had the chance to (10) _____ all the options.

Jessica: Don't worry. I'll (11) _____ it secret. You can (12) _____ me not to tell anyone.

Sophie: Yes, not even (13) _____ friends, like Sam and Daisy. I need to (14) _____ some
more information about the company, too.

Jessica: Yes, you need to (15) _____ the positive and negative effects before deciding.

Sophie: Oh, it's so difficult!

11 – 15 correct: I can talk about problems and making decisions.
0 – 10 correct: Look again at the vocabulary sections on pages 70 and 75.   SCORE: /15

**A   Complete the conversation with the correct third conditional form of
the verbs in brackets. (8 points)**

Aaron: Back to work tomorrow! It was a nice break, but I don't want to go back!

Dan: I know. Three days in New York was much too short! If we (1) _____ (take) a week off,
we (2) _____ (be) able to stay longer and we (3) _____ (do) more.

Aaron: Yes, if we (4) _____ (think) about it before, we could (5) _____ (take) two weeks
off and might (6) _____ (go) to Washington DC to visit Romy as well as New York.

Dan: Actually, we could (7) _____ (spend) a week in New York if we (8) _____
(not leave) on Tuesday.

Aaron: Well, we didn't, so there's no point discussing it. We'll just do that next time!

**B   Rewrite the sentences so that they have the same meaning, using the words
in brackets. (7 points)**

1   Pete would like to have more free time. (*wish*)
2   I want tomorrow to be sunny. (*hope*)
3   Are you having a good time? (*hope*)
4   I want you to be here. (*wish*)
5   Did you enjoy the concert last night? (*hope*)
6   You don't live near me. (*if only*)
7   She never phones me. (*wish/would*)

11 – 15 correct: I can use the third conditional. I can use *hope*, *wish* and *if only*.
0 – 10 correct: Look again at the grammar sections on pages 70–71 and 73–74.   SCORE: /15

SPEAKING WORKSHOP

talking about hopes and wishes

A   Read the conversation below and answer the questions.

1   What is Sarah looking for at the moment?
2   What does Keira advise Sarah to do?
3   Who feels more optimistic about the future?

Sarah: I'm sending out job applications this week. I hope I get several interviews!

Keira: I think you'll be lucky to get one. Companies aren't taking on new people at the moment.

Sarah: I suppose not, but I think the situation is a bit better now than last year.

Keira: That's true, but I wish it would improve faster. Just think, if the banks hadn't made all those bad loans, there wouldn't have been a recession. Anyway, I hope it's better by the time I leave uni.

Sarah: You still have two years, so if the economy keeps improving, it should be much better by then.

Keira: I hope so. Anyway, what will you do if you don't get a job?

Sarah: Keira, I'm not going to think that way! Not yet, anyway.

Keira: Look, I'm just being realistic. I wish I could tell you that everything will be fine, but I'm not so sure. I just think you should consider some different options in case you don't get a job straightaway.

Sarah: OK, I see your point. That's probably a good idea, but I'm going to see what happens with these applications first.

B   Read the conversation again and find these things.

1   three phrases to say you would like something to happen in the future
2   two phrases to express dissatisfaction with a situation in the present
3   a phrase to agree with someone
4   a phrase to say you understand what someone is saying

C   Think of a current situation or problem that you are dissatisfied with. Answer these questions.

1   What is the situation or problem? What could have prevented it?
2   How do you wish it were different now?
3   In what ways do you hope the situation will improve in the future?

D   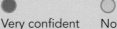 Work in pairs. Tell your partner about your situation. Find out if they agree or disagree with your assessment of the situation. Offer advice to your partner about their situation.

E   Find a new partner and talk about the problem with them.

HOW ARE YOU DOING?

Think about your speaking and tick the statements that are true.

I feel confident …

○ describing a situation or problem.
○ talking about how I would like a situation to be different.
○ using phrases of agreement and disagreement.

How do you feel about your speaking generally?

● ○ ●
Very confident   Not sure …   Need to practise

UNIT 7 THINK AGAIN!

SPEAKING
speculating
What kinds of phrases do we use to indicate that we are speculating (guessing)?

READING
distinguishing fact and opinion
In which ways, apart from using specific phrases, do people convey their opinion about things?

LIFE SKILLS

STUDY & LEARNING

thinking logically
How can thinking logically help us in our personal and professional lives?

A 🗣 Work in pairs. Do the quiz.

ARE YOU A RIGHT-BRAIN *or* LEFT-BRAIN THINKER?

Read the questions and tick *Yes* or *No*.

▶ Add up the number of green boxes and orange boxes.

▶ Look at your score to find out what kind of thinker you are!

	Yes	No	
1	☐	☐	I wear a watch.
2	☐	☐	I like to draw.
3	☐	☐	I'd rather draw a map than give someone directions.
4	☐	☐	When I get something new, I usually read the instructions.
5	☐	☐	I play or would like to play a musical instrument.
6	☐	☐	I've considered becoming a politician, an artist or an architect.
7	☐	☐	I hate following a schedule.
8	☐	☐	I make 'to-do' lists.
9	☐	☐	I generally do well in maths and science.
10	☐	☐	I've considered becoming a lawyer, a doctor or a journalist.

Your score

More orange boxes: You are more of a left-brain thinker.

More green boxes: You are more of a right-brain thinker.

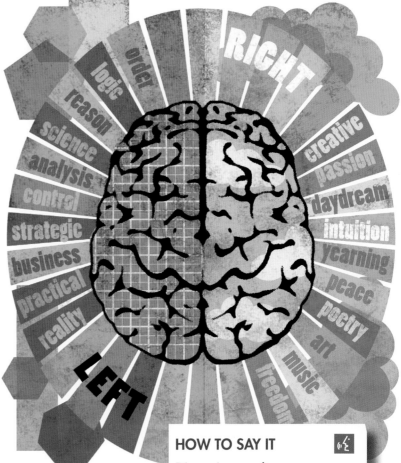

HOW TO SAY IT 🗣

Discussing results

I think the quiz is saying that left-brained people like …, while right-brained people prefer …

I think left/right-brained people are …

According to the quiz, I'm left/right-brained, but I like/don't like …

B 🗣 Work in groups. Discuss the results of the quiz. Are there more right-brain or left-brain thinkers in your group? What do the quiz questions suggest are some characteristics of left- and right-brain thinkers?

A: *Are you a left-brain or a right-brain thinker?*
B: *Left-brained, according to the quiz.*
A: *So how many are left-brained, how many are right-brained?*

Writers often use specific phrases to let the reader know whether something is a fact or an opinion. In addition, opinions are often expressed through the use of adjectives like *good, bad, great,* etc. Look for specific phrases, as well as positive and negative adjectives, to identify opinions in a text.

A Look at these people. Do you recognise any of them? What do you think they have in common?

Leonardo da Vinci

Marie Curie

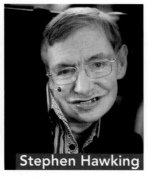
Stephen Hawking

Helen Keller

Albert Einstein

B Read this article and check your ideas.

BEYOND
THE ORDINARY

Everyone agrees that the scientists Albert Einstein and Marie Curie were geniuses, and so was Leonardo da Vinci, who was a scientist, an inventor, a writer and an artist. Mozart was clearly a genius and what about the incredibly talented scientist Stephen Hawking? Or Helen Keller, the amazing woman who became a writer, even though she was deaf and blind? Are they geniuses? What makes a genius?

According to one definition, a genius has a high IQ. Studies show that normal IQs range from 85 to 115, and a genius has an IQ over 140. However, this seems to me to be a poor definition. 'Genius' is a complicated concept, involving many different factors, and intelligence tests usually measure only logical thinking. A better definition of 'genius' would include other things, like creativity. The artist Picasso produced thousands of beautiful works of art. Was he a genius?

One very useful definition of 'genius' states that originality is the defining factor. A genius puts things together in new ways – ways that ordinary people have never thought of – and creates something new. It might be a new idea, a new work of art or a new way of working. Geniuses change the world they are born into. That raises another question: Are geniuses born that way?

The writer Malcolm Gladwell has written about geniuses in his book *Outliers: The Story of Success*, and he feels that there is an important factor we often overlook: hard work. 'The people at the very top don't just work much harder than everyone else,' he says. 'They work much, much harder.' You have to be born with talent, but then you have to develop that talent. According to research, the minimum for this is 10,000 hours, about three hours a day for ten years. By studying examples ranging from Mozart to Bill Gates, Gladwell shows that they all did an enormous amount of work before becoming successful. So, while talent and IQ are crucial, it seems that geniuses work very hard to achieve their success.

C Read these sentences and phrases from the article in Exercise B. For each one, decide if it expresses a fact or an opinion. Underline the word(s) or phrase(s) in the article that helped you decide.

1 … the incredibly talented scientist Stephen Hawking …
2 … Helen Keller, the amazing woman who …
3 Studies show that normal IQs range from 85 to 115 …
4 … this seems to me to be a poor definition.
5 A better definition of 'genius' would include other things …
6 One very useful definition of 'genius' …
7 … he feels that there is an important factor we often overlook: hard work.
8 According to research, the minimum for this is 10,000 hours …
9 By studying examples ranging from Mozart to Bill Gates, Gladwell shows …

D Work in pairs. Think of other geniuses you know of. Which one do you admire the most? Why?

A 🎧 **2.01 LANGUAGE IN CONTEXT** Listen to the conversation below. Do Ben and Morgan get the right answer?

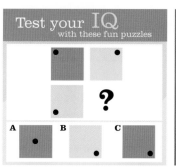
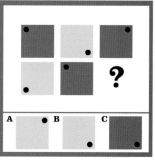

Test your IQ
with these fun puzzles

Morgan:	Hi Ben. What are you doing?
Ben:	Oh, hi Morgan. I'm just doing some logic puzzles in this magazine. I'm not doing very well, though!
Morgan:	Let me see. Which symbol is missing? Hmm … OK. Well, the missing square **must** be red.
Ben:	Yes, that's what I think. So the answer **can't** be B. It **could** be A, though.
Morgan:	No, it **can't** be A. Look where the dot is. It **must** be on the right at the bottom. The answer **must** be C.
Ben:	Oh, yes. You're right. Hey, you're good at these things! Let's try the next question. Oh, this one is different. I think it **might** be B, but it **could** be A.

B ANALYSE Read the conversation in Exercise A again.

NOTICE!
Look at the modal verbs in bold. What form of the verb always follows a modal?

Form Complete the table with examples from Exercise A.

		Function	
subject + modal + base form	☐	The missing square (1) _____ be red. It (2) _____ be on the right at the bottom. The answer (3) _____ be C.	
	☐	The answer (4) _____ be B. No, it (5) _____ be A.	
	☐	It (6) _____ be A. I think it (7) _____ be B.	

Function Read the rules below and write the number of each function in the correct place in the table.
1 We use this to say that it's impossible that something is true.
2 We use this to say that we are sure that something is true.
3 We use this to say that something is possibly true.

WHAT'S RIGHT?
○ It might be the last one.
○ It could be the last one.
○ It can be the last one.

C PRACTISE Read the first sentence in each pair. Write an appropriate modal to complete the second sentence.

1 You're expecting Nicole to call. The phone rings.
   That _____ be Nicole.
2 You are certain the answer isn't D.
   The answer _____ be D.
3 It's possible your mobile phone is at home.
   My mobile phone _____ be at home.
4 You don't think it's possible that John is sick.
   John _____ be sick.
5 You are sure this is Emma's house.
   Emma _____ live here.
6 It's the middle of summer. You don't believe it when someone says it's snowing.
   It _____ be snowing!

D 🗣 **NOW YOU DO IT** Work in pairs. For each puzzle, decide what comes next.

1 red, orange, yellow, green, ?
2 1, 4, 9, 16, ?
3 M, T, W, T, ?
4 January, March, May, July, ?
5 0, 1, 1, 2, 3, 5, 8, ?
6 M, V, E, M, J, ?

HOW TO SAY IT 🗣

Making deductions
What does 'V' stand for?
I think it stands for …
What do they all have in common?
They're all …
The answer might be …
No, it can't be … because …
I think it must be …

⚙ We often use a noun (e.g. *pain*) + a suffix (e.g. *-less*) to make an adjective (e.g. *painless*). We often use *-ful* to form adjectives that mean 'with' or 'full of' and *-less* to form adjectives that mean 'without'.

A Complete each sentence with the correct adjective formed from the noun in brackets.

1 I was never very good at maths because I was _____. (*care*)
2 Some kids get into trouble because they are _____ and they take too many risks. (*fear*)
3 Intelligence is _____ on its own – you need to understand people, too. (*use*)
4 Very intelligent people are often very lonely and this can be _____ for them. (*pain*)
5 Einstein had a very _____ brain. (*power*)
6 I feel _____ about the future. I think good things will happen! (*hope*)
7 Nadine is very _____ and always considers her friends' feelings. (*thought*)
8 Most people believe that without government, we would have a very _____ society. (*law*)

B Choose *Agree* or *Disagree* for each statement.

1 Logic is useless for understanding other people and their emotions.   Agree / Disagree
2 Highly intelligent people are often thoughtless.   Agree / Disagree
3 We shouldn't be fearful of the future.   Agree / Disagree
4 Life shouldn't be painless. We learn from difficult experiences.   Agree / Disagree

C 🗣 Work in pairs. Compare your answers with your partner's. Explain your choices.

A You are going to listen to a lecture. Before you listen, look at the photo and try to guess what the lecture is going to be about.

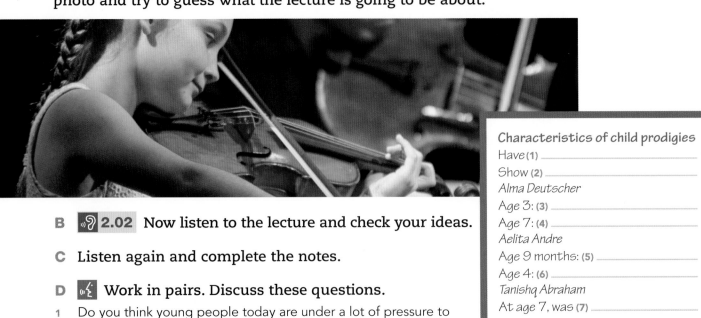

B 🎧 **2.02** Now listen to the lecture and check your ideas.

C Listen again and complete the notes.

D 🗣 Work in pairs. Discuss these questions.

1 Do you think young people today are under a lot of pressure to be successful?
2 Do you know someone who had an exceptional talent as a child? What happened to him/her?
3 What do you think a child prodigy's life must be like?

Characteristics of child prodigies
Have (1) _____
Show (2) _____
Alma Deutscher
Age 3: (3) _____
Age 7: (4) _____
Aelita Andre
Age 9 months: (5) _____
Age 4: (6) _____
Tanishq Abraham
At age 7, was (7) _____
Now: (8) _____
Difficulties for child prodigies
1 Have (9) _____
2 (10) _____

GRAMMAR: question tags

A 🎧 **2.03** **LANGUAGE IN CONTEXT** Listen to the conversation below. What job does Justin want to do?

Penny: Justin, I've just read an interesting article about brain hemispheres. You're left-handed, aren't you?

Justin: Yeah, why?

Penny: Well, apparently left-handed people are often good at maths and music. Do you think that's true?

Justin: Hmm, interesting … I suppose I am good at maths. And I love music! But that can't be true for everyone, can it? I mean, you play in a band, don't you? So you must be good at music. But you aren't left-handed, are you?

Penny: You're right. I don't think it's a hard and fast rule. The article just says there are some links between handedness and certain abilities. But people don't always develop them. In fact, you didn't start playing the guitar until quite recently, did you?

Justin: Yeah, although I've always wanted to. And I've being playing the keyboard since I was really little. I would really like to have a career in music, but my dad doesn't like that idea. I should just tell him that I was born to be a rock star, shouldn't I?

Penny: Definitely!

NOTICE!
Underline the question phrases at the ends of sentences in the conversation above. Are they *yes/no* or information questions?

B **ANALYSE** Read the conversation in Exercise A again.

Function **Tick the completions for the rule that are true.**
We use question tags to …
a) confirm information that we are almost certain about.
b) check information we're not sure about.
c) ask for further information.

Form **Complete the table with question tags from Exercise A.**

	Affirmative main verb, negative question tag	Negative main verb, affirmative question tag
main verb *be*	You**'re** left-handed, (1) _____ ?	You **aren't** left-handed, (2) _____ ?
simple tenses	You **play** in a band, (3) _____ ?	You **didn't start** playing the guitar until quite recently, (4) _____ ?
modals	I **should** just **tell** him that I was born to be a rock star, (5) _____ ?	That **can't be** true for everyone, (6) _____ ?

For question tags with perfect and continuous tenses, see the Grammar Reference on p.161.

C **PRACTISE** **Complete the question tags.**
1 You didn't do well on the test, _____?
2 Alastair is really clever, _____?
3 We aren't late for the test, _____?
4 Tom could read when he was three, _____?
5 I won't see you tomorrow, _____?
6 The bus leaves at 5.30pm, _____?
7 Claudia's got a new car, _____?
8 I shouldn't do it like this, _____?

WHAT'S RIGHT?
◯ It starts at nine, isn't it?
◯ It starts at nine, doesn't it?
◯ They don't study chemistry, do they?
◯ They don't study chemistry, don't they?

have got uses *have* in question tags:
We haven't got a test tomorrow, have we?

D 🎤 **NOW YOU DO IT** Work in pairs. Use question tags to check your knowledge about these areas of your partner's life. Ask other questions to find out more.

• family • interests • ambitions • experiences

You've got three brothers, haven't you? What are their names?

A 🎧 **2.04** Listen to the sentences. In which sentences does the speaker sound certain? In which sentences does the speaker sound less certain?

		certain	less certain
1	I'm not late, am I?	☐	☐
2	I'm not late, am I?	☐	☐
3	Today's the 27th, isn't it?	☐	☐
4	Today's the 27th, isn't it?	☐	☐

B 🎧 **2.05** Listen to these sentences and answer the questions.

1 In which two sentences does the speaker sound certain? Does the voice go up or down on the question tags?

2 In which two sentences does the speaker sound less certain? Does the voice go up or down on the question tags?

1 We've done this wrong, haven't we?   ↓
2 You're German, aren't you?   ↑
3 You didn't work on that project, did you?   ↓
4 You've studied art, haven't you?   ↑

C 🗣 Work in pairs. Practise saying the question tags in Exercises A and B.

SPEAKING: speculating

⚙ We speculate when we aren't sure about something, and have to guess or make a deduction. In order to speculate, we can use modals of deduction and question tags. We can also use phrases such as *Maybe it's a …, If you ask me, …, It could be a …,* and *It looks like a …* to show we are uncertain.

A 🎧 **2.06** Listen to the conversation. Underline the phrases that the speakers use to speculate about the photo.

Jonny: Look at this picture. What do you think it is?
Ally: Well, if you ask me, it could be a dry riverbed.
Jonny: I don't think it can be a riverbed. It's the wrong shape. It looks like a tree trunk to me.
Charlie: Let me see. It's part of an animal, isn't it?
Ally: Hmm … It could be, I suppose. Maybe it's a lizard.
Charlie: No, I don't think so. What about a rhinoceros?
Jonny: Of course! It must be a rhino. It's obvious now!

B 🗣 Work in pairs. Look at these photos of everyday things. Speculate about what each photo might be.

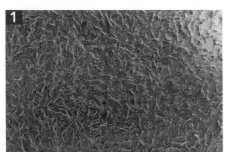

C 🗣 Compare your ideas with another pair. Who has the best ideas?

HOW TO SAY IT 🗣

Speculating

It could be a …, couldn't it?
Maybe. It looks to me like it might be a …
It can't be a …, can it? What about …?

A Match the verbs 1–6 with the nouns a–f to make collocations.

1 explore
2 find
3 develop
4 solve
5 challenge
6 learn

a) a solution
b) (all) the possibilities
c) a problem
d) yourself
e) your abilities
f) new skills

B Complete these sentences with the correct form of the phrases in Exercise A.

1 You need to practise regularly to _____ in a new skill.

2 I try to _____ to do something new and different every day.

3 You should always _____ before making a decision.

4 When I have to _____, I try to look at it from different angles.

5 I think it's important to _____ to keep your brain active.

6 When I have a problem, my friends usually help me _____.

C Work in pairs. Say which statements in Exercise B you agree with and explain why.

A Read the text. What are the main arguments in favour of varying your study environment? What are the main arguments against it? Which side do you agree with more?

Should you vary your study environment?

Some scientists and neurologists say that to improve your thinking skills, you should vary where and how you work or study. For example, don't always work at your desk. Instead sit in your favourite chair or lie on the sofa, with your family talking around you or even with the TV on! There are several reasons for this theory.

First, the brain works better if it has variety. A variety of stimuli causes the brain to be more alert, so more learning takes place. Another reason is that if you are studying and listening to music at the same time, you are multi-tasking. Asking your brain to do more than one thing at a time is good brain training. Finally, always studying in the same place is boring, and if you are bored, your level of concentration is lower.

On the other hand, many educators recommend always studying at the same time in the same place for several reasons. First, this creates a routine, and if you have a routine, it is easier to develop the habit of studying for a certain amount of time every day. Second, you have all your books close by and organised in one area. Finally, you can be away from distractions like TV or other people, and many educators believe this is necessary for good concentration.

B Read this list of arguments for and against the argument 'Are video games good for brain training?'. Put a tick next to the arguments for using video games and a cross next to the arguments against.

☐ Antisocial activity – little interaction with friends or family

☐ Develops problem-solving skills – players have to think of creative ways to solve puzzles or problems

☐ Improves eye-hand coordination – in visual games, eyes see images and hands have to react quickly

☐ Not enough physical activity – leads to obesity and other physical problems

☐ Possible addiction – not enough sleep; poor school work

☐ Improves memory – in many games players have to remember words or images

☐ Unbalanced skills development – players don't learn other things such as sports or hobbies

☐ Reduces stress – games are fun; playing releases aggression and frustration

C 'Are video games good for brain training?' Use these notes to write your for and against text:

There is disagreement about whether or not playing video games is a good way to train your brain.

• arguments for (at least three)
• arguments against (at least three)

THINKING LOGICALLY

- Question your assumptions.
- Approach the problem differently.
- Think of new ideas and test them.

A Do this puzzle. Connect these dots by drawing four straight lines, without lifting your pencil off the paper and without going back over a line. You have two minutes.

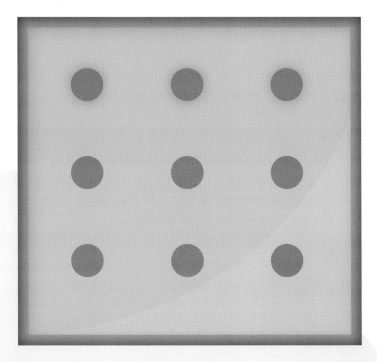

B If you solved the puzzle, well done! If you didn't, it might help you to question your assumptions. To do this, decide whether these sentences about the puzzle are true (T) or false (F).

1 The instructions say each line has to start and end on a dot. T / F
2 Your lines can go further than the rows of dots. T / F
3 Each line has to go through three dots. T / F

C Now try the puzzle in Exercise A again. If you still can't work out the answer, find someone who has the answer and ask them to show you how to do it.

D Do this puzzle. Look at this fish made out of matchsticks. Move three matchsticks only so that the fish is swimming in the opposite direction. You have one minute.

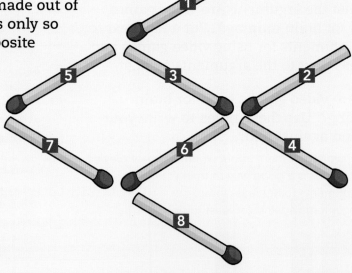

E If you solved the puzzle in Exercise D, read this text and decide if it describes how you think. If you didn't solve the puzzle, read the text and think about how you should approach the puzzle in Exercise D differently.

Logical thinking

There are times in all our lives when we need to think more logically. It might be in a real-life situation, such as making a business decision. Or it might be when we are doing a test or puzzle of some kind. The problem some of us have when it comes to thinking logically is that we think certain limits exist, when in fact they don't. It's all about our assumptions.

We all have lots of assumptions – things we think are correct, even if there's no reason to. To illustrate, take a look at this well-known puzzle using matchsticks. The coin looks as if it is inside a 'glass' formed by four

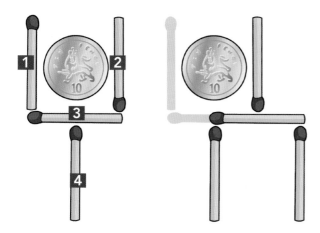

matchsticks. You have to move just two matchsticks to get the coin outside the glass. You cannot move the coin! It seems impossible … and it is impossible, as long as you assume that the glass has to stay the same way up. However, the puzzle becomes very easy if you think about making an 'upside-down' glass. To do this, all you have to do is move matchstick 3 to the right a little and move matchstick 1 down.

The key to solving this problem is to question your assumptions. And questioning your assumptions is a big part of logical thinking.

Logical thinking is not just about the artificial world of puzzles. This same kind of thinking can be very useful in real life, too. If we aren't careful, we can assume things about ourselves, other people and the world around us, which limit our thinking. By analysing and questioning our assumptions, we can think more logically and systematically about a problem, and perhaps find solutions that we simply couldn't see before.

F Now try the puzzle in Exercise D again. Use what you learnt in the article to help you.

G Work in pairs. Brainstorm a list of real-life problems and how logical thinking might help to solve them. Then explain your ideas to the rest of the class.

Problem: *How to get a huge new sofa into your house*

How logical thinking might help: *It can help you think of different ways, e.g. through the window.*

HOW TO SAY IT

Discussing logical thinking

One problem which could be solved using logical thinking is …

Do you think logical thinking would help if …?

How would logical thinking help in that situation?

If …, logical thinking could help you to …

REFLECT … How can improving your logical thinking help you in **Self and Society** and **Work and Career**?

Language wrap-up

1 VOCABULARY

Choose the correct words. (15 points)

One of the most **(1)** powerful / powerless and **(2)** useful / useless techniques for training your brain is visualisation. Whether you're trying to **(3)** develop / learn abilities you already have, or trying to **(4)** develop / learn a new skill, visualisation can help you. It can also help you **(5)** find / solve a solution to stopping unhealthy habits, such as smoking, when you think you've **(6)** explored / challenged all the possibilities and you're feeling **(7)** hopeful / hopeless. In fact, visualisation can work in any situation where you are trying to **(8)** challenge / solve yourself to improve, or if you are trying to **(9)** find / solve a difficult problem. The technique involves forming a picture in your mind, like a picture on a movie screen. You have to be **(10)** careful / careless to create a really vivid picture of what you want to achieve. Imagine yourself feeling **(11)** fearful / fearless and strong. Then add sound and make it come to life. Then, make a small black and white picture of yourself feeling **(12)** fearful / fearless and failing. Quickly replace that **(13)** painful / painless image with your bright, happy image. Do that five or six times. Now, every time you feel **(14)** powerful / powerless and think you are going to fail, the positive image will come to mind. Difficult situations become much less **(15)** painful / painless and you are more likely to succeed. Why not give it a try?

11 – 15 correct: I can use adjectives with -*ful* and -*less* and use collocations connected to improving your brain.

0 – 10 correct: Look again at the vocabulary sections on pages 84 and 87.   **SCORE:**   /15

2 GRAMMAR

A   Complete the conversation with *must, can't* or *might/may/could*. (7 points)

Andy: I can't finish this crossword puzzle. Do you know a country with a five-letter name?

Kelly: There **(1)** _____ be hundreds! It **(2)** _____ be 'China'.

Andy: No, it **(3)** _____ be 'China' because it begins with the letter *I*.

Kelly: Why didn't you say that? Well, it **(4)** _____ be 'Iran'. That only has four letters. It **(5)** _____ be 'Italy'.

Andy: No. It **(6)** _____ be Italy because it ends with the letter *a*.

Kelly: It **(7)** _____ be 'India' then.

Andy: Brilliant! Thanks.

B   Complete the question tags. (8 points)

1   They can't solve the puzzle, _____ ?
2   She's very good at puzzles, _____ ?
3   You'll help me, _____ ?
4   We didn't pass the test, _____ ?
5   She hasn't got an exam today, _____ ?
6   We shouldn't buy that car, _____ ?
7   You don't have a motorbike, _____ ?
8   Paula doesn't like dogs, _____ ?

11 – 15 correct: I can use modals of deduction to express degrees of certainty. I can use question tags to check information.

0 – 10 correct: Look again at the grammar sections on pages 83 and 85.   **SCORE:**   /15

WRITING WORKSHOP

A Read the text. Does the writer give a balanced answer to the question, or one particular view?

IS DOING SPORT GOOD FOR THE MIND?

While some scientists say that doing sport is good training for both the mind and the body, others criticise organised sport. One reason for this is that contact sports like football or rugby can cause permanent brain damage if players get injured. Another reason is that doing sport can also lead to emotional problems. There is often too much pressure to win, and players sometimes suffer from a great amount of stress. Finally, the enormous competition to win or to be the best player on the team can cause some players to have strong feelings of aggression.

On the other hand, recent studies indicate that exercise can actually help your brain work better. First, physical activity stimulates the brain to produce new stem cells, so exercise literally makes your brain grow. Second, you need mental as well as physical skills to do some sports. You have to solve problems, plan strategies and adapt to different situations, and you have to do it all at lightning speed! Finally, if you play a team sport, you are also developing good teamworking skills.

B Read the article again and find these things for each paragraph.

1 the topic sentence
2 the main arguments – how many are there in each paragraph?
3 phrases that link arguments together

C You are going to write a for and against text with the title 'Is watching television good for young children?'. First, read these arguments and decide if they are for or against the question.

- Some TV programmes are educational.
- Many TV programmes are not appropriate for young children.
- Watching too much TV can lead to inactivity and health problems.
- Watching TV can help children relax and have quiet time.
- Parents can control how much TV their children watch.
- Children aren't being creative when they're watching TV.

D Write a two-paragraph text. Use your notes from Exercise C to help you. Include:

- a topic sentence for each paragraph.
- at least three arguments for and against the topic.
- sequencing words and phrases to introduce the arguments and link them together.

HOW ARE YOU DOING?

Look back at your writing and tick the statements that are true.

- ◯ I have stated the main idea of each paragraph in a topic sentence.
- ◯ I have given at least three arguments for and against the question.
- ◯ I have used sequencing words and phrases to link my arguments together.

Now ask a partner to look at your writing and tick.

Does the text present a good balance of for and against arguments?

● Well done! ◯ Nearly! Look at the unit again. ● Think again! Ask your teacher for help.

UNIT 8 STORIES WE TELL

IN THIS UNIT YOU

- learn language to tell stories and anecdotes
- tell a personal anecdote
- read a traditional African legend
- listen to a traditional North American story
- write a legend or anecdote from your country
- learn how to use past experiences to make better decisions for the future
- ▶ watch a video about myths and legends

LISTENING
predicting
When you read a book or watch a film, do you find yourself guessing what will happen next? How do you feel when you get it right/wrong?

WRITING
checking your work
How many drafts of a writing task do you usually make? What kind of things do you check every time?

LIFE SKILLS
SELF & SOCIETY

learning from experience
'We learn from failure, not from success!' What does this statement mean? Do you agree with it?

A Look at these three stills from online videos. What do you think each person might be talking about?

A

B

C

B 🔊 **2.07** Now listen to each person talking. Were any of your predictions correct?

A: *My prediction about the man with the computer was more or less right, but the other two were completely wrong!*

B: *I thought the girl was going to talk about her friends, but …*

VOCABULARY: embarrassing events

A Write the correct phrase under each picture.

> arrive late   click on 'Reply to all'   forget someone's name   get lost   get the wrong day
> say the wrong thing   send a text to the wrong person   spill a drink on someone

1 _____
2 _____
3 _____
4 _____

5 _____
6 _____
7 _____
8 _____

B Complete these sentences with the correct form of phrases in Exercise A.

1 John's meeting was a disaster. Halfway through, he _____ the client's _____ and had to ask him.
2 I wished Lorena 'Happy Birthday', but I _____. It was last month!
3 Sofia _____ to the interview because she overslept and missed the train.
4 At a business dinner, I _____ on my boss! Her skirt was soaked.
5 I missed Pete's birthday party. I _____ and couldn't find his house!
6 I _____ to Vicky. I asked her how her boyfriend was, but they had just split up.
7 I sent an email complaining about my boss. The problem was that I _____ and accidentally sent the email to him, too!
8 I wanted to send a message to my girlfriend saying 'I love you', but I _____ it _____. It went to my colleague instead!

C 🗣 Work in pairs. Which situation in Exercise A do you think is the most/least embarrassing? Why?

GRAMMAR: relative clauses

A LANGUAGE IN CONTEXT Read the comments and decide which moment was the most embarrassing.

NOTICE!

Underline the words that often introduce questions, e.g. *when*. Are they used to introduce questions in this case?

WHAT WAS YOUR most embarrassing moment?

SUZIE: It was the time when I spilt a drink all over someone that I really liked!

ANDY: I'd just started a new job, and I had responsibility for a report that was going to be discussed in a big meeting. During the meeting, I found out that the data which I had used was completely wrong!

EVAN: Once, I thought the person who answered the phone was my girlfriend, so you know, I started saying romantic things. The person who I was talking to was my girlfriend's mother!

MARISA: It happened at the place where I used to work. I made a joke that involved my boss, and he was standing right behind me!

B ANALYSE Read the comments in Exercise A again.

Form Complete the table with examples from Exercise A.

Relative pronoun	Examples
who	I thought **the person** (1) _____ was my girlfriend.
when	It was **the time** (2) _____ all over someone.
where	It happened at **the place** (3) _____ .
which/that	I found out that **the data** (4) _____ was completely wrong.
	I had responsibility for **a report** (5) _____ in a big meeting.

Function Choose the correct option to complete the rule.
We use relative clauses to …
a) ask an indirect question about a person, thing, time or place.
b) give more information about a person, thing, time or place.

C PRACTISE Rewrite the sentences to include relative clauses about the underlined words.

1 It was my worst moment. I forgot my new boss's name!
  <u>My worst moment</u> was _____ !
2 I ran into that man on my bicycle a couple of days ago!
  That's <u>the man</u> _____ !
3 I had an accident on this street.
  This is <u>the street</u> _____ .
4 Celia started that rumour.
  Celia is <u>the person</u> _____ .
5 That news story caused the politician to resign.
  That was <u>the news story</u> _____ .

D NOW YOU DO IT Work in pairs. Think about how you would complete the phrases below. Explain your choices to your partner.

The person who I admire the most is …
The time when I was the happiest was …
A place where I would love to live is …
One thing that makes me really happy is …

> **WHAT'S RIGHT?**
> ○ The report that it has all the information is on your desk.
> ○ The report that has all the information is on your desk.
> ○ The man which donated a lot of money is a billionaire.
> ○ The man who donated a lot of money is a billionaire.

SPEAKING: telling an anecdote

A 🎧 **2.08** Listen to this anecdote. What two embarrassing things happened in the story?

B Work in pairs. Think about a funny or embarrassing thing that happened to you or to someone you know. Then ask and answer these questions to help you prepare to tell your anecdote.

1 What are you going to talk about?
2 When did it happen?
3 Who else was there?
4 What happened first?
5 What happened after that?
6 What happened in the end?

C Work with a different partner. Tell each other your anecdotes. Ask questions to find out more information.

> **HOW TO SAY IT**
>
> **Telling an anecdote**
> *The funniest / most embarrassing thing was the time when …*
> *What happened was …*
> *It happened at a restaurant/party/place where …*
> *She/He was the person who/that …*

VOCABULARY: adjectives for describing stories

A Match each definition to the correct word.

If a story …

1 makes you feel uncomfortable, it's …
2 affects you emotionally, it's …
3 has lots of new, creative ideas, it's …
4 is fun to read or watch, it's …
5 is only for children (in a negative way), it's …
6 seems irrelevant and uninteresting, it's …
7 makes you think, it's …
8 isn't realistic, it's …
9 is exciting, it's …
10 makes you want to find out how it ends, it's …

a) entertaining.
b) gripping.
c) thrilling.
d) disturbing.
e) pointless.
f) unbelievable.
g) imaginative.
h) moving.
i) thought-provoking.
j) childish.

B Work in groups. For each adjective in Exercise A, think of a story you know that the adjective describes. It could be a book, a fairy tale, a film or another kind of story. Say why you would characterise the story that way.

A: *Gripping.*
B: *The film World War Z! I couldn't wait to get to the end to see if the zombies took over the world!*

READING: a story

A Look at the pictures. What do you think this African legend is about?

Long ago, there lived a woman named Manzandaba and her husband Zenzele. They had many children and during the day they were happy. They spent their days making baskets and hunting. But in the evenings, they were unhappy. 'Mama,' the children cried, 'Please, tell us some stories!' But she and Zenzele didn't know any stories. There were no stories, no dreams, no magical tales back then.

One day, Zenzele asked Manzandaba to go out and find stories, and she agreed. Manzandaba decided to ask every animal she passed if they knew any stories. The first animal Manzandaba met was the hare, but he didn't have any stories. The next animal was the baboon. 'Baboon!' she called. 'Do you have any stories that I could take back to my people?' The baboon laughed. 'I have no time for stories!' Next she came upon the elephant. 'Oh, kind elephant,' she asked, 'Do you know where I might find some stories?' 'I don't know any stories,' he said, 'but why don't you ask the eagle?'

So Manzandaba searched for the great fish eagle, and found him near the river. 'Eagle, my people are hungry for stories. Where can I find some?' 'Well,' he said, 'I know someone who may be able to help you. Wait here.' So Manzandaba waited.

Finally, the eagle came back and said, 'My friend, the big sea turtle, will take you to the story place!' 'Climb onto my back,' said the sea turtle. 'I will carry you to the bottom of the ocean, the Land of the Spirit People.' The sea turtle took Manzandaba to the King and Queen, and Manzandaba told them that she was looking for stories. 'We have many stories,' they said. 'But what will you give us for those stories, Manzandaba?' 'What do you want?' Manzandaba asked. 'A picture of your home and your people,' they said. 'Can you bring us that?' 'Yes!' Manzandaba answered. 'I can!'

Manzandaba returned home and told her family everything. When she got to the end of her story, her husband said, 'I can make a beautiful picture in wood for the Spirit People.' And he did. Finally, Manzandaba returned to the Spirit Kingdom. When they saw the picture, the King and Queen were very happy! In return, the King and Queen gave Manzandaba the most beautiful shell she had ever seen. 'Whenever you want a story,' they said, 'hold this shell to your ear and you will have your story!' And that is how stories came to the world.

B Read the legend and answer the questions.

1 At the beginning of the story, why were the people unhappy in the evenings?
2 What did Manzandaba do to try to find stories?
3 How did the eagle help Manzandaba?
4 Why didn't the Spirit People give Manzandaba the stories on her first visit to them?
5 In what form did stories come to the world?

C Work in groups. Discuss these questions.

1 Which adjectives from the vocabulary section would you use to describe this story? Why?
2 Why do you think cultures have legends?
3 Can you think of any legends from your country that are similar to this one?

PRONUNCIATION: /ə/ in multisyllable words

A 2.09 Listen to these words. Can you hear the /ə/ sound of the underlined unstressed vowels?

/ə/   child<u>r</u>en   anim<u>a</u>l   imagin<u>a</u>tive   husb<u>a</u>nd   simil<u>a</u>r

B 2.10 Say these words aloud and underline the /ə/ sound of the unstressed vowels. Then listen and check.

negative elephant picture legend magical

C 2.11 Listen to these sentences. Now work in pairs and practise saying the sentences.

1 Her husband gave her a magical picture of an animal.
2 The African elephant is similar to the Indian elephant.
3 The children listened to the storyteller telling legends from Peru.

A LANGUAGE IN CONTEXT Read the blurb from the back cover of a book. Who might be interested in reading this book?

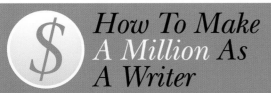

How To Make A Million As A Writer

Advice and tips from the experts! Are you <u>hoping</u> to earn big money as a writer? This book will show you how!

- Do you <u>enjoy</u> writing? Do you <u>want</u> to write full time?
- Do you find it difficult to <u>begin</u> writing? When you <u>start</u> to write, do you run out of ideas quickly?
- Have you <u>decided</u> to start a novel but can't <u>continue</u> writing? Then this book is for you!

Best-selling authors offer a few simple steps to get rid of the writer's block that's holding you back. Learn all about character, plot and the winning formula for success! Our experts <u>discuss</u> creating stories that really sell!

NOTICE!

Look at the underlined verbs. Which ones are followed by a *to*-infinitive and which ones by a gerund (*-ing* form)?

B ANALYSE Read the text in Exercise A again.

Form Complete the table with examples from Exercise A.

	Examples	Other verbs
verb + gerund	Do you (1) _____? Our experts (2) _____ stories that really sell!	admit, avoid, deny, dislike, finish
verb + infinitive	Are you (3) _____ big money as a writer? Do you (4) _____ full time? Have you (5) _____ a novel …	agree, help, invite, manage, offer, plan, promise, refuse, seem
verb + gerund/ infinitive	…but can't (6) _____? Do you find it difficult to (7) _____? When you (8) _____, do you run out of ideas quickly?	hate, like, love, prefer

C PRACTISE Complete each sentence with the verb in brackets in the correct form.

1 He admitted _____ (*copy*) the story from another book.
2 Have you finished _____ (*read*) that book I lent you yet?
3 I thought the story seemed _____ (*end*) a bit suddenly.
4 Traditional stories sometimes teach people _____ (*behave*) in the right way.
5 Why do so many young people dislike _____ (*write*)?
6 I hope _____ (*become*) a full-time writer by the time I'm 30.
7 My parents advised my sister _____ (*take*) that job.
8 I want to avoid _____ (*work*) full time as long as possible!

WHAT'S RIGHT?

○ We discussed to read that new novel.
○ We discussed reading that new novel.
○ The story was long, but I managed to finish it.
○ The story was long, but I managed finishing it.

D NOW YOU DO IT Work in small groups. Choose at least five of the phrases below and think of how you would finish them. Tell your group.

I never finish …	I really dislike …	I have decided …
I have promised …	I enjoy …	It was difficult, but I managed …
I usually avoid …	I hope …	

LISTENING: predicting page 73 ⚙

As well as predicting before you listen, you can also predict as you listen. Try to predict what the speaker is going to say next. You might not be right, but it will help to prepare you.

A You are going to listen to a traditional North American story. Look at the pictures. What do you think the story is about?

B »⑨ **2.12** Listen to the first part of the story. Answer the questions.

1 Why did Rabbit invent a story to tell the other animals?
2 How did the animals react to the story?

C »⑨ **2.13** Circle what you think is going to happen next. Then listen and check.

a The sun is going to disappear, and the animals are going to be cold and hungry.
b The animals are going to look for food so that they can survive when the sun disappears.
c Rabbit is going to tell the animals that it was only a joke.

D Listen again and answer the questions. Then say what you think is going to happen next.

1 Why did Kluskap think something was wrong?
2 What did he think when he heard the story?

E »⑨ **2.14** Listen to the final part of the story and check your answers. Then answer these questions.

1 What did Kluskap do?
2 Why does Rabbit have long ears today?

F What did you think of the story? Do you have stories about animals in your culture?

WRITING: checking your work page 75 ⚙

⚙ When you write a story or an essay, use a checklist to help you check your work. Include reminders to check grammar, vocabulary, spelling and punctuation. Also include reminders to check that you have done what the task asked you to do and you have included all the necessary information.

A 〔✍〕 Work in pairs. Read this advert for a story competition and complete the checklist with the correct information.

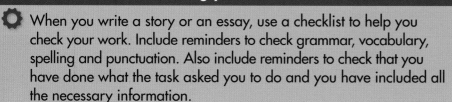

CHECKLIST FOR WRITING A STORY

1 Type of story: _____ or _____ Not _____ ◯
2 Introduction states _____ and _____ ◯
3 Maximum number of words: _____ ◯
4 Rules for folk tales: _____ ◯
5 Rules for original stories: _____ ◯
6 Information to include in the email: _____ ◯

B Write a short story for the competition. When you have finished writing, use your checklist to check your work.

WE WANT TO HEAR YOUR STORIES! SEND US A STORY FROM YOUR COUNTRY AND WIN A TRIP TO VISIT OUR OFFICES IN LONDON!

The story can be a traditional folk tale or an original story. It cannot be a summary of a film or a book. The introduction should state clearly what kind of story it is and in general what it is about. The story should have a maximum of 200 words. If you use a folk tale, you must write the story in your own words. If you write an original story, it should not be a personal anecdote, so you should write the story in the third person (*he, she, it, they*, but not *I* or *we*). Remember to include your full name, email address and phone number on your entry. Ready? Start writing!

LifeSkills

LEARNING FROM EXPERIENCE

- Tell someone about a bad experience.
- Let them help you understand what happened and analyse why things went wrong.
- Together, think of ways to avoid a similar situation in the future.

A  **Work in small groups. Read about a bad experience in a person's life. Then discuss these questions.**

1 Do you think Don is telling the whole story? If not, what questions would you ask him to understand what happened?
2 Did Don make any mistakes or incorrect assumptions? If so, what did he do wrong?
3 What seems to be Don's attitude about what happened? Did he admit to making any mistakes?
4 What should Don do differently in a similar situation in the future?

DON DAWSON works for a large advertising company. He is the creative director of several important accounts. The company recently lost one of Don's biggest accounts. Here is his story.

'We have worked with the airline Jet Stream for about five years. At the end of each year, we create the advertising strategy for the next year. The goal is to create an image concept and to design ads to project that image. In the past year, Jet Stream has had three near-accidents and several other incidents that were related to airline safety. In response to this, my team and I decided that Jet Stream needed to build an image of safety. We created a series of ads around the slogan 'Safety first. Nothing else matters.'

When we presented the concept to the airline executives, they hated it. They said the ads would make people think of the problems they had had. They wanted us to change the concept, and their idea was to have typical ads with smiling passengers receiving meals from smiling flight attendants. I told them that ads like that would insult people's intelligence because everyone knows that their airline has had safety issues. I said that the types of ads they were suggesting were unimaginative and pointless and that I was sure that a very junior, inexperienced person in their marketing department had come up with that approach. I told them not to worry because our agency would create a much more sophisticated ad campaign with real messages.

After I had said all of that, I found out that the person who had suggested their approach was their new marketing director, and he was in the meeting! He said that he had created the concept and that maybe I didn't understand the airline business. I said that I understood what sells products, airlines or anything else, and boring, pointless ads do not. Their guy said we didn't have anything else to talk about, and they cancelled the contract and left the meeting. You know, they say the client knows best, but at least in this case, I don't think so!'

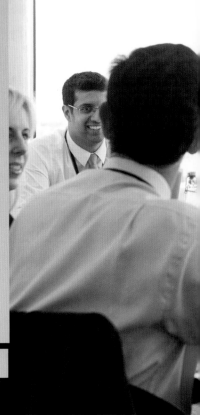

B 🗣 **Think of a bad experience you had in the past. You are going to tell a partner about it. First, think about what you're going to say. Use these questions as a guide.**

1 What was the background or context of the situation?
2 What happened? What was the sequence of events?
3 How did the situation end?

C 🗣 **Work in pairs. Tell your partner about your bad experience. Listen carefully to your partner's experience. Ask questions to understand what happened.**

D Think about your partner's experience and make notes. Use these questions as a guide.

1 Did your partner make any mistakes or incorrect assumptions?
2 What did he/she do wrong?
3 What was his/her attitude during the experience? What is his/her attitude now?
4 What should your partner do differently in a similar situation in the future?

E Now follow the same process to reflect on your own experience.

F 🗣 **With your partner, discuss your analysis of your partner's experience and your experience.**

• Did you both reach similar conclusions? Discuss any differences and try to come to an agreement.
• What did you learn from analysing your experience?
• Was it helpful to talk about the experience with another person? Why or why not?
• What would you do differently in a similar situation in the future to avoid making the same mistake?

A: *I learnt that I shouldn't assume I can do everything myself!*
B: *Yes, because you did that, you didn't have time to do the job well.*
A: *I realise now that I was wrong to do the presentation alone. Next time, I'll ask a colleague to help me.*

REFLECT ... How can learning from experience help you in **Work and Career** and **Study and Learning**?

Language wrap-up

1 VOCABULARY

A Read what the people said. Use the phrases from the box to describe the mistake each person made. (7 points)

1 'I realised that I didn't know where I was.' – Pete
Pete _____ .

2 'I thought the party was on Friday, but when I arrived, no one was there.' – Janie
Janie _____ .

3 'I didn't think when I sent the email that it would go to everyone.' – Katy
Katy _____ .

4 'I was supposed to be there at seven, but I didn't get there until eight.' – Elena
Elena _____ .

5 'I wish I hadn't mentioned the wedding because Julie got really upset.' – Mark
Mark _____ .

6 'In the meeting, I couldn't remember if he was Mr Wilkins or Mr Williams!' – Josh
Josh _____ .

7 'I meant to send the text message to my mum, but I sent it to my boss!' – Josh
Josh _____ .

> arrived late
> clicked on 'Reply to all'
> forgot someone's name
> got lost
> got the wrong day
> said the wrong thing
> sent a text to the wrong person

B Choose the correct words. (8 points)

1 The movie was thrilling / childish. Nobody over ten years old would like it.
2 It was a fun, unbelievable / entertaining story, and I think everyone would enjoy it.
3 It was a bit thrilling / unbelievable at the end. It just wouldn't happen in real life.
4 If you're going to write for children, you need to be really disturbing / imaginative.
5 The book is really thought-provoking / pointless. It talks about important issues.
6 That was a childish / gripping news story! I couldn't stop watching it.
7 I didn't see the purpose of that story. It seemed moving / pointless to me.
8 It was so moving / entertaining when the family finally met again. I was in tears!

> **11 – 15 correct:** I can talk about embarrassing events and use different adjectives to describe stories.
> **0 – 10 correct:** Look again at the vocabulary sections on pages 94 and 96. **SCORE:** /15

2 GRAMMAR

Complete the text with the correct forms of the verbs in brackets and the correct relative pronouns. (15 points)

Finally, it was the day **(1)** _____ all the students were going home for the holidays! I wanted to avoid **(2)** _____ (spend) too much money, so I decided **(3)** _____ (get) the bus. I bought a ticket for a bus **(4)** _____ went directly to my town. The bus station was really crowded, but I managed **(5)** _____ (find) someone **(6)** _____ could show me the right bus stop. He even offered **(7)** _____ (help) me with my luggage. He was the only person **(8)** _____ seemed **(9)** _____ (have) any information, so I followed him to the bus and got on. I had finished **(10)** _____ (take) my last exams that morning, and I was really tired, so I fell asleep as soon as the bus started **(11)** _____ (move). When I woke up, I saw that all the other passengers **(12)** _____ had been on the bus had gone, and we were in a town **(13)** _____ I had never been before! Obviously, the bus **(14)** _____ I had got on was the wrong one! Fortunately, the bus company agreed **(15)** _____ (let) me get another bus, and I finally got home!

> **11 – 15 correct:** I can use relative pronouns and the gerund or infinitive form after verbs.
> **0 – 10 correct:** Look again at the grammar sections on pages 94–95 and 98. **SCORE:** /15

SPEAKING WORKSHOP

telling an anecdote

A ⏺ **2.15** 🗣 Listen to someone telling an anecdote about an experience. Then work in pairs and talk about what happened. Try to remember as many details as possible. Use these questions to help you.

1 Where did the story happen?
2 What happened when Lily went to get her car?
3 What did she do?
4 How did the story end?

B Listen again and number these phrases in the order you hear them.

a The most awful thing happened to me the other day! ___
b So what happened? ___
c What did you do? ___
d Really? ___
e I'm getting there! ___
f Oh, no! ___
g That's terrible! ___
h So then what did you do? ___

C Match the phrases in Exercise B with their functions below.

1 introduces an anecdote _____
2 encourages the speaker to continue _____ _____ _____
3 expresses disbelief or surprise _____ _____ _____
4 tells the speaker not to be impatient _____

D Think of an experience that you or someone you know had. Think about how you would answer the questions below to help you prepare to tell your anecdote.

1 When and where did it happen?
2 Who was there?
3 What happened first?
4 What happened next?
5 How did the situation end?
6 How would you describe the experience in general?

E 🗣 Work in pairs. Tell your anecdote. As you listen to your partner's anecdote, ask questions and make comments. Use some of the expressions from Exercise B.

F 🗣 Find a new partner and tell your anecdote again.

HOW ARE YOU DOING?

Think about your speaking and tick the statements that are true.

I feel confident …

○ telling an anecdote about an experience.
○ expressing disbelief and surprise.
○ encouraging someone to continue speaking.

How do you feel about your speaking generally?

Very confident   Not sure …   Need to practise

UNIT 9 BODY TALK

IN THIS UNIT YOU

- ⚙ learn language to describe situations and regrets
- ⚙ talk about what to do for health problems and injuries
- ⚙ listen to a medical consultation
- ⚙ write a persuasive email
- ⚙ read about someone's regrets
- ⚙ learn to develop your memory
- ▶ watch a video about health

SPEAKING
asking for clarification
When you don't understand what someone has said, what can you say? Make a list of phrases.

READING
speed reading
Is it useful to be able to read quickly? Why? In what situations?

LIFE SKILLS STUDY

developing your memory
Do you have a good memory? Do you think it's possible to improve your memory? How?

A 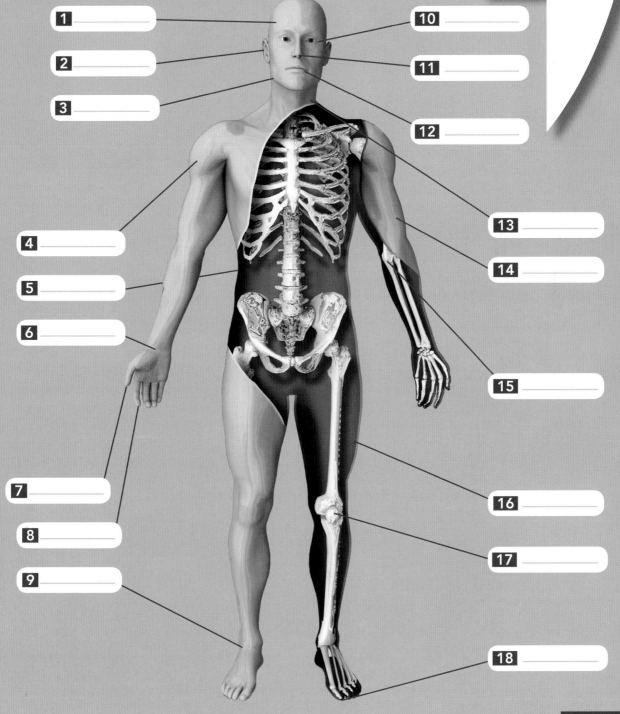 Work in groups. Label as many parts of the human body as you can using the words in the box. You have two minutes!

ankle arm back ear elbow eye finger head jaw knee
leg mouth neck nose shoulder thumb toe wrist

B))2.16 Listen and check. Did any of the groups label all the body parts correctly?

A: *I thought 7 was finger, but it's thumb.*
B: *We labelled most of the body parts correctly, but not all of them.*

HOW TO SAY IT

Speculating and guessing
I think 4 is arm.
It might be shoulder.
It can't be elbow.
It must be shoulder.

1 _____

2 _____

3 _____

4 _____

5 _____

6 _____

7 _____

8 _____

9 _____

10 _____

11 _____

12 _____

13 _____

14 _____

15 _____

16 _____

17 _____

18 _____

VOCABULARY: injuries

A Match each injury from the box with the correct picture.

> break your leg · burn yourself · cut your finger
> hurt your knee · hurt your shoulder · injure your back
> pull a muscle · sprain your ankle

B 🔊 Complete each phrase with other parts of the body. Compare your answers with a partner.

1 break your _____
  break your _____
2 sprain your _____
  sprain your _____
3 cut yourself
  cut your _____
  cut your _____
4 hurt yourself
  hurt your _____
  hurt your _____

C 🔊 Have you, or has someone you know, ever had any of the injuries in Exercise A? What happened? Tell a partner.

A: *I broke my arm when I was five. I fell out of a tree.*
B: *Really? I pulled a muscle dancing last month.*

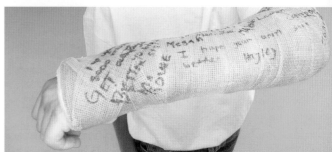

GRAMMAR: infinitive clauses with impersonal *it*

A LANGUAGE IN CONTEXT Read this advice from a health website. Does Ian need to see a doctor?

B ANALYSE Read the text in Exercise A again.

Form Complete the table with examples from Exercise A.

It's (not)	adjective	infinitive clause
It's	essential	to rest the muscle.
It 1) _____	_____	_____ the shoulder relaxed.
It 2) _____	_____	_____ a doctor.
It 3) _____	_____	_____ to a professional.

Function Tick the two correct functions. Cross out the incorrect function.

We use *it's* (not) + adjective + infinitive clause when we want to …
a) use the adjective to describe a person.
b) use the adjective to describe an action.
c) use the adjective to describe a situation.

It means the same as using the gerund as a subject.
It's essential to rest the muscle. = Resting the muscle is essential.

✚ eMED
MEDICAL ADVICE

I think I've pulled a muscle in my shoulder. Is there anything I should or shouldn't do? – *Ian*

Healthcare worker Sue Atkins replies:

Hi Ian. Well, it's essential not to strain the muscle even more. When you injure yourself like this, it's important to keep the shoulder relaxed. Don't try to do too much exercise. Generally, if you pull a muscle, it's not necessary to see a doctor. But if you are in severe pain, it's better to speak to a professional because it could be something more serious. Hope you get well soon!

NOTICE!

Find the adjective *essential* in the text. What comes before this word? What comes after it?

C PRACTISE Match the problems 1–6 to the advice a–f. Then write complete sentences using the words in brackets. Start each sentence with *It's*.

1 I burnt my hand cooking dinner.
2 I hurt my knee playing football.
3 I feel depressed after my accident.
4 I hurt my arm yesterday.
5 My sister cut her hand badly.
6 I'm going to do exercise at the gym every day!

a) (*better / lift things with the other arm*) _____
b) (*important / see a doctor*) *It's important to see a doctor.*
c) (*good / get fit*) _____
d) (*essential / take her to hospital*) _____
e) (*better / stop playing for a while*) _____
f) (*common / feel like that*) _____

D 🔊 **NOW YOU DO IT** Work in pairs. Talk about what you should do for the medical problems in the box. Use the prompts below to help you.

a broken leg   a sprained wrist   a minor burn   a pulled muscle   a minor cut

- go to hospital
- rest
- call an ambulance
- put some ice on it
- put a plaster on it

A: *Well, with a broken leg, it's essential to go to hospital immediately.*
B: *Yes, and it's important not to move too much.*

WHAT'S RIGHT?
- ◯ It's important to rest.
- ◯ Is important to rest.
- ◯ It's better to go to hospital.
- ◯ It's better go to hospital.

SPEAKING: asking for clarification

⚙ If you didn't hear or didn't understand what someone said, it's better to let them know immediately. Then they can either repeat what they said, or explain it to you.

A Write R next to the phrases used to ask for repetition and E next to the phrases used to ask for an explanation.

1 Can you explain what you mean? _____
2 Sorry, what was that? _____
3 I didn't understand the last part. _____
4 Excuse me? _____
5 Pardon me? _____
6 Sorry, I'm not sure I follow you. _____

B 🔊 Work in pairs and follow the instructions.

- Student A, you have sprained your wrist. Listen to Student B's advice. Ask for clarification where necessary. Then swap roles. Look at pictures 5–8 and give Student B advice.
- Student B, look at pictures 1–4 and give Student A advice. Then swap roles. You have burnt your hand. Listen to Student A's advice. Ask for clarification where necessary.

A: *It's important to elevate the area.*
B: *Sorry, I'm not sure I follow you. What does 'elevate' mean?*

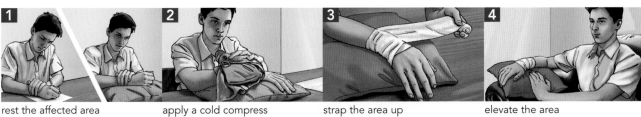

1 rest the affected area
2 apply a cold compress
3 strap the area up
4 elevate the area

5 remove the person from the source of heat
6 cool the burn with lukewarm water
7 regulate the person's temperature
8 cover the burn with cling film

A Look at the pictures and complete the people's symptoms with these words.

> cough   dizzy   headache   itchy   sore   temperature   vomit   breathing

1 'I sneeze a lot and my eyes are red and _____.'

2 'I have a _____ – I feel hot and cold – and my muscles ache.'

3 'I feel sick. I think I'm going to _____.'

4 'My ear hurts and I feel _____.'

5 'My nose is running and I have a bad _____.'

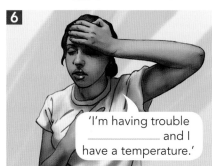

6 'I'm having trouble _____ and I have a temperature.'

7 'I have a terrible _____ and my vision is blurred.'

8 'My throat is _____ and it really hurts when I swallow.'

B Match the symptoms in Exercise A with these health problems.

a) He's got a migraine. _____

b) He's got hay fever. _____

c) She's got a chest infection. _____

d) She's got a sore throat. _____

e) He's got an ear infection. _____

f) He's got the flu. _____

g) He's got a cold. _____

h) She's got food poisoning. _____

C Work in pairs. Take turns choosing one of the health problems from Exercise A and acting out the symptoms. Your partner has three chances to diagnose the problem.

A Work in pairs and discuss these questions.

1 In your country, is it common to speak to a doctor over the phone? Does it depend on what problem you have?

2 Do doctors make house calls in your country?

3 Would you go to a private surgery, a medical centre or a hospital to see a doctor? Is it easy to get an appointment? How long would you usually spend with the doctor?

A: *I'd usually go to my local surgery.*   B: *It's not common to speak to a doctor over the phone.*

B 🎧 **2.17** Listen to a conversation between a patient and a doctor. Tick the problems the patient has now.

C Listen again and tick the treatments the doctor suggests.

D 🗣 Roleplay a conversation like the one you heard. Student A, you are the patient. Student B, you are the doctor.

 1 ☐
 5 ☐
 4 ☐
 6 ☐
 2 ☐
 8 ☐
 3 ☐
 7 ☐

HOW TO SAY IT 🗣

Asking and answering about symptoms
What seems to be the problem?
I've got a problem with my …
I see. Let's have a look.
When did you notice the symptoms?
I first noticed it when I …

WRITING: a persuasive email

A Read this email. Which of these problems do you think Olivia has asked for advice on?

loneliness ☐   eating properly ☐   getting fit ☐
an injury ☐   her family life ☐

● ● ○ subject: Feeling down

Hi Olivia!
It was great to get an email from you. Sorry to hear you've been feeling unhappy recently. You asked for my advice, so here goes!
First of all, you should make sure you know what a healthy diet is. Make sure you eat plenty of healthy foods and only eat sweet foods occasionally! You'll look and feel great in no time!
Secondly, I think you should find a cookery course. It's fun to cook and you'll learn how to make tasty, healthy meals. You'll learn all about healthy eating, and that really helps when you want to lose weight.
Finally, why not join a gym? It's a great way to get fit! It's good to have a regular routine and go maybe three evenings a week. It can be a bit expensive, but you never know – you might make some new friends!
I hope you find some of my advice helpful. Write soon and let me know how you get on.
Love, Jade

B 🗣 Work in pairs. You have received an email from a friend who wants to get fit and wants to make new friends. Decide which three of these pieces of advice you would give to them and say why.

find more time for your friends ☐   spend more time online ☐   take up a sport ☐   get a new job ☐
see a doctor ☐   join a gym ☐   eat a healthy diet ☐   join a club ☐

C Write an email to your friend. Give them your advice, and give reasons to persuade them to follow it.

PRONUNCIATION: /ɜː/

A 🎧 **2.18** Listen to this sound and the words. Can you hear the /ɜː/ sound? Now listen again and repeat.

/ɜː/   hurt   worse   girl

B 🎧 **2.19** Listen and circle the two words in each group that contain the /ɜː/ sound. Practise saying the words.

1 nerve   sister   verb   error   3 work   store   door   word
2 bird   first   hair   iron   4 our   burn   hurt   your

C 🗣 Work in pairs and practise saying the sentences.

1 My back really hurts.
2 The girl hurt her knee.
3 What's the English word for this part of the body?
4 Burns are a common household injury.

A LANGUAGE IN CONTEXT

Read this extract from an actor's autobiography. Did the woman have a healthy lifestyle when she was young?

NOTICE!

Look at the two underlined sentences in the text. Which one refers to the present and which one refers to the past? What is the tense of the main verb in each case?

Chapter 4

Looking back

As far as my health goes, I think I've been quite lucky over the years. It's important to eat well, and I eat lots of fruit and vegetables now. But it hasn't always been like that. <u>For example, I wish I had eaten better food as a young woman.</u> I hardly ever sat down to eat a proper, healthy meal, so I always got colds and flu because I had a poor immune system. And I smoked for years. If only I hadn't started smoking! I gave up smoking five years ago, but I often get chest infections now, and I'm sure it's because of smoking. I also wish I'd done more exercise, and I definitely wish I hadn't put on so much weight. Being overweight can cause lots of health problems and as you get older, it's much more difficult to lose it. <u>I wish I had a time machine</u> to go back and change things!

B ANALYSE Read the text in Exercise A again.

Form Complete the table with examples from Exercise A.

	Examples
Subject + *wish* + past perfect	I wish I (1) _____ better food.
	I also wish I (2) _____ more exercise.
	I definitely wish I (3) _____ weight.
If only + past perfect	If only I (4) _____ smoking!

WHAT'S RIGHT?
- ◯ I wish I hadn't broken my leg when I was a teenager.
- ◯ I wish I didn't break my leg when I was a teenager.
- ◯ If only I hadn't left my job.
- ◯ If only I haven't left my job.

Function Choose the correct option to complete the rule.

We use *wish / if only* + past perfect to talk about …
a) things we would like to change in the present.
b) things we want to change in the future.
c) things we would like to change about the past.

C PRACTISE Complete the second sentence using the word in brackets so that it means the same as the first.

1 My doctor gave me good advice. I didn't listen.
   I wish I had listened to my doctor's advice. (*wish*)

2 I ate a huge breakfast this morning. Now I feel sick.
   _____. (*only*)

3 Terri wanted to go to college, but she didn't go.
   _____. (*wish*)

4 James stayed up late last night. This morning, he's really tired.
   _____. (*wish*)

5 I didn't work at school. I failed my exams.
   _____. (*only*)

6 My parents drove to France. The journey was terrible.
   _____. (*wish*)

D NOW YOU DO IT Tick the areas of your life that you have regrets about. Then explain your regrets to a partner.

- ☐ family
- ☐ boyfriend/girlfriend
- ☐ studies
- ☐ friends
- ☐ money and work
- ☐ health

I wish I'd eaten healthier food when I was younger and I also wish I'd done more exercise.

Speed reading can help you get information from a long text quickly. When you speed read, keep your eyes moving forwards. Don't stop and don't read anything twice. Look at groups of words, not individual words.

A Quickly read this text about one woman's regrets. You have one minute. Then close your book and make notes about everything you can remember in your notebook.

MYBLOG

About   Achieve   Contact

September 21st   comments (2)

So, what big regrets do I have in my life so far? Well, I left school when I was 18 and immediately got a job in a bank because I wanted to start earning my own money. It seemed like a good idea at the time, but I really don't enjoy it. Now I wish I'd been to university before starting work. I'd really like to study fashion because I've always been interested in clothes. Last month, I finally decided to do something about it, and I'm going to do a part-time course on the internet. I hope it's the start of a brand new career for me.

And then last June I did something that I really regret now. I got a rose and my boyfriend's name tattooed on my upper arm. And well, guess what? We split up a few weeks ago and now I'm really embarrassed about the tattoo. Of course my mum didn't want me to get a tattoo, and now I really wish I'd listened to her. It will cost a lot of money to get it removed, and I've also heard it can be very painful. I really wish I hadn't got it.

I have a few other smaller regrets, too. In December, I had a big argument with my mum and dad, and I moved out of their house into my own flat. Although I like having my own place, I wish I'd stayed at home because the rent is really expensive, and now I never have any money to go out with my friends. Also, I can't cook, and I wish I didn't have to make my own dinner every evening. I really miss my mum's cooking! I also wish I had learnt to drive when I was younger. I never did and now I can't afford to have driving lessons. I have to take the bus everywhere, and it's so slow and usually very crowded, too. I wish I had known then what I know now!

B Read your notes and try to answer these questions.

1 What does the woman regret about her career choice?
2 What is she going to do about it?
3 What does she regret about her tattoo?
4 Why does she not like living on her own?

C Work in pairs. Compare your answers to the questions in Exercise B and compare your notes. How much of the information did you understand after only reading the text quickly once? Read the text again more slowly, and check how much you remembered.

LifeSkills

DEVELOPING YOUR MEMORY

- Select the information you need to remember.
- Create a memory tool.
- Use the memory tool to help you remember the information.

A Work in groups. Think about when you have an exam or test. What techniques do you use to help you remember information? Make a list.

B Read this information about what a 'memory tool' is and how it can help you develop your memory.

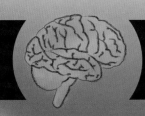

REMEMBER MORE
with a memory tool

HOME NEWS ABOUT ARTICLES CONTACT

Do you need an easy way to remember key information? One of the most effective ways is to use a memory tool. A memory tool is a technique that helps you remember information easily and effectively.

One example of a memory tool is to take the first letter of each word in a list of words you need to memorise and make a new word from these letters. For example, you can use the name Roy G. Biv to remember the colours of the rainbow: red, orange, yellow, green, blue, indigo, violet. Another example is to use hand gestures to remember something. For example, when children learn their left from their right, they should hold their fingers like this:

They'll see that their left hand forms the letter L, but their right hand does not!

Experts believe that the human brain can only remember a limited number of things, but that putting these items into groups can help the brain to remember more things. Try it for yourself and see if it works!

C Imagine that you have an important biology exam next week. Read this information about the human brain. Underline in the text where the four different parts of the brain shown in the diagram are found.

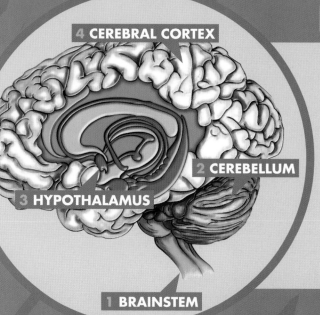

All human brains HAVE THESE PARTS:

4 CEREBRAL CORTEX

2 CEREBELLUM

3 HYPOTHALAMUS

1 BRAINSTEM

BRAINSTEM: The brainstem controls automatic functions (heartbeat, breathing, blood pressure). It is located in front of the cerebellum.

CEREBELLUM: The cerebellum takes information about your position and uses this to move your arms and legs together. It is behind the brainstem.

HYPOTHALAMUS: This is found above the brainstem. It controls visceral body functions (body temperature, behaviour, eating, drinking, etc).

CEREBRAL CORTEX: The cortex gets information from all of the sense organs (eyes, nose, ears, etc). It controls emotions and thought. It is the outer layer of the brain.

D Look at this example of a memory tool to help you remember the different parts of the brain. Complete the memory tool.

Boys	Hate	Chocolate	Cake
r	Y		
a	p		
a	o		
i	t		
n	h		
s	a		
t	l		
e	a		
m	m		
	u		
	s		

E Now think of a memory tool that you can use to help you remember the functions that the four different parts of the brain control. Make a note of it and try to learn it.

F Work in pairs. Close your books and test your partner on what they remember about the functions of the brain.

A: *This part of the brain controls eating and drinking.*
B: *The hypothalamus!*
A: *Correct!*

REFLECT ... How can the skill of developing your memory help you in **Self and Society** and **Work and Career**?

Language wrap-up

1 VOCABULARY

Read the symptoms. Match each sentence to the phrases from the box to describe the injury or health problem. (15 points)

> break your leg   burn yourself   cut your finger   have a chest infection   have a cold
> have a migraine   have a sore throat   have an ear infection   have the flu   have food poisoning
> have hay fever   hurt your shoulder   injure your back   pull a muscle   sprain your ankle

1   'I think I've eaten something bad. I'm going to vomit.' _____
2   'The knife slipped, and there was blood everywhere.' _____
3   'It hurts when I swallow.' _____
4   'Every summer, I sneeze a lot and my eyes get red and itchy.' _____
5   'I had an accident and now I can't walk for six weeks.' _____
6   'I lifted a heavy box and now I have to rest until it gets better.' _____
7   'I was cooking and spilt very hot water on my hand.' _____
8   'I have a really high temperature and my muscles ache.' _____
9   'My ear hurts and I feel dizzy.' _____
10   'I was running and my foot went in a hole. It hurts a bit.' _____
11   'I have a terrible headache and my vision is blurred.' _____
12   'I can't breathe and I have a temperature. My chest hurts.' _____
13   'I fell and now I can't move my arm properly!' _____
14   'I exercised without warming up and now my leg hurts.' _____
15   'My nose is running and I have a cough.' _____

> **11 – 15 correct:** I can talk about injuries, health problems and symptoms.
> **0 – 10 correct:** Look again at the vocabulary sections on pages 106 and 108.

SCORE: /15

2 GRAMMAR

Complete the texts with the correct form of the verbs in brackets. (15 points)

'It's common (1) _____ (want) to change your appearance. But it's not easy (2) _____ (get) your parents to agree to it! When I was 18 I got a tattoo, but I didn't tell my mum. I wish I (3) _____ (tell) her because she was really angry when she found out. It's awful (4) _____ (think) that I hurt her feelings. If only I (5) _____ (not be) so selfish. I wish I (6) _____ (think) about her feelings. It's not hard (7) _____ (do), but I just don't stop and think sometimes.'

'I wish I (8) _____ (have) children earlier. It's difficult (9) _____ (imagine) life without my daughter now. It's impossible (10) _____ (describe) how I felt when she was born. If only I (11) _____ (take) more photos of her when she was really small! It's easy (12) _____ (forget) to take photos when your life suddenly becomes so busy. It's great (13) _____ (be) a parent. I just love it! I wish now that I (14) _____ (understand) my own mother a bit better. It's so easy (15) _____ (not think) about how other people feel when you're young.'

> **11 – 15 correct:** I can use infinitive clauses with *it*. I can use *wish* and *if only* to talk about regrets.
> **0 – 10 correct:** Look again at the grammar sections on pages 106–107 and 110.

SCORE: /15

WRITING WORKSHOP
a persuasive email

A Read this email and answer these questions.

1 What does Rachel want to do? _____
2 What does Becky say about the changes Rachel wants to make? _____
3 What three practical things does Becky advise Rachel to do? _____

---

subject: catching up

from: b.williams@personalmail.com

Hi Rachel!

How are you? I'm sorry I haven't written sooner, but I've been so busy!

I was sorry to hear you've been having a few problems. Do you mind if I offer you some advice? I hope you understand that it's because I care about you.

First of all, stop worrying! It's easy to let things get on top of you. You should make an action plan and take it one step at a time. You say you want to get fit and get a new job and make new friends. It's hard to do so many things at once!

Secondly, you need to choose what's most important. Why not concentrate on getting fit and feeling better about yourself? You say you want to join a gym. It's never too late! Go on – join one! You should start now, and maybe you'll meet some new people that way. I know it's not easy to change your life. I'm here to help if you need some encouragement! Maybe I could come and visit you next month and cheer you up?

Lots of love,

Becky

B Read the email again and find the sentences where Becky does these things.

1 She apologises for not writing sooner.
2 She refers to her friend's email.
3 She explains the first thing her friend should do.
4 She makes a suggestion for something her friend should join.
5 She explains that she understands how hard it is.
6 She offers to do something practical to help.

C Read this extract from an email from a friend. Make notes on some ideas for advice you can give your friend.

1 How are you going to start your email?

_____

2 What two pieces of advice are you going to give your friend?

_____

3 What reasons will persuade your friend to follow your advice?

_____

4 What can you suggest you can do to help your friend?

_____

5 How are you going to end your email?

_____

I don't know. Recently, I've been feeling really down. I'm bored at work and need to find a new job. I just don't have any ideas about how to do it. It might be better to stay where I am and just hope things improve.

D Write a persuasive email to your friend. Use your notes from Exercise C to help you.

UNIT 10 STAGE AND SCREEN

IN THIS UNIT YOU

- ⚙ learn language to talk about performers and live events
- ⚙ talk about a show or live event you've seen
- ⚙ read an article about live event broadcasts in cinemas
- ⚙ listen to a lecture
- ⚙ write a descriptive paragraph
- ⚙ learn to work effectively as part of a team
- ▶ watch a video about award ceremonies

LISTENING
taking notes

When might you take notes as you listen? Make a list of as many situations as you can.

WRITING
descriptions

What do you think makes good descriptive writing?

LIFE SKILLS

SELF & SOCIETY

working as part of a team
There's a saying that 'there's no "I" in "team"'. What do you think that saying means?

A Are you a fan of stage and screen? Tick the activities that you do regularly.

go to the cinema ☐

stay in and watch a film ☐

see a stand-up comedian ☐

go to the theatre ☐

watch videos online ☐

go to the opera ☐

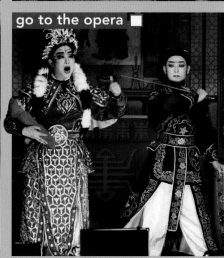

HOW TO SAY IT

Expressing and explaining preferences

The thing I like to do the most is …

I'm a big fan of …

I spend a lot of my free time …

That's probably because …

The reason for that is that I …

B Work in pairs. What is your favourite activity in Exercise A? Why?

A: *The thing I like to do the most is watch videos online. They're really funny.*

B: *I'm a big fan of the theatre. That's because I love seeing plays.*

VOCABULARY: at a live performance

A Match the words in the box to their definitions.

admission charge   audience   costumes   crowd   director   lighting
orchestra   row   scenery   venue

1	people watching a concert	_____	6	amount you pay to see a show	_____
2	clothes worn by actors	_____	7	people watching a play/film, etc	_____
3	large group of musicians	_____	8	place where shows often happen	_____
4	lights used in a show	_____	9	furniture and decoration on stage	_____
5	line of seats in a theatre	_____	10	person who tells actors what to do	_____

B Complete the sentences with the words from Exercise A.

1 The show was great, but the _____ was too high for a lot of people.
2 The _____ started cheering when the band came on stage.
3 I loved the show, particularly the colourful _____ everyone was wearing.
4 When the _____ started to play, the show began.
5 They used really dramatic _____, and I think it worked very well.
6 We couldn't see very well because we were in the back _____ .
7 The _____ loved the show and clapped for a very long time.
8 The Arena is such a great _____. There's always a great atmosphere.
9 I thought the _____ was awful! It looked cheap and badly made.
10 The _____ explained that the scene needed lots of feeling and emotion.

C 🔊 Which of the things in Exercise A are most important to you when you go to a live performance? Discuss with a partner.

A: *For me, the venue is really important. The seats should be comfortable.*
B: *Really? I think the actors and their costumes are more important.*

NOTICE!
Underline a clause which gives you extra information about the Bolshoi Ballet School. What relative pronoun comes at the beginning of the clause?

GRAMMAR: non-defining relative clauses

A LANGUAGE IN CONTEXT Read this biography of a ballerina. What is remarkable about her?

Polina Semionova, who was born in Russia in 1984, is one of the youngest ballerinas to become a principal dancer. A principal dancer, who is also called a prima ballerina, is one of the stars of a ballet company. Semionova studied at the Bolshoi Ballet School, which is in Moscow, and she won many prizes for her dancing before joining the Ballet Staatsoper Berlin as a principal dancer at the age of just 18. A year later, she won praise for her appearances in *Swan Lake*, which she performed with the English National Ballet. She continues to demonstrate her exciting talent to ballet audiences around the world.

B ANALYSE Read the text in Exercise A again.

Form Complete the examples with phrases from Exercise A. Then tick the statements that are true. Cross out the statements that are not true.

Polina Semionova, (1) _____, is one of the youngest ballerinas to become a principal dancer. A principal dancer, (2) _____, is one of the stars of a ballet company. Semionova studied at the Bolshoi Ballet School, (3) _____, and she won many prizes for her dancing. A year later, she won praise for her appearances in Swan Lake, (4) _____.

Non-defining relative clauses …

1 are separated from the rest of the sentence by commas. ☐
2 do not need commas to separate them from the rest of the sentence. ☐
3 can only come after the noun they refer to. ☐
4 can come before or after the noun they refer to. ☐
5 can use *who* to refer to people, and *which* or *that* to refer to places and things. ☐
6 can only use *who* to refer to people, and *which* to refer to places and things. ☐

Polina Semionova

Function Choose the correct option to complete the sentences.

1 A non-defining relative clause …
   a) identifies the subject of the sentence.
   b) gives us extra information about a noun.
2 We … which person or thing we are referring to.
   a) don't already know
   b) already know

3 The relative clause … without affecting the basic meaning.
   a) could be removed from the sentence
   b) could not be removed from the sentence

C PRACTISE Write sentences with non-defining relative clauses using the information given.

WHAT'S RIGHT?
- ○ Tchaikovsky, who wrote *Swan Lake*, was born in 1840.
- ○ Tchaikovsky, he wrote *Swan Lake*, was born in 1840.
- ○ This car, which we bought last year, is from Italy.
- ○ This car, that we bought last year, is from Italy.

1 The Paris Opera Ballet is the world's oldest ballet company. It was founded in 1669.

The Paris Opera Ballet, which was founded in 1669, is the world's oldest ballet company.

2 Harry Houdini was born in 1874 in Budapest. He was a famous magician.
3 *Swan Lake* was based on Russian folk tales. It was written by Tchaikovsky.
4 The Sydney Opera House was designed by Jørn Utzon. It opened in 1973.
5 The first opera was called *Dafne*. It was performed in 1598.

D NOW YOU DO IT Use the information below or find information about another performer you want to write about. Write a short biographical paragraph about the performer, using non-defining relative clauses to connect facts together where appropriate.

David Blaine

David Blaine, magician
b. 1973 in New York
became famous for *Street Magic*; the show was broadcast 1997

1999: spent 7 days in plastic box; box was buried under tank of water
2000: spent over 63 hours in a block of ice; ice was in Times Square, New York
2002: stood on top of tall pillar for 35 hours; pillar was 30m high
2012: spent 72 hours inside a million volts of electricity; broadcast on YouTube

PRONUNCIATION: /æ/ vs /ʌ/

A »♫ **2.20** Listen to these sounds and words. Can you hear the difference? Now listen again and repeat the sounds and words.

/æ/ ankle   /ʌ/ uncle

B »♫ **2.21** Is the underlined sound /æ/ or /ʌ/? Put the words from the box in the correct row. Then listen and check. Practise saying the words.

~~uncle~~ ~~ankle~~ b<u>a</u>t b<u>u</u>t beg<u>u</u>n beg<u>a</u>n c<u>a</u>ts c<u>u</u>ts d<u>o</u>ne D<u>a</u>n

/æ/	ankle, _____, _____, _____, _____
/ʌ/	uncle, _____, _____, _____

C »♫ **2.22** Listen to these sentences and complete them with the words from Exercise B that you hear. Practise saying the sentences.

1 Did you see the documentary about a woman with 40 _____?
2 My _____ was a stand-up comic when he was younger.
3 The scenery for this show was _____ by a friend of my dad's.
4 *Dream Date* _____ 30 minutes ago, so you've missed most of it.
5 I love soaps, _____ I don't enjoy reality TV shows too much.

SPEAKING: talking about a live event

A))) **2.23** Listen to two friends talking about a show. Tick the topics below that they mention.

admission charge ☐   costumes ☐   crowd ☐   lighting ☐
orchestra   ☐   scenery ☐   venue ☐

B Listen again and complete the questions the first woman asks about each of the following things.

1 the event   _____ was it?
2 the type of event   What _____ show was it?
3 the venue   What was the venue _____?
4 the costumes   _____ the costumes?
5 the admission charge   How much _____?
6 her friend's opinion   Would _____ it?

C Complete each area of the word web with at least one more question to ask a partner.

D Think of a show or other live event you saw recently. Think about the topics in Exercise A and use the questions in Exercises B and C to help you decide what to say.

E 🗣 Work in pairs. Ask and answer questions with your partner about the show or live event you saw.

> **PERFORMERS**
> How many musicians were there?
> _____ ?
>
> **OTHER**
> _____ ?
>
> **EVENT**
>
> **ADMISSION CHARGE**
> Was the show worth the money?
> _____ ?
>
> **EVENT VENUE**
> Was the venue big or small?
> _____ ?

VOCABULARY: at the Oscars

A Read these facts about the Oscars. Find a word or phrase to match each definition.

THE OSCARS

- In 1929, the first Oscar for leading actor went to Emil Jannings for two films, including *The Way of All Flesh* (1927). Unfortunately, no copies of the film exist. At the same ceremony, the Oscar for Best Picture went to the World War I drama, *Wings*, which also won an award for the special effects in the war scenes.
- Tatum O'Neal was the youngest ever winner of an Oscar for best supporting actress. She won in 1974 at the age of 10 for her role in *Paper Moon*. The film was also nominated for Best Screenplay, written by Alvin Sargent, but didn't win.
- The most successful director in Oscar history is John Ford. He won four Oscars for Best Director and was also nominated twice: in 1940 for Best Director for *Stagecoach* and in 1953 for Best Picture for *The Quiet Man*.
- *Up* won the Oscar for Best Animated Feature in 2010 and was also nominated for Best Picture. That Oscar went to *The Hurt Locker*, but *Up* also won the Oscar for Best Original Score, for music written by Michael Giacchino.

1 the actor/actress who plays the main part in a film: _____ actor/actress
2 impressive visual images added to a film: special _____
3 an actor/actress who plays a secondary part in a film: _____ actor/actress
4 the script for a film: _____
5 the person who is in charge of the creative side of film making: _____
6 a film made of images created by hand or on a computer: _____ film
7 the music in a film: _____

B 🗣 Work in pairs. Think about the films you've seen. Which film or person would you nominate for an Oscar? Why?

Best Picture   Best Director
Best Original Score   Best Actor/Actress
Best Visual Effects   Best Animated Feature
Best Screenplay

A: I saw the new *Iron Man* film recently, and I would nominate it for Best Visual Effects.
B: Why is that?
A: Well, there's a lot of action, and it all looks real. They've done a really good job.

GRAMMAR: defining relative clauses

A 🎧 **2.24 LANGUAGE IN CONTEXT** Listen to this dialogue.

Daisy: Oh, I love that actress who just came on! What's her name?

Angela: Do you mean the one with red hair?

Daisy: No. I mean the one who's talking now. She was in <u>the film that we saw last week</u>. Remember?

Angela: Oh, her! That's Jennifer Lawrence. She was in that film which had Bradley Cooper in it … What was it called …? Oh, yes – *Silver Linings Playbook*. She won an Oscar for it, didn't she?

Daisy: Yes! That's right. She's so talented!

B **ANALYSE** Read the conversation in Exercise A again.

Form Complete the examples with phrases from Exercise A. Then tick the statements that are true.

*I love **that actress** (1)* _____ .
*I mean **the one** (2)* _____ .
*She was in **the film** (3)* _____ .
*She was in **that film** (4)* _____ .

Defining relative clauses …

1 are separated from the rest of the sentence by commas. ☐
2 do not need commas to separate them from the rest of the sentence. ☐
3 can only come after the noun they refer to. ☐
4 can come before or after the noun they refer to. ☐
5 can use *which* or *that* to refer to things. ☐
6 can only use *which* to refer to things. ☐

> **NOTICE!**
> Look at the underlined text. What is the object of the underlined text?

Function Choose the correct option to complete the sentences.

1 A defining relative clause …
  a) identifies the subject of the sentence.
  b) gives us extra information about a noun.
2 The relative clause … without affecting the basic meaning.
  a) could be removed from the sentence
  b) could not be removed from the sentence

> **Subject and Object relative clauses**
> A noun can either be the subject or the object of a defining relative clause:
> *I love that actress who just came on!*
> (*that actress* is the subject of *who just came on*)
> *She was in the film that we saw last week.*
> (*the film* is the object of *that we saw last week*)
>
> When the noun is the object of the relative clause, the relative pronoun can be left out:
> *She was in the film **that** we saw last week.*
> *She was in the film we saw last week.*

C **PRACTISE** Rewrite the sentences using defining relative clauses. Start with the words given. If the relative pronoun can be left out, write it in brackets.

1 Jennifer Lawrence played a character called Tiffany in the film.
The character *(that) Jennifer Lawrence played in the film was called Tiffany.*

2 I saw a man in the supermarket. I'm sure he was a well-known actor.
I'm sure the man _____ .

3 I loved one film more than any other as a child. It was *The Lion King*.
The film _____ .

4 I really admire Al Pacino. He's an actor.
An actor _____ .

5 *Schindler's List* changed my life. It's a film.
A film _____ .

D 🎙 **NOW YOU DO IT** Work in pairs. Choose one of the following to talk about with your partner. Ask each other questions and use defining relative clauses where appropriate.

- an actor/actress who I admire
- a film that changed my life

A Read this extract from a magazine article and answer the questions.

1 Why do some people not go to live events?
2 Where has the idea of showing live events in cinemas become popular?
3 What are the advantages to arts organisations of live events at the cinema?
4 What are the advantages to members of the public of live events at the cinema?
5 What disadvantage is mentioned?

LIVE ... AT A CINEMA NEAR YOU!

We all know what a live event is. You go to a venue, sit or stand with other members of the audience or crowd, and watch real people on stage acting, singing or dancing. It involves travelling to the venue, which is often difficult for people who don't live in major cities, and often means paying a high admission charge. It isn't surprising, therefore, that some people think live events are only for people who have plenty of money, or who live in a big city.

But what if we could bring live events to more people closer to where they live? That's exactly the question organisations like the New York Metropolitan Opera and the National Theatre in the UK have asked themselves. Their answer is events which are broadcast live in cinemas.

The idea has taken off around the world. Apart from the advantages to the public, the organisations themselves also benefit. This kind of live event attracts new people who wouldn't normally walk into an opera house or a theatre. Perhaps after seeing and enjoying a performance at their local cinema, they may be inspired to travel to see a live opera, play or ballet in person. It also means that the organisations can make much more money from a performance than by just selling tickets to one audience in one room.

Some people say that watching a live event at the cinema can't possibly be as good as being there in person. They argue that you'll never experience the atmosphere of a live event in a great venue unless you're there. That might be true, but with some events, watching live in the cinema may, in different ways, be better than actually being there. Different cameras can offer different viewpoints, including close-ups, which isn't possible from one seat in the theatre. In addition to that, the show may include interviews with performers or a tour of the venue before the main live event. It all adds up to a wonderful night at the theatre, opera or ballet at your local cinema.

B Work in pairs. Discuss your opinions of live events at the cinema. Decide which of the following live events you would rather see at the cinema and explain why. Say what you think the experience would be like.

- an opera
- a play
- a ballet
- a classical concert
- a rock or pop concert
- a sports match
- a dance show

A: *In my view, showing live events at the cinema is a fantastic idea because …*
B: *I'm not so sure. I think something is lost. For example, …*

LISTENING: taking notes

⚙ When you take notes, don't try to write down everything you hear. Listen for and note down the main ideas and important points related to those ideas. To help you identify the important information, listen for phrases like *The important thing is …*

A))) 2.25 Listen to the beginning of a lecture. Choose what you think the lecture is going to be about.

a) the history of television
b) the present state of television
c) the future of television

B 🎧 **2.26** Listen to more of the lecture and read the notes. Correct any notes that are wrong.

> Smart TVs
> - technology dates from: 1984
> - show television shows only
> - provide interactive services (e.g. games), but not including on-demand
> - advertisers enthusiastic about on-demand TV

C 🎧 **2.27** Listen to the rest of the lecture. Complete the remaining notes. Then check with a partner.

> 3D TVs
> - 3D film popular in USA in (1) _____
> - problem 1: 3D film and TV involves
>   (2) _____, which are (3) _____
> - problem 2: 3D TVs can be (4) _____
> - experts say they will become more popular when (5) _____

D Work in pairs. Using your notes, take it in turns to summarise what the lecturer said. Then discuss these questions.

• In your opinion, will smart TVs continue to develop in the future? In what ways?
• What about 3D TVs? Will they become more popular, or not?

WRITING: descriptions

⚙️ A descriptive paragraph gives the reader a general impression. Good descriptive paragraphs contain adjectives and key details to interest the reader.

A Read this description of a woman's favourite TV programme and follow the instructions below.

1 Find and underline the topic sentence.
2 Circle the adjectives.
3 Underline the details that serve to create interest in the reader.

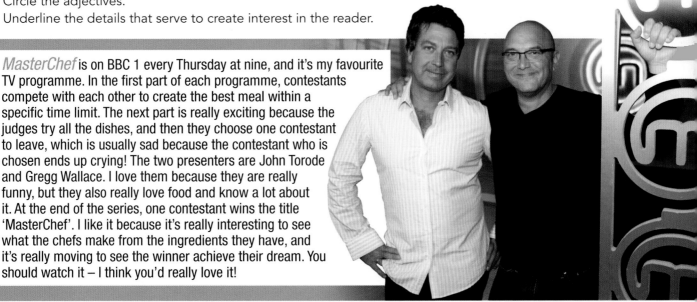

MasterChef is on BBC 1 every Thursday at nine, and it's my favourite TV programme. In the first part of each programme, contestants compete with each other to create the best meal within a specific time limit. The next part is really exciting because the judges try all the dishes, and then they choose one contestant to leave, which is usually sad because the contestant who is chosen ends up crying! The two presenters are John Torode and Gregg Wallace. I love them because they are really funny, but they also really love food and know a lot about it. At the end of the series, one contestant wins the title 'MasterChef'. I like it because it's really interesting to see what the chefs make from the ingredients they have, and it's really moving to see the winner achieve their dream. You should watch it – I think you'd really love it!

B You are going to write a description of your favourite TV show. Before you start, answer these questions in your notebook.

1 What's the title of the programme?
2 What channel is it on? When?
3 What type of programme is it?
4 What happens in each programme?
5 Who is the presenter of the programme / your favourite person in the programme? What is he/she like?
6 What do you like about the programme, and why?

C Now write your descriptive paragraph. When you have finished, read several of your classmates' descriptions. Do they make you want to watch the programme? Why or why not?

LifeSkills

WORKING AS PART OF A TEAM

- Participate equally.
- Be positive and encourage others.
- Listen actively to others.
- Regularly review whether you're being a good team player.

A Work in pairs. Look at these photos of different kinds of teams. What do they have in common? What characteristics do you think the members of these teams have?

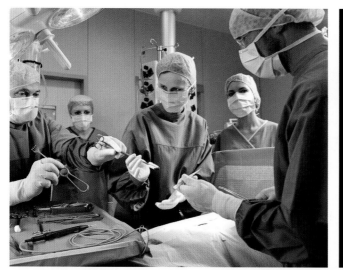

B Work in pairs. Tick which of these characteristics you think a good team player needs to have. Then discuss which of these characteristics you think you have.

- ☐ a good sense of humour
- ☐ good active listening skills
- ☐ patience
- ☐ good writing skills
- ☐ an understanding of personal strengths and weaknesses

- ☐ a strong personality
- ☐ good communication skills
- ☐ academic qualifications
- ☐ an ability to persuade others
- ☐ a positive attitude

C 〔🗣〕 Work in groups. You belong to a local theatre group. You are planning to do a show based on a film or TV programme. You are going to work as a team to prepare a new scene involving the characters from the film or TV programme that you choose. First, choose a film or TV programme and decide who is going to play which role, and appoint a director. Choose from these, or think of another.

How I Met Your Mother

The Dark Knight

D 〔🗣〕 In your team, write the dialogue for your scene and practise acting it.

E Stop what you are doing when your teacher asks you to, and reflect on whether you are being a good team player. Complete the progress form.

Individual progress form	Yes	No
Up until now:		
I have participated fully.	☐	☐
I have had a positive attitude.	☐	☐
I have encouraged others.	☐	☐
I have listened actively to others.	☐	☐
I have communicated effectively with others.	☐	☐
To be a better team player during the rest of this activity, I need to _____		

F 〔🗣〕 Now continue practising your scene with your group.

G 〔🗣〕 Act out your scene for the rest of the class. Vote on the best one.

H 〔🗣〕 In your groups, reflect on your individual and team performance. Answer these questions.
- What went well / didn't go so well?
- How well did you work as part of a team?
- What could you do better next time?

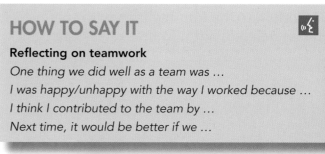

HOW TO SAY IT 〔🗣〕

Reflecting on teamwork
One thing we did well as a team was …
I was happy/unhappy with the way I worked because …
I think I contributed to the team by …
Next time, it would be better if we …

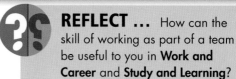

REFLECT … How can the skill of working as part of a team be useful to you in **Work and Career** and **Study and Learning**?

Language wrap-up

1 VOCABULARY

Complete the sentences with the words from the box. (15 points)

admission charge animated audience costumes director leading actor lighting
orchestra row scenery score screenplay special effects supporting actor venue

1 The performance was good, but I didn't like the _____ the actors were wearing.
2 The _____ was beautiful in the play. It shone onto the stage like moonlight.
3 Ben Stiller is an actor, but he's also worked as a _____ on a few films.
4 The _____ is the music in a film.
5 An _____ film is a film made of images created by hand or on a computer.
6 We have seats in _____ 34 at the back.
7 The _____ is the script in a film.
8 We saw that show at a great _____ in London.
9 The show was great, but the _____ was very expensive.
10 The _____ in that film were amazing. I felt as if I was flying!
11 The _____ played fantastic music. They were really talented.
12 The _____ plays the main part in a film.
13 The _____ clapped loudly at the end of the play.
14 The _____ had been painted by a famous artist. It was beautiful.
15 The _____ plays a secondary part in a film.

> **11 – 15 correct:** I can talk about a live performance and use adjectives to describe the Oscars.
> **0 – 10 correct:** Look again at the vocabulary sections on pages 118 and 120.

SCORE: /15

2 GRAMMAR

A Combine the information in each pair of sentences in one single sentence. Use a non-defining relative clause. Keep the information in the same order. (7 points)

1 This book is my favourite. It was my uncle's. _____
2 My sister is 21. She's at university. _____
3 *Starry Night* is very famous. It was painted by Van Gogh. _____
4 St Paul's Cathedral was designed by Christopher Wren. It was finished in 1675. _____
5 My grandmother lives in Greece. She was born in 1940.
6 This room is at the back of the house. It's my office. _____
7 The vase was expensive. It was stolen last week. _____

B Complete the film taglines with *that*, *which* or *who*. If the relative pronoun can be deleted, put it in brackets. (8 points)

1 He was a man _____ died … and then came back.
2 Dreamland was a place _____ you visited and then never left.
3 In a world _____ is a cruel place, love is the only thing to believe in.
4 This year, all the people _____ are destined to be together will meet.
5 When the people _____ you work with are your girlfriend's parents, watch out!
6 Even the best of friends can have problems _____ are hard to solve.
7 The thing _____ she most wanted was the thing she couldn't have.
8 He was a man working in a place in _____ no one knew him.

> **11 – 15 correct:** I can use defining and non-defining relative clauses to give extra information.
> **0 – 10 correct:** Look again at the grammar sections on pages 118–119 and 121.

SCORE: /15

SPEAKING WORKSHOP talking about a live event

A Read and complete the conversation with the words and phrases from the box.

absolutely amazing atmosphere better friendly fun worth it

Anna: How was the festival?

Jon: Oh, it was (1) _____! We had such a lot of (2) _____! The venue was really great. There were four different stages, which each played a different kind of music. I loved the rock stage!

Anna: What was the admission charge like?

Jon: You know what festivals are like these days! It cost a fortune, and I couldn't afford to do it all the time, but it was (3) _____.

Anna: What about the bands?

Jon: The Lizards, who came on last, were (4) _____ brilliant!

Anna: Was there a good crowd?

Jon: Yeah. There were loads of people, and everyone was really (5) _____. There was a really good (6) _____.

Anna: What's happening next year?

Jon: Well, the people who organised it said that it'll be even (7) _____ next year! Why don't you come? We could book tickets in advance!

Anna: Great idea!

B Read the conversation again and find the questions Anna asks about these things.

1 the performances
2 the cost
3 the people who attended
4 the event generally
5 the future of the event

C Think of a live event you went to recently, or imagine one. For example, a music festival, a ballet, a concert or a play. Using key words only, make notes about the event. Think about:

- the event generally
- the cost
- the performances
- the people who attended
- the future of the event

D 🗣 Work in pairs. Tell each other about your events, and ask and answer questions.

HOW ARE YOU DOING?

Think about your speaking and tick the statements that are true.

I feel confident …

◯ talking about live events.
◯ asking questions about live events.
◯ using adjectives to describe live events.

How do you feel about your speaking generally?

⬤   ◯   ⬤
Very confident   Not sure …   Need to practise

UNIT 11 BREAKING THE RULES

IN THIS UNIT YOU

- ⚙ learn language to talk about regrets, mistakes and behaviour
- ⚙ listen to an argument between friends
- ⚙ read an article about a TV programme
- ⚙ talk about problems and give advice
- ⚙ write a short story
- ⚙ learn to understand graphs
- ▶ watch a video about unusual laws

READING
speed reading
Do words and phrases you don't know slow you down? What can you do about it?

SPEAKING
using softening language for criticism
When was the last time you criticised someone or gave someone advice? What happened? Did they accept your criticism or advice?

LIFE SKILLS

WORK & CAREER

understanding graphs
Where might you see graphs in your everyday life? What kind of information might be presented in a graph?

A Look at the picture. Find as many examples of rule-breaking as you can.

KEEP OFF THE GRASS

ONE WAY

DISABLED PARKING

NO ENTRY

DO NOT FEED THE BIRDS

NO FOOD OR DRINK

HOW TO SAY IT

Talking about offences

You can't …

You mustn't …

He/She/They shouldn't be + gerund

You're not allowed to + base form

I think the worst offence is … because …

B Compare your answers in pairs. Then say which example of rule-breaking in the picture is the worst and why.

A: *You're not allowed to walk on the grass, but that person is walking her dog there.*

B: *Yes, and you can't turn right there, but that person is doing it. I think that's the worst offence, because it's really dangerous.*

VOCABULARY: breaking the rules

A Match each offence to the correct picture (A–H).

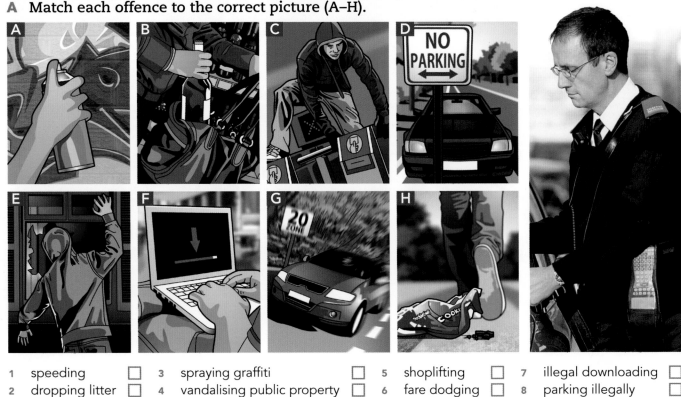

1	speeding ☐	3	spraying graffiti ☐	5	shoplifting ☐	7	illegal downloading ☐
2	dropping litter ☐	4	vandalising public property ☐	6	fare dodging ☐	8	parking illegally ☐

B Number the offences in Exercise A in order of seriousness from 1 (the most serious) to 8 (the least serious).

C Work in pairs. Compare your lists and explain the reasons for your opinions.

A: *I think illegal parking is the most serious because it can be really dangerous for cyclists. How about you?*

B: *Yes, I suppose so, but I think it's OK in an emergency.*

GRAMMAR: *should/shouldn't have*

A))) 2.28 **LANGUAGE IN CONTEXT** Listen to the conversation below. What is the topic of the conversation?

Josh: Can I talk to you about something, Tessa?

Tessa: Of course. What's the matter?

Josh: This is just between you and me, but I saw Chris taking a DVD from a music shop without paying the other day.

Tessa: Wow, that's terrible! Did you say anything to him about it?

Josh: Well, that's the problem, I didn't say anything, and I feel really bad. I should have told him to put it back and not be so stupid, shouldn't I?

Tessa: Yeah, you probably should have said something. But don't feel bad. It's not your fault. He shouldn't have left the shop without paying for it.

Josh: I know.

Tessa: Well, let's go and talk to him about it.

NOTICE!
Find *should* and *shouldn't* in the conversation.
Are Josh and Tessa talking about the present or the past?

B **ANALYSE** Read the conversation in Exercise A again.

Function **Choose the two correct options to complete the sentence.**
We use the perfect modal *should/shouldn't have* to …
a) criticise things that people did or didn't do in the past.
b) express uncertainty about things that people did or didn't do in the past.
c) express regret about things that people did or didn't do in the past.

Form Complete the table with examples from Exercise A.

	Examples
should have + past participle	(1) _____ (2) _____
shouldn't have + past participle	(3) _____

C PRACTISE Complete the sentences with *should have* or *shouldn't have* and the correct form of the verb in brackets.

1   Maddie _____ (*call*) the police as soon as she saw the boys vandalising the club.
2   I _____ (*drive*) at 60 km/h instead of 75 km/h. Then I wouldn't have got a speeding ticket.
3   You _____ (*lie*) to the police about spraying graffiti. They know you did it.
4   Dad _____ (*park*) illegally on the pavement.
5   James _____ (*download*) those music files. It's wrong and the sound quality was terrible!
6   We _____ (*tell*) a security guard that we saw those girls shoplifting.
7   Beth _____ (*drop*) litter in the town centre. A police officer saw her and she was fined.
8   I know you were in a hurry, but you _____ (*dodge*) the train fare.

> **WHAT'S RIGHT?**
> What did Pierre do wrong?
>
> ○ He shouldn't have hit the other guy.
> ○ He shouldn't hit the other guy.

D 🔊 NOW YOU DO IT Make a note of two things you did in the past and feel bad about now, and two things you didn't do in the past, but now wish you had done. Then tell a partner and describe the consequences.

I should have prepared for a big maths test, but I didn't. I failed, and I had to repeat the course.

LISTENING: to an argument

A 🔊 2.29 Listen to an argument between two friends.
Tick which of these things Noah says he did or didn't do.

	he did	he didn't
1 see someone do something wrong	☐	☐
2 inform someone about an offence	☐	☐
3 tell someone a lie	☐	☐
4 cheat in an exam	☐	☐
5 listen to an explanation	☐	☐

B 🔊 2.30 Listen to the rest of the argument and tick which of these things Finn says Noah should or shouldn't have done.

	should have done	shouldn't have done
1 listen to an explanation	☐	☐
2 hurt someone's feelings	☐	☐
3 ask to see a book	☐	☐
4 assume that someone is doing wrong	☐	☐
5 inform someone about an offence	☐	☐

C 🔊 Work in pairs. Say what you think Noah and Eva should or shouldn't have done. Explain why. Say what you think Noah and Eva should do now. Do you agree?

A: *He shouldn't have told Eva what he had seen.*
B: *Why do you say that?*
A: *Well, it wasn't really his business.*
B: *I disagree. I think …*

To improve your reading speed, quickly scan the whole text before reading to get an idea of the overall meaning. Then read through the text quickly, ignoring any words or phrases you don't know.

A Quickly scan this article about the reality TV show *Brat Camp*. Can you say what the show was about before you read the article?

B Quickly read this article about *Brat Camp*. You have three minutes.

Brat Camp

Brat Camp was a reality show that used to run on American and British TV. It was about teenagers who caused their families a lot of trouble. Their parents, who had had enough of them and their rule-breaking, sent them to a tough camp for problem teenagers. Some of the teenagers had been in trouble for behaviour such as shoplifting, spraying graffiti and vandalising public property. The purpose of the camp? To help them understand how bad their behaviour was, and to challenge them to improve it through discipline and hard work.

One of the teenagers in the second UK series, Ed, was causing his mum so many problems that he'd left the family home. Ed was always arguing with his family and had stolen money, credit cards and a laptop computer from them. Ed's mum said: 'When I threw him out, I told him, "I've got to throw you out, you are not living here anymore. The fact that I am doing this shows you how desperate I am."'

The teenagers were sent to Turn-About Ranch in Utah. At the ranch, teenagers discovered the great rewards of working within a family of people, developing trust and earning respect. The staff worked side-by-side with the teenagers to share the tasks that needed to be done, while building strong relationships and teaching the teenagers real-life skills. The ranch took them out of their environment of television, music and video games and got them excited about the natural environment, learning and their physical and mental abilities.

The animals on the ranch played a vital role in teaching the teenagers to think outside themselves, to love and care for others and to give without expecting something in return. They learnt to work together with peers and adults and they began to understand the impact their behaviour had on others. After living at the camp, teenagers often realised that they shouldn't have treated their families so badly and should have shown them more respect.

The camp, and her horse there, made a big difference to Jenni, a sixteen year old. At first, Jenni was scared of the horses, but that changed towards the end. 'I love my horse. I really have to get back to Utah in the summer. I miss everyone so much!' said Jenni once she was back in the UK. Her parents said that Jenni came back happy and she was fun to be with, but she was still messy!

The team that ran Turn-About Ranch said that it was successful because it gave teenagers the chance to take responsibility for their behaviour. They knew from the beginning what the house rules were, and if they chose to break them, they would be punished. The rules were relaxed if the teenager's behaviour improved. It was as simple as that.

C Now try to answer these questions without looking back at the text.

1 What was the purpose of Turn-About Ranch?
2 What rules had Ed broken before he went on the show?
3 Did Jenni like her experience at Turn-About Ranch?
4 What effect did being at the ranch have on Jenni?
5 Why did Turn-About Ranch appear to work?

D 🎤 Work in pairs. Do you think that a place like Turn-About Ranch is good for problem teenagers? Why or why not?

PRONUNCIATION: /ʧ/ vs /ʃ/

A 🎧 **2.31** Listen to these sounds and words. Can you hear the difference? Now listen again and repeat the sounds and words.

/ʧ/ watch   /ʃ/ wash

B 🎧 **2.32** Is the underlined sound /ʧ/ or /ʃ/? Put the words from the box in the correct column. Then listen and check. Practise saying the pairs of words.

| chip | sheet | watch | shoes | cheat | wash | choose | ship |

/ʧ/	/ʃ/
watch	wash
1 _____	4 _____
2 _____	5 _____
3 _____	6 _____

C Practise saying these sentences. Make sure you pronounce the /ʧ/ and /ʃ/ sounds correctly.

1 I took off my watch to wash my hands.
2 It's against the rules to use a cheat sheet in the exam.
3 They loaded the ship with bags of chips.
4 I want to choose the right pair of shoes.

VOCABULARY: good and bad behaviour

A Read each sentence and choose the correct option in the definition for the words and phrases in bold.

1 Could you **do me a favour** and pass me that book? — talk to / help me
2 Don't **tell lies**! I know you took the money! — say something true / false
3 I hadn't studied so I decided to **cheat** in the test. What a mistake! — break / follow the rules of a game/test, etc
4 You should **think twice** before you decide to break the law. — act quickly / consider something carefully
5 Dan really **hurt my feelings** when he said he'd told people my secret. — made me feel bad / good
6 I know I should **be considerate**, but I often forget about other people's feelings. — act in a mean and unkind / kind and thoughtful way
7 You can trust me because I never **break a promise**. — do / not do what you agreed to do
8 Don't you know that when you **spread gossip** it can hurt a lot of people? — talk about other people's private lives / tell people about your private life

B Complete each sentence with the correct form of one of the phrases in Exercise A.

1 Can you _____ to your neighbours and turn your music down?
2 I think Ben _____. I saw him looking at Elizabeth's exam paper.
3 I haven't spoken to Lisa since I heard she was _____ about me to other people.
4 Julio said he would _____ before taking the job in Spain because of his fiancée.
5 Can you _____ and lend me £20 until I get paid?
6 Yolanda _____ to her mum. Instead of studying like she said she would, she went out.
7 You said you were going to take me to the cinema tonight and you're cancelling again! Why are you always _____ your _____?
8 I'm sorry I _____ when I said I didn't like the poem you wrote. You know I'm not very good with poetry!

A LANGUAGE IN CONTEXT Read this conversation. What has the young woman done wrong?

Security guard:	Hey, you! Stop!
Woman:	What?
Security guard:	I saw you putting something in your bag. Let's have a look.
Woman:	It's just some sunglasses. I was going to pay for them.
Security guard:	I'm afraid you'll have to come with me.
Woman:	Look, I was going to see what they looked like in daylight. And then I was going to take them to the cashier. I wasn't going to steal them, if that's what you're thinking!
Security guard:	I don't care what you say you were going to do. You were supposed to pay for them before you left the shop. Come on. You'll have to speak to the manager.

B ANALYSE Read the conversation in Exercise A again.

Function Choose the correct option to complete the sentences.

1 We use *going to* in the past to talk about plans and intentions that happened / didn't happen.

2 We use *supposed to* in the past to talk about things we were expected to do that we did / we didn't do.

Form Complete the table with examples from Exercise A.

	Examples
was/were going to + base form	I (1) _____ for them.
	I (2) _____ what they looked like in daylight.
was/were supposed to + base form	(3) You _____ for them before you left the shop.

NOTICE!

1 Underline all the examples of *was/were going to* in the conversation.

2 What form of the verb follows *was/were going to*?

WHAT'S RIGHT?

○ I was going to go shopping, but it started raining.

○ I was to go shopping, but it started raining.

C PRACTISE Match the two parts to make correct sentences.

1 Trisha and I were going to be friends forever, but …
2 Irma was going to say the wrong thing, but …
3 Mum and dad were supposed to fly at 3pm, but …
4 Malcolm was supposed to move out, but …
5 We were going to ask John to do us a favour, but …
6 I was going to spend the money I won on myself, but …

a) then I decided not to be so selfish!
b) she thought twice before she spoke.
c) he changed his mind at the last minute.
d) then she started telling me lies.
e) they lost their passports at the airport!
f) then we decided we didn't need his help.

D NOW YOU DO IT Think about things that you were going to do or were supposed to do in the past but didn't, and why. Tell a partner using these ideas and phrases.

ideas	• events or meetings you missed
	• education or career choices you didn't make
	• hobbies or interests you didn't start
	• places you didn't visit
phrases	was/were going to was/were planning to was/were supposed to

A: *I was supposed to go to Pete's party last night, but I didn't in the end.*
B: *Oh, why not?*
A: *Well, I was planning to finish work early but …*

SPEAKING: using softening language to give criticism

We use softening language when we want to criticise something somebody has done, but we don't want to appear too critical or rude.

A))) **2.33** Listen to two versions of a conversation. In which one does Erin react better to John's criticism?

B))) **2.34** Listen to the second conversation again. Tick the phrases that John uses to give criticism.

1 Maybe you should have … ☐
2 I wonder whether you could have … ☐
3 I just think it's possible that … ☐
4 I'm not sure that was the best way to handle this. ☐
5 Did you think about … *-ing* …? ☐
6 Did you try … *-ing* …? ☐

C Work in pairs. Student A, read Situation A, then explain to Student B how you feel about it. Student B, use softening language to give criticism. Then switch roles and repeat.

Situation A
You were going to spend half-term with your family, but you decided to go on holiday with some friends. You hurt your mum's feelings.

Situation B
You were planning to go to a concert with some friends. You had promised to give everybody a lift, but at the last minute you decided you didn't want to drive and everybody was late.

WRITING: a short story

A Answer these questions. Work in pairs and compare your answers.

In a short story, …
1 is it better to have lots of characters or very few characters? Why?
2 is it better to have lots of different incidents and action or just a few key moments? Why?
3 is it important to use paragraphs, or are they not so important? Why?
4 What is the effect of using the first person to tell a story?

B Read the beginning of a short story. Is it written in the first person or the third person? Choose a title for the story from the titles below. Explain why you chose it.

a) It was my own fault!
b) Breaking the rules
c) The biggest mistake of my life
d) A false accusation!

C Work in pairs. Brainstorm ideas for how the story might continue. How many possibilities can you think of?

D Now work on your own. Write the rest of the story. Make your writing as descriptive as you can. When you have finished, read your story to your classmates. Vote on which story you enjoy the most.

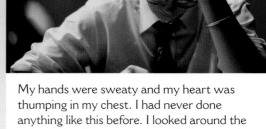

My hands were sweaty and my heart was thumping in my chest. I had never done anything like this before. I looked around the exam room. There were lots of other people, some looking nervous, others looking relaxed. I closed my eyes and waited.

I was going to revise for the exam, I really was. I had got all my notes together the night before and I was planning to go through them one last time. I decided to have one quick game online before I started, but one game became two, and the next thing I knew, it was midnight. I had run out of time! There was only one thing to do – I decided to write some of the information on my arm and on my leg. I know it was cheating, but I really had to pass that exam!

I opened my eyes. The examiner was handing out the exam papers, face down, one on each desk. I looked at mine in front of me.

'OK', said the examiner. 'You can turn your papers over and begin'.

LifeSkills

UNDERSTANDING GRAPHS

- Look at the important elements in the graph, such as the title, key and axes.
- Identify the pattern.
- Analyse what the information means.

A Write the correct name under each type of graph.

> bar chart   line graph   pie chart

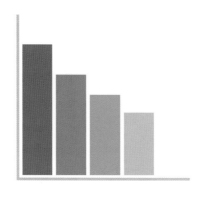

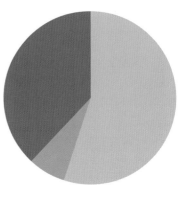

1 _____

2 _____

3 _____

B Match each profession 1–6 with a graph a–f which that person might need to understand as part of their work.

1 a doctor   _____
2 an architect   _____
3 a business manager _____
4 a teacher   _____
5 a scientist   _____
6 an economist   _____

a) a bar chart showing the costs of different building materials
b) a line graph showing how the average temperature of the Earth is changing
c) a line graph showing a person's temperature on different days
d) a pie chart showing where a country's income comes from
e) a pie chart showing different costs a business faces
f) a bar chart showing someone's marks on a series of tests

C Look at this pie chart which gives information about problems a business is facing. What problem is shown by the red part of the chart? What problem is shown by the yellow part?

D Look at the pie chart in Exercise C again. Tick the two statements which are true.

1 Shoplifting is a bigger problem than theft by staff. ☐

2 Staff absences are a bigger problem than shoplifting. ☐

3 Mistakes with orders are a bigger problem than theft by staff. ☐

4 Damaged stock is a bigger problem than mistakes with orders. ☐

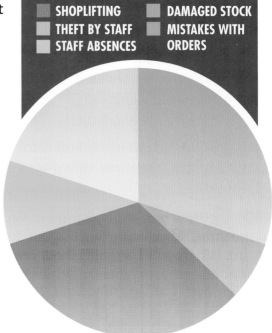

■ SHOPLIFTING   ■ DAMAGED STOCK
■ THEFT BY STAFF   ■ MISTAKES WITH ORDERS
■ STAFF ABSENCES

E A business manager wants to try to deal with the problem of shoplifting. Look at this bar chart. Choose the correct title, a, b or c.

> **a) The cost of shoplifting**
> **b) Shoplifting in different countries**
> **c) Different ways of preventing shoplifting**

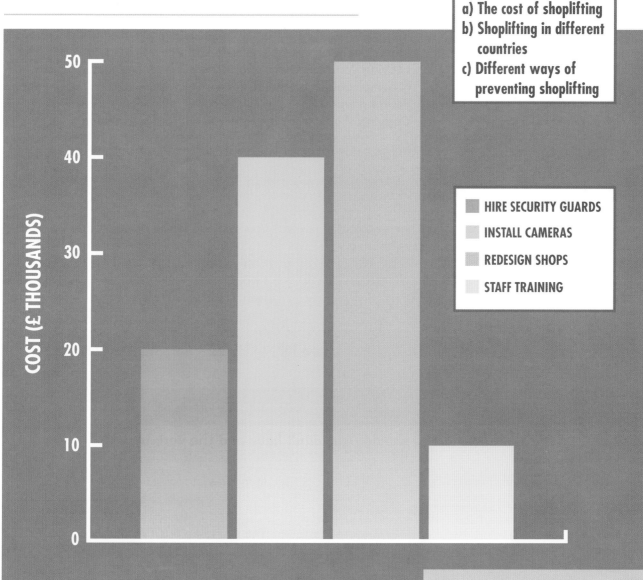

HIRE SECURITY GUARDS
INSTALL CAMERAS
REDESIGN SHOPS
STAFF TRAINING

COST (£ THOUSANDS)

F   Work in pairs. The business manager has got a budget of £60,000. Discuss what they should do, based on the information in the bar chart in Exercise E.

G Choose two measures you think might be effective.

H Tell the class what you decided. Compare your ideas and explain the reasons for your opinions.

HOW TO SAY IT

Talking about charts
The chart shows that ... would cost ...
We can see from the chart that ...
According to the chart, ...
If you look at the key, the red bar shows ...

REFLECT ... How can the skill of understanding graphs be useful to you in **Self and Society** and **Study and Learning**?

Language wrap-up

VOCABULARY

A Match the phrases to the words in bold in the sentences below. (8 points)

a dropping litter
b fare dodging
c illegal downloading
d parking illegally
e shoplifting
f speeding
g spraying graffiti
h vandalising public property

1 **Damaging buildings in town** should be punished.
2 I was fined for **driving too fast** on the motorway.
3 Is prison the right punishment for **stealing something from a shop**?
4 I think **going on the bus or train without a ticket** is wrong.
5 **Leaving your car where you shouldn't** happens a lot in my city.
6 **Leaving rubbish on the street** isn't allowed.
7 **Painting words** on trains is very common in New York.
8 **Copying things from the internet without permission** is very common.

B Complete the sentences with the correct form of the words from the box. (7 points)

be considerate   break a promise   cheat   do (someone) a favour
hurt (someone's) feelings   spread gossip   think twice

1 Sam likes to _____. Don't tell her anything!
2 It was nice of you to _____ and offer to give Grandma a lift.
3 You really _____ by not inviting her to your party.
4 You shouldn't _____ in your exams.
5 You said you would help me, and you can't _____.
6 Can you _____ and feed the cat?
7 I would _____ before telling your secret to Ivan. He'll tell everyone!

11 – 15 correct: I can talk about breaking rules and good and bad behaviour.
0 – 10 correct: Look again at the vocabulary sections on pages 130 and 133.   SCORE: /15

2 GRAMMAR

A Complete the sentences using *should / shouldn't have* and the verb in brackets. (8 points)

1 They missed the train. They _____ (*be*) at the station by 10.
2 You _____ (*make*) a promise you couldn't keep.
3 Dad got a speeding ticket. He _____ (*go*) so fast.
4 The traffic was terrible. We _____ (*walk*) to the party.
5 Immy was late for school. She _____ (*go*) to bed early and _____ (*sleep*) late.
6 The sound on this TV isn't good. We _____ (*buy*) the other one.
7 The cake was for Jake. You _____ (*eat*) it!

B Rewrite the sentences using the word in brackets. (7 points)

1 We planned to leave at nine, but we didn't. (*supposed*) _____
2 Ollie wanted to have a party, but he was ill. (*going*) _____
3 I wasn't sure about going to the party, but I did. (*going*) _____
4 I wanted to go shopping yesterday, but I finished work late. (*supposed*) _____
5 They intended to move to the USA, but they didn't. (*going*) _____
6 You shouldn't have told Julia about the surprise. (*supposed*) _____
7 The weather forecast said it would rain today. (*going*) _____

11 – 15 correct: I can use *should/shouldn't have* to criticise past behaviour, and *was/were going to* and *was/were supposed to* to talk about plans and intentions in the past that didn't happen.
0 – 10 correct: Look again at the grammar sections on pages 130–131 and 134.   SCORE: /15

WRITING WORKSHOP

writing a short story

A **Read this short story and answer these questions.**

1 Why was the writer driving so fast?
2 Why didn't the writer get a fine?

Caught speeding!

One day, it was raining and I was driving home from work. The traffic can be bad, and that day it was terrible. I got stuck for an hour!

When we started moving, I was late for dinner. I started to drive faster. I shouldn't have done, but I was tired and hungry. Suddenly, I saw a flashing light behind me. It was the police! I stopped and a police officer walked to my window.

'Do you know what speed you were doing, Madam?' he said. I didn't know and he told me I had been speeding. I started to apologise when another car went past going very fast! The police officer ran to his car.

'It's your lucky day,' he called. 'Don't do it again!' He got into his car and chased the other car. I didn't get a fine, and now I always drive very carefully!

B **Read the story again. Choose *T* (true) or *F* (false) for each statement.**

1 The first paragraph gives background detail.   T / F
2 The writer uses the past continuous to describe the opening situation. T / F
3 The writer uses the past simple to describe the main action of the story. T / F
4 The writer creates drama by using direct speech.   T / F
5 The story has lots of characters and different incidents.   T / F
6 The story is simple and is told in a simple, direct way.   T / F

C **Look at this title for a short story. Read the two plots and choose one to use for the story.**

It wasn't me!

Plot 1
Some money goes missing from a shop and one of the workers is blamed. She denies it and starts crying, and finally another worker admits that they did it.

Plot 2
A man is arrested by the police, who think he is an escaped criminal because he looks like the photos of the wanted man. Finally, other officers catch the wanted man and the innocent man is set free.

D **Make notes to answer these questions.**

1 What is the background situation at the start of the story?
2 Who are the characters in your story?
3 What happens first and how does the main character react?
4 What happens next?
5 What happens at the end? How does your main character feel?

E **Write a short story (less than 150 words) in your notebook. Use your notes from Exercise D to help you.**

HOW ARE YOU DOING?

Look back at your writing and tick the statements that are true.

◯ I have told the story in a simple, direct way.
◯ I have used direct speech to show what people said.
◯ I have described how my characters felt.
◯ I have used the past simple and the past continuous.

Now ask a partner to look at your writing and tick.

Is the story entertaining and interesting?

●   ◯   ●

Well done!   Nearly! Look at the unit again.   Think again! Ask your teacher for help.

UNIT 12 JUST THE JOB!

IN THIS UNIT YOU

- learn language to talk about work and jobs
- read job advertisements
- listen to a lecture about work
- talk about your ideal job
- write a description of a workplace
- learn to prepare for a job interview
- ▶ watch a video about careers

LISTENING
taking notes
When do you need to take notes? Do you usually write full sentences? Or just key words?

WRITING
descriptions
What keeps our interest when we hear or read a description of something?

LIFE SKILLS

WORK & CAREER

preparing for a job interview
Think of five things you need to do before going to a job interview. Why is it important to prepare?

A Match the pictures to the unusual jobs.

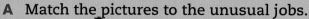

A

B

C  **D** 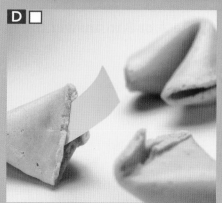 **E**

F

1   ice cream taster: tastes different ice cream flavours to see which ones people will buy
2   laughter therapist: helps other people become happier by making them laugh
3   golf ball diver: finds the golf balls that have landed in the lakes on golf courses
4   cartoon mascot: wears a cartoon costume at a theme park or fair
5   snake milker: extracts venom from snakes
6   fortune cookie writer: writes the fortunes inside the cookies you get with Chinese food

HOW TO SAY IT

Talking about unusual jobs

I think it would be fun to be a … because …

The most interesting job is being a …

Another unusual job is being a …

Some people work as …, which is very unusual.

B Work in pairs and compare your answers. Which is the strangest job? Which is the most interesting job? What other unusual jobs do you know?

A: *I think the strangest job is golf ball diver.*
B: *Really? I think it would be fun to be a laughter therapist.*
A: *Yes, but the most interesting job is ice cream taster!*

VOCABULARY: the world of work

A Read the sentences and match the phrases in bold with these phrases.

apply for a job
be unemployed
get on with your colleagues
earn a good salary
get a part-time job
~~have a career~~
work for a company
write a CV

1 I'd love to **work** in advertising when I leave university. *have a career*

2 If you are a lawyer, you can **be very well paid**. _____

3 Do you **have a good relationship with the people you work with**? _____

4 John will **not have a job** if the company closes down. _____

5 To apply for a job, you need to **write down information about yourself**. _____

6 When I finish university, I'd like to **ask for the chance to work** in the army. _____

7 Would you like to **have a job in a place** like Apple, for example? _____

8 Why don't you **work for a few hours a day** as a hairdresser? _____

B 🗣 Work in pairs. Ask and answer these questions.

1 Have you ever applied for a job?

2 What career do you hope to have?

READING: job adverts

A Read these adverts for jobs. Write A or B to answer the questions.

Which job requires someone who …

1 is a good listener? _____

2 enjoys being alone? _____

3 has travelled a lot? _____

4 can make decisions? _____

5 has a good sense of style? _____

6 has the ability to write well? _____

A

WANTED: ISLAND CARETAKER

We're looking for someone fit, active and ambitious to do the best job in the world! You'll live on a tropical island, with just the fish and birds for company! You'll blog about your adventures, and keep the world up to date on what a fantastic area the island is in. Apart from informing the public, you'll also inform us, by keeping an eye on the wildlife and reporting on the levels of fish in the area.

We are offering a great salary and free accommodation, with the best view in the world! The successful applicant will have a CV full of adventure and will be an experienced traveller. He or she will also have an interest in the natural world and the environment, as well as excellent communication skills.

Contact us at bestjob@totaltropics.com and we'll send you an application form. What are you waiting for?

B

Personal Shopper Required

Our clients are busy people who don't always have time to go shopping. That's where you come in! The successful applicant will work for an individual client in order to understand their personal style, in terms of clothes, furniture, decoration – or whatever else the client desires! You will then go shopping for your client, selecting items that you think will match their style.

We welcome applications from people from a broad range of backgrounds. You might currently work in a boutique or have a proven interest in designer brands and high-end fashion. Experience in the fashion industry is an advantage but not essential. In return, we offer training, a good salary and the opportunity to travel to meet clients.

Send a CV, together with a personal statement explaining why you think you would make a great personal shopper, to jobs@personalshoppers.co.uk.

B 🗣 Work in small groups. Discuss these questions.

1 Which things you would like or dislike about each job?

2 Would you be interested in doing one or both jobs?

3 Which job you would prefer, and why?

A: *One thing I'd like about the first job is that you'd get away from it all.*

B: *Really? I'm not sure. It sounds a bit lonely to me but I suppose I'd have the internet.*

GRAMMAR: *so, such, too, enough*

A LANGUAGE IN CONTEXT Read this conversation. What is Grace finding difficult?

Ella: Grace, how's your first week with the company been? Do you like the job?

Grace: Hmm. It's too early to say, really. I mean, it's really interesting here. I love the company. And the people are so friendly! But there's a lot to learn and there isn't enough time to do everything. It's such a big job that I'm not sure where to begin.

Ella: Don't worry. I think you're doing really well.

Grace: Oh, thanks. But I'm worried that I'm not learning quickly enough. And everyone else in the department is always too busy to help me. I feel bad asking them.

Ella: It's not always like this. Everyone has too much work this week.

Grace: Talking of that … The figures aren't ready for the presentation. They were so complicated that I couldn't understand them!

Ella: Don't worry. I'll help you with those.

Grace: Thanks, Ella. You're such a great colleague!

> **NOTICE!**
> Underline *so, such, too, enough* in the conversation. What part of speech follows *so*, a noun or an adjective?

B ANALYSE Read the conversation in Exercise A again.

Function Match the two halves of the sentences to complete the explanations.

1	We use *so*	a)	with (adjectives +) nouns to mean *very, really* or *extremely*.
2	We use *such*	b)	with adjectives and adverbs to say that there is more of something than we need.
3	We use *too*	c)	with adjectives and adverbs to mean *very, really* or *extremely*.
4	We use *not … enough*	d)	with adjectives and adverbs to say that there is less of something than we need.
5	We use a *that* clause	e)	after *too* and (*not*) … *enough* to show results or consequences.
6	We use an infinitive clause	f)	after *so* and *such* to show results or consequences.

Form Complete the table with examples from Exercise A.

	Examples
so + adjective/adverb	*The people are* (1) _____ !
such + adjective + noun	*You're* (2) _____ *colleague!*
so/such … that …	*It's such a big job* (3) _____ *where to begin.*
	They were so complicated (4) _____ *them!*
too + adjective/adverb	*It's* (5) _____ *to say, really.*
not + adjective/adverb + enough	*I'm not learning* (6) _____ .
too/(not) … enough … to …	*Everyone else is always too busy* (7) _____ *me.*
	There isn't enough time (8) _____ *everything.*

> **WHAT'S RIGHT?**
> ◯ It's such hot!
> ◯ It's so hot!

C PRACTISE Correct the mistakes in the sentences.

1 He's too young that he works here. _____
2 You aren't working enough fast. _____
3 This is such great job. _____
4 All my colleagues are such helpful. _____
5 I'm so tired to work today. _____
6 We don't have enough time to finish the job. _____

D 🔊 NOW YOU DO IT Roleplay a conversation like the one in Exercise A. Use the information below to help you.

Student A
You work in an office. You meet Student B during a break. You want to make them feel welcome and find out how the new job is going. Ask questions about their first day on the job and answer any questions they may have about the job, the office or your colleagues.

Student B
This is your first day in your new job. You meet Student A during a break. You want to make friends. Answer their questions about your day so far, and ask Student A questions about the job, the office or your colleagues.

When you listen to a lecture, concentrate on understanding the speaker rather than on taking detailed notes. Keep notes short and simple by using abbreviations and symbols like + instead of the word *and*, or *incl* instead of the word *including*. You can also invent your own abbreviations.

A Match these common abbreviations to their meanings.

1	b/c	a)	for example
2	≠	b)	more than / greater than
3	→	c)	with
4	e/	d)	is the same as / is equal to
5	b4	e)	is different from / is not equal to
6	w/	f)	because
7	=	g)	approximately
8	e.g.	h)	every
9	>	i)	before
10	approx	j)	causes

B 🎧 **2.35** You are going to listen to the first part of a lecture whose title is 'No one should ever work'. Listen and complete the notes below.

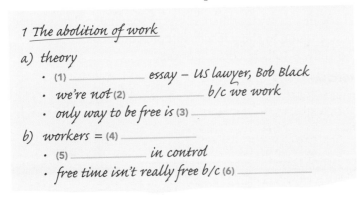

1 The abolition of work

a) theory
- *(1) _____ essay – US lawyer, Bob Black*
- *we're not (2) _____ b/c we work*
- *only way to be free is (3) _____*

b) workers = (4) _____
- *(5) _____ in control*
- *free time isn't really free b/c (6) _____*

C 🗣 Work in pairs. Use the outline to tell each other the main points of the lecture.

D 🎧 **2.36** 🗣 Listen to the final part of the lecture. Take notes under the following headings, using abbreviations where possible. Then compare your notes with a partner and combine them to make them more complete.

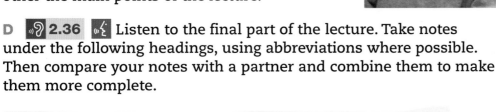

c) work kills
- *(7) _____*
- *(8) _____*

2 Criticism of theory
a) Schleuning,
- *(9) _____*

E 🗣 Work in small groups. Read the notes you took and talk about whether you agree or disagree with the key ideas that the speaker mentioned.

A: *I agree with the idea that people shouldn't have to work.*
B: *I disagree. I think that working is important because …*

A 🎧 **2.37** Listen to two men, Oscar and Daniel, talking about their ideal jobs. Match each man to an appropriate job below.

computer programmer

zoo-keeper

lawyer

pilot

farmer

B Who said each phrase? Tick the correct column. Then listen again and check.

		Oscar	Daniel
1	I couldn't work in an office.	☐	☐
2	Earning a high salary isn't really important to me.	☐	☐
3	The thing I'm looking for is adventure.	☐	☐
4	The key thing for me would be relationships with people.	☐	☐
5	It would be good to be outside.	☐	☐
6	I think my ideal job would probably include that.	☐	☐

C 🗣 Work in pairs. Describe what your ideal job would be like. Ask and answer questions to find out more information. Together, make a list of two or three jobs that would be close to your ideal.

A Read the sentences. Match the meanings of the phrasal verbs in bold with their definitions in the box.

> answer   complete with information   do something that should have been done before
> investigate   make less progress   participate in   return someone's phone call
> send a copy of an email or letter

1 Don't forget to **copy in** Jake when you send the email.   _____
2 Could you just **fill in** this form, please?   _____
3 Can you **pick up** the phone? I'm talking to Mr Jones on the other line.   _____
4 I'm trying to **catch up** with all the work I didn't get done yesterday.   _____
5 I'd like to **join in with** your meeting, if that's OK.   _____
6 I'll ask Kyle to **look into** this problem further.   _____
7 Did you **call** Mr Wilkinson **back**?   _____
8 I'm worried that I'm going to **fall behind** with my work.   _____

B 🗣 Work in groups. Discuss these questions.

1 How often do you send emails? Do you usually have to copy other people in?
2 What are some ways to catch up with your work when you start to fall behind? For example, one way might be not to pick up the phone every time it rings.
3 Do you tend to join in with conversations in class or at work? Why or why not?

GRAMMAR: separable and inseparable phrasal verbs

A LANGUAGE IN CONTEXT Read this review of the reality TV series *Job Swap*. Which of the women enjoyed her experience on the show?

Tuesday's *Job Swap* (8:30pm, Channel 9) was fantastic! Zoe, a hairdresser from Edinburgh, swapped jobs with Jemma, a part-time office secretary from Brighton. Zoe was very positive about the experience and said she'd learnt new skills. 'At the salon, I don't have to write information down or fill in forms, so that was new for me.' In contrast, Jemma had problems with some of the other hairdressers. 'I didn't get on with them,' she said. 'They talked about famous celebrities all the time. I'd never heard of any of them, so I didn't join in with their conversations.' She didn't like the customers, either. 'Dealing with them was so boring!' she said. Boring maybe, but it did make great TV!

> **NOTICE!**
> 1 Underline all the phrasal verbs in the review.
> 2 How do these two phrases differ in terms of word order? *write information down* and *fill in forms*?

B ANALYSE Read the text in Exercise A again.

Form Choose the correct option to complete the sentences. Then complete the table with examples from Exercise A.

With separable phrasal verbs, you **(1)** can / can't put a noun between the verb and the particle. With inseparable phrasal verbs, you **(2)** can / can't. With separable phrasal verbs, we **(3)** always / never separate the verb and the particle when the object is a pronoun (*you*, *it*, *them*, etc).

> Phrasal verbs with a particle plus a preposition are always inseparable.
> *I didn't get on **with** them.*

	Form	Example
Separable phrasal verbs	verb + particle + noun verb + noun/pronoun + particle	**(4)** _____
Inseparable phrasal verbs	verb + particle (+ preposition) + noun/pronoun	*I didn't get on with the stylists.* **(5)** _____

C PRACTISE Choose the correct answer to complete the sentences. Choose both answers if they are both correct.

1. A: Did you remember to turn off the lights before you left the office?
   B: No, I forgot to turn them off / off them. Sorry.
2. Peter called. I said you'd call him back / back him.
3. The people I work with are really nice. I get along with them / them with.
4. A: What should I do with this form?
   B: Just write your information down / write down your information and sign it.
5. I ran into John Carver / John Carver into at a meeting today.
6. A: Have you heard of the company called Nike?
   B: Yes, of course I've heard it of / of it!

D 🗣 **NOW YOU DO IT** Work in pairs. Think of a business that you'd like to set up. Tell your group about the things you'd like and dislike about having your own business.

A: *Setting a clothing shop up would be cool.*
B: *Maybe, but I don't think I'd like dealing with angry customers.*

A 🔊 **2.38** Listen and repeat these sentences. With each phrasal verb, is the stress on the main verb or on the particle?

1 When you've filled in the form, please hand it in to reception.
2 I've fallen behind with my work a bit, but I'm hoping to catch up next week.
3 I copied Helen in when I sent the email but she didn't get back to me.

B 🔊 **2.39** Practise saying these sentences with the correct stress. Then listen and check.

1 We need to look into the poor sales figures and come up with solutions.
2 When you call Rob back, ask him to come up to my office.
3 I didn't pick the phone up because I was writing up my notes from the meeting.

WRITING: descriptions page 123 ⚙

⚙ To make your descriptions interesting, use adjectives which tell the reader how something feels, sounds, tastes, looks or smells. Try to create a picture in your reader's mind.

A Which of the adjectives in the box can you use to describe these different workplaces? Write four adjectives for each picture. Then compare your answers in pairs.

bright busy chaotic colourful comfortable dirty
fun noisy repetitive smelly stressful unsatisfying

B Read this description of a workplace. Underline the adjectives. What does the writer like and dislike about their workplace?

About me! | My photos | My friends | My groups

I work in a busy office. It can be quite stressful at times, but it's also a fascinating place to work. My colleagues and I all work together in one huge room, so we can easily share interesting ideas.

The thing I enjoy the most is that we have a fun, relaxing area where we can take a break, play games, talk to people from other departments and get new ideas. It's unusual, but it really works.

On the down side, the staff restaurant is quite old-fashioned, dark and depressing, and not many of us eat there. It's such a shame because the rest of the place is bright, colourful and modern.

C If you work, write a description of your workplace. If you don't work, write a description of your ideal workplace. Use a variety of descriptive adjectives.

D Work in groups. Read your description to your group. When everyone has finished, vote on the description which created the best picture in your mind.

PREPARING FOR A JOB INTERVIEW

- Think about questions you may be asked.
- Prepare answers that emphasise the key points you want to make.
- Practise your responses.

A Look at these pictures. How do you think the people who are being interviewed feel and why? Tell a partner.

1

2

B 2.40 Now listen to the interview with the man from picture 1. Would you give him the job? Why or why not?

C Read the careers advice. Which of the questions do you think is the most difficult to answer?

CAREERS ADVICE

INTERVIEW QUESTIONS

Whatever type of job you're applying for, it's always a good idea to be prepared.
Here is a list of FAQs in job interviews and advice on how to answer them.

- **Tell me about yourself.**

This is your chance to say who you are. Find out about the company to get an idea of the skills, experience and personalities they're looking for. In the interview, talk about things that show you would be the best person for the job!

- **What do you do in your current job?**

Be positive about what you do in your current (or previous) job. Try to link your past experience to the job you are being interviewed for.

- **What are your strengths and weaknesses?**

You can talk about your ability to stay calm, your prioritising skills, problem-solving skills, how good you are as a team player, how confident/reliable/motivated, etc, you are. Give real-life examples! Be honest about a weakness, but don't focus on it. Say what you are doing to change it.

- **Why do you want to work for this company?**

Be positive. Find out about the company and explain how what they offer is connected to your ambitions and hopes for the future.

- **When can you start?**

Be enthusiastic! Say 'Immediately' or 'I need to give x weeks' notice to my current employer.'

- **Have you got any questions?**

Before the interview, always prepare one or two questions to ask at the end of the interview which show you're interested in the company, for example:
How many people work in the department?
Do you offer training?
How is performance evaluated and rewarded?
Good luck!

D 🎧 **2.41** Now listen to a woman being interviewed for the same job as the man in Exercise B. As you listen, think about whether you would give her the job, and why / why not.

E Work in pairs. Talk about whether you would give the job to the man or the woman, and why.

F Think of a job you would be interested in applying for. Then work on your own to prepare complete and positive answers to the interview questions in Exercise C.

G Work in pairs. Take turns roleplaying a job interview. Student A, ask the questions from Exercise C. Student B, give the answers you prepared. Then switch roles.

HOW TO SAY IT

Describing work experience
I have experience in …
One of my main strengths is …
I really enjoy …
Working as part of a team interests me because …
I'd like to work for your company because …

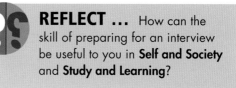

REFLECT … How can the skill of preparing for an interview be useful to you in **Self and Society** and **Study and Learning**?

Language wrap-up

A Choose the correct phrases. (7 points)

If you've **(1)** been unemployed / applied for a job for some time one of the most important things you should do is **(2)** earn a good salary / write a good CV. It's also important to make sure you are **(3)** applying for a job / having a career that is right for you. There's no point **(4)** getting on with your colleagues / working for a company if you want to run your own business. If you need to be at home to look after children, it's probably more important to **(5)** get a part-time job / have a career than work all the time. If **(6)** earning a good salary / applying for a job is important to you, you will need to work hard and be prepared to work long hours, too. Whatever job you get, you should make an effort to **(7)** work for a company / get on with your colleagues. We can't choose the people we work with!

B Complete the sentences with the phrasal verbs from the box. (8 points)

call back	1 Could you please _____ this form with your information?
catch up	2 Always be polite when you _____ the phone.
copy in	3 Please could you _____ the customer who left a message?
fall behind	4 I don't want to _____ with my work while I'm away on holiday.
fill in	5 Don't worry. Jenny will help you _____ with your work when you get back.
join in	6 Can you _____ the accounts department when you send this message?
look into	7 I need to _____ the problem in some more detail.
pick up	8 Are you going to _____ with tomorrow's meeting or not?

11 – 15 correct: I can talk about the world of work and use phrasal verbs for talking about work.
0 – 10 correct: Look again at the vocabulary sections on pages 142 and 145.   **SCORE:**   /15

A Complete the sentences with so, such, too or enough and the adjective in brackets. (7 points)

1 It was _____ (good) idea to have the meeting in a café.
2 Was my report _____ (detailed)?
3 This meeting has been going on _____ (long). It should have finished at three.
4 It's _____ (difficult) to get a job in TV. But I'm not going to give up.
5 Ella is _____ (brilliant) teacher. All her students love her.
6 It's _____ (nice) working here. Everyone is very friendly.
7 The room isn't _____ (big) for the meeting. We'll have to find a bigger one.

B Tick the sentences that are correct. Rewrite the incorrect sentences. (8 points)

1 I was listening to my MP3 player, but a colleague asked me to turn off it.

2 John Brown phoned. Can you call back him? _____
3 Filling in forms is a large part of my job. _____
4 If you don't want to forget something, write down it. _____
5 Some colleagues were having a discussion, but I didn't join in. _____
6 I've never heard of this new company. _____
7 As a doctor, I have to be very good at getting on patients with.

8 If you go to the theatre, you might run Mary into. _____

11 – 15 correct: I can use so, such, too and enough, and separable and inseparable phrasal verbs to talk about work.
0 – 10 correct: Look again at the grammar sections on pages 143 and 146.   **SCORE:**   /15

SPEAKING WORKSHOP talking about ideal jobs

A Read and complete this conversation with the phrases from the box.

> I couldn't work   is important to me   my ideal job would be one   my ideal job would have to include that
> the key thing for me   the thing I'm looking for   would love to

Rees: I'm so bored working here that I might start looking for another job.

Hamish: Really? That's interesting.

Rees: Yes, (1) _____ where I can be creative.

Hamish: What would you like to do?

Rees: I like to make things, so (2) _____.

Hamish: Oh, I know what you mean! I find it very satisfying when I make things with my own hands. Would you like to be your own boss or work for someone else?

Rees: A good salary (3) _____, so I think I'd want to work for a company. I think (4) _____ would be to look forward to going to work every morning. Job satisfaction is very important.

Hamish: I agree. I'd like to get a new job, too – something completely different. (5) _____ is working with the general public, instead of being stuck in an office all the time.

Rees: Oh, that's not for me. (6) _____ with the public all the time. I need peace and quiet! I prefer working on my own, or in a small team.

Hamish: Oh, I (7) _____ help people if I could. Maybe something like nursing would suit me.

Rees: Yes, I can see you as a nurse. Anyway, I guess it's time to get back to work.

Hamish: Yeah, for now. Who knows? One day, we might find our ideal jobs!

B Read the conversation again and find these things.

1 a phrase to encourage the speaker to say more
2 two questions to ask for more information
3 a phrase to agree with someone
4 a phrase to disagree with someone

C Look at this list of aspects of a job. Choose the four that are most important to you and number them from 1 (most important) to 4 (least important).

- [ ] being creative
- [ ] earning a high salary
- [ ] helping people
- [ ] job satisfaction
- [ ] job security
- [ ] using practical skills
- [ ] working in an office
- [ ] working outside
- [ ] working with animals
- [ ] working with children
- [ ] working with computers
- [ ] working with the public

D 🔊 Work in pairs. Imagine you work for the same company and you are both thinking about a change of career. Roleplay a conversation like the one in Exercise A. Ask and answer questions about your ideal jobs. Use the phrases from the box in Exercise A to help you.

E 🔊 Find another partner and repeat your conversation.

HOW ARE YOU DOING?

Think about your speaking and tick the statements that are true.

I feel confident …
- ⃝ describing my ideal job.
- ⃝ agreeing and disagreeing with someone.
- ⃝ using questions to ask for more information.

How do you feel about your speaking generally?

⬤ Very confident   ⃝ Not sure …   ⬤ Need to practise

Grammar reference

PRESENT PERFECT + *YET/ALREADY/JUST*

Form

We use *already* in affirmative statements and questions. We use *yet* in negative statements and questions. We use *just* in affirmative statements and questions. The position of *already* and *just* in a sentence in the present perfect is immediately before the past participle. We use *yet* at the end of a sentence.

	Affirmative	Negative	Question
already	*I've already read the book so I know what happens.*		*Have you already read the book?*
just	*I've just sent the email five minutes ago.*		*Have you just spoken to Maria?*
yet		*I haven't eaten lunch yet.*	*Have you found a job yet?*

Function

We use *yet* to say that something hasn't happened, but it will happen soon.
We use *just* to say that something has happened in the immediate or very recent past.
We use *already* to say that something happened sooner than expected, or to emphasise that it has happened.

1 Tick the correct sentences. Rewrite the incorrect sentences.

Lyndsey: (1) ☐ Have you found a new job yet? _____

Michelle: No, I haven't. (2) ☐ But a company just has called me about an interview. _____

Lyndsey: Fantastic! (3) ☐ Have you yet researched the company? _____

Michelle: (4) ☐ Yes, I've just looked at their website. _____

Lyndsey: What about clothes? You'll need to wear something smart.

Michelle: (5) ☐ I've already bought a new suit _____ (6) ☐ but I haven't already got a bag. _____

Lyndsey: I can lend you one. It's new. (7) ☐ It has been used yet. _____

2 Complete the sentences with *yet, just* or *already*.

1 I've _____ seen Rebecca. She was here two minutes ago.
2 We're going to see the new James Bond film. Have you _____ seen it?
3 I'm really hungry. Is dinner ready _____?
4 They haven't arrived _____. Maybe their train is late.
5 We're really full. We've _____ eaten a big bowl of ice cream.
6 Have you spoken to Adam _____? He's been waiting for your call.

PRESENT PERFECT CONTINUOUS

Form

	have/has + been + -ing form of the verb	Short answers
Affirmative	*I have been checking my emails all afternoon.*	
Negative	*She hasn't been cleaning the room so it's very dirty.*	
Questions	*Have you been working here for a long time?* *How long have you been working here?*	Yes, I have. No, I haven't.

Function

We use the **present perfect continuous**:
• to talk about an activity that started in the past and is still in progress now.
• to talk about the result of a recent continuing activity.
• with questions starting with *How long* …?
We use the **present perfect simple** to talk about something that happened at an unspecified time in the past.

1 Complete the conversation with the correct form of the verbs in brackets. Use the present perfect continuous when possible.

Lucy: Where have you been? I (1) _____ (wait) here for ages.

Aiden: I'm sorry. I (2) _____ (call) you but you didn't answer.

Lucy: Oh, sorry. My phone's been switched off. I've been in the library for a few hours.

Aiden: (3) _____ (revise) for the exam all this time?

Lucy: No, I (4) _____. I've been with Sue. We (5) _____ (try) to look at websites for our holiday.

Aiden: Did you find anything?

Lucy: No, the internet (6) _____ (work) all morning.

2 Complete the sentences with the present perfect simple or present perfect continuous of the verbs in brackets.

1 Recently, Ellie _____ (think) about changing her career.
2 We _____ (not have) time to download the music for the barbecue.
3 Jon and Susie _____ (see) each other on and off for three years.
4 I _____ (not watch) that film for a long time.
5 I'm really hot because I _____ (jog).
6 How long _____ (rain)?

UNIT 2

USED TO

Form

Affirmative	Negative	Questions	Short answers
used to + base form of verb	**didn't use to + base form of the verb**	**Did you use to + base form of verb** **What did you use to …?**	
I used to play rugby. It used to rain all the time.	I didn't use to drink milk. He didn't use to eat meat.	Did you use to wear glasses? What music did she use to listen to?	Yes, I did No, I didn't.
You can use *never* and *always* with *used to*.		My brother always used to get up really early. I never used to get up before 11am at weekends.	

Function

We use *used to* to talk about things that were true in the past, but are not true in the present.

1 Tick the correct sentences. Rewrite the incorrect sentences.

1 ☐ She used have long hair, but now it's short. _____
2 ☐ I used to eat meat, but now I'm a vegetarian. _____
3 ☐ Did Rachel and Eva used to play in a band when they were younger? _____
4 ☐ They used to have a dog? _____
5 ☐ Dad didn't use to have a beard. _____
6 ☐ What time did you use to wake up on Sundays? _____
7 ☐ It didn't used to snow a lot in the winter. _____
8 ☐ We didn't use to see our friends during the week. _____

2 Complete the sentences with the verbs in brackets and *used to*.

1 Tom's sister _____ (play) in a band but now she doesn't have time.
2 I _____ (drink) coffee because I didn't like it.
3 A: _____ (go out) with my sister?   B: Yes, when we were at school.
4 Alex _____ (eat) meat at all. He was a strict vegetarian.
5 A: Where _____ (work)?   B: In a consultancy firm.
6 My parents _____ (speak) Spanish fluently, but they don't now.

PAST PERFECT

Form

Affirmative	Negative	Questions	Short answers
had + past participle	*had not* + past participle	*Had (you)* + past participle	
I had left the party when he arrived.	*We hadn't heard about that restaurant before.*	*Had you visited London before you moved here?*	*Yes, I had.* *No, I hadn't.*

Function

We use the **past perfect** to talk about something that happened before a specific time in the past.

1 Complete the sentences with the past perfect of the verbs from the box.

> see   (not) save   visit   (not) eat   become   leave

1 Our friends _____ Hungarian food before, but they really liked it.
2 Kim's computer crashed and she lost all the work she _____.
3 By the time he was 28, Tony _____ the manager of his department.
4 A: _____ London before?   B: No, they hadn't.
5 I _____ already _____ the first film, so I downloaded the sequel.
6 The waiter collected the empty glasses they _____ on the table.

2 Complete the sentences with the past simple or past perfect of the verbs in brackets.

1 We _____ (*know*) exactly what to do because we _____ (*read*) the instructions beforehand.
2 The play _____ (*start*) when I _____ (*arrive*) at the theatre.
3 The garden _____ (*be*) very dry because it _____ (*not rain*) all summer.
4 They _____ (*tell*) me they _____ (*not have*) time to go on holiday this year.
5 Sue was surprised. She _____ (*not know*) her husband _____ (*organise*) a birthday party for her.
6 Sara _____ (*remember*) the message her brother _____ (*give*) her.

UNIT 3

DEFINITE ARTICLE *THE* / ZERO ARTICLE

Function

We use the definite article *the*:	Examples
when something has been mentioned before.	*I can see a man and a woman in a café. The woman is wearing a blue coat.*
when there is only one of something or the reference is to a whole group.	*the world, the labour party, the BBC*
with some country names that have plural nouns or the words States, Kingdom or Republic in the name.	*the Netherlands, the United States, the United Kingdom*
with geographical features.	*the Pacific Ocean, the Andes, the Mississippi River*
when the noun answers the question *which?* or *what?*	*A: Which jacket is yours? B: The red one.*

We don't use articles:	Examples
with plural countable nouns when talking about them generally.	*Dogs are good pets. Apples are a healthy snack.*
with uncountable nouns when talking about them generally.	*money, wood, water*
with names of people, months, cities, most countries, products, etc.	*David Beckham, New York, January*

1 Complete the sentences with *the* or – (no article).

1 _____ Serengeti is an important ecosystem in East Africa.
2 _____ young people spend a lot of money on technology.
3 There is a hotel and two restaurants in the town. _____ hotel is next to _____ sea.
4 _____ company's research found that _____ women enjoy shopping with friends.
5 Many people download _____ music from _____ internet.
6 _____ North Pole reaches temperatures of -45°C.

2 Complete the text with *the* or – (no article).

(1) _____ sport has always played an important role in (2) _____ society and it is constantly evolving. We know (3) _____ first Olympic Games took place in (4) _____ Greece in 776 BCE. Monuments from (5) _____ Ancient Egypt tell us that (6) _____ Pharaohs enjoyed swimming in (7) _____ River Nile 2000 years ago. In 1940, (8) _____ archaeologists found (9) _____ cave paintings in Lascaux, France, which show (10) _____ men wrestling and running. (11) _____ cave paintings date back 17,000 years. More recently, (12) _____ Industrial Revolution increased the amount of (13) _____ leisure time people had to play and observe different sports. Nowadays, (14) _____ extreme sports are popular. Perhaps they reflect a need to escape the routine of everyday life in (15) _____ modern era.

INDIRECT QUESTIONS

Function
We use indirect questions to be more polite.

Form

	Direct question Use normal question order	**Indirect question** Use affirmative word order
Information question	*What's her email address?* *How much will it cost?* *Why is it the wrong colour?* *When did you order my new laptop?*	*Can you tell me what her email address is?* *Do you have any idea how much it will cost?* *I wonder why it is the wrong colour?* *Could you tell me when you ordered my new laptop?*
Yes/No question	*Do you have a bigger size?* *Can I exchange it for a different one?* *Is it expensive?*	*Do you know if you have a bigger size?* *Do you think I could exchange it for a different one?* *Could you tell me if it's expensive?*

1 Write the words in the correct order to make sentences.

1 costs / know / you / do / how / the / much / camera / ?

_____

2 phone / you /could / do / order / a / me / think / you / mobile / new / ?

_____

3 is / where / nearest / could / tell / ATM / you / the / me / ?

_____

4 idea / you / do / any / have / arrive / when / will / it / ?

_____

5 credit / can / accept /you / me / tell / whether / cards / you / ?

_____

6 why / didn't / she / wonder / I / the / job / apply / for / ?

_____

2 Complete the indirect questions using the prompts.

1 When will the laptop be ready?
Can you tell me _____?

2 What time did the bank close?
Do you have any idea _____?

3 Is this tablet available in black?
Do you know _____?

4 Do you sell this model online?
Could you tell me _____?

5 Where can I get my car fixed?
Do you think you could tell me _____?

6 Why is the shop closed on Saturdays?
I wonder _____?

CAUSATIVE *HAVE* AND *GET*

Form

get/have + direct object + past participle	*have* + indirect object + base form	*get* + indirect object + infinitive form
I want to get my hair cut.	*I'm going to have the plumber fix the shower.*	*I got the mechanic to fix the car.*

Function

To have/get something done means that another person does something for you.
Have someone do something and *get someone to do something* also mean you ask/hire someone to do something for you.

1 Complete the sentences with the correct form of *get/have* and a verb from the box.

manicure   install   cut   deliver   repair   do

1   Let's _____ a pizza _____ to the house.
2   I'm _____ the grass _____ tomorrow.
3   Can you _____ your laptop _____ at work?
4   Jennifer _____ a telephone line _____ last week.
5   What are you going to _____ _____ to the house before you sell it?
6   I might _____ my nails _____ at the new salon.

2 Complete the conversation with one word in each space.

Luisa: Jane, do you have Jack's telephone number?

Jane: Yes, of course. Are you going to (1) _____ the shower fixed?

Luisa: Yes, I'm also going to get (2) _____ to repair the roof.

Jane: He's really reliable. You could (3) _____ him paint the fence in the garden, too.

Luisa: What are you doing this afternoon?

Jane: I'm going to the hairdresser's to (4) _____ my hair coloured. Then I have to take my laptop to the service centre. I want to (5) _____ the technician to install anti-virus software.

Luisa: Do you mind if I come with you to the hairdresser's? I'd like to get my hair (6) _____, it's grown a bit too long.

ADJECTIVES ENDING IN *-ED/-ING*

Form/Function

-ed participles used as adjectives describe an effect on a person or thing.
I was very interested in the detective story.
I was really frustrated by what happened.
-ing participles used as adjectives describe the person or thing that causes an effect.
The book was very interesting.
That situation was really frustrating.

1 Choose the correct adjective form to complete the sentences.

1   The end of the film was surprising / surprised.
2   I haven't done much work today. I'm not very motivating / motivated.
3   The news about Caroline's grandma was really depressing / depressed.
4   Users of the company's online website were dissatisfying / dissatisfied with the service they received.
5   A: What's that noise outside? It's really annoying / annoyed.
     B: I can't hear anything.
6   Running a business requires a lot of hard work and it can be tiring / tired.

2 Complete the text with -*ing* or -*ed* adjectives formed from the verbs in the box.

complicate exhaust frustrate disappoint excite interest bore fascinate

The situation is **(1)** _____. Jim wants to move to Australia and live on farm. He thinks his job as an accountant in the UK is **(2)** _____. Every night he feels **(3)** _____ because he works long hours. He's been wanting a career change for a while but his wife, Anita, really likes her job as a nurse. She might feel **(4)** _____ if she moves to another country and can't find work. However, Anita is very **(5)** _____ in Aboriginal history, she finds the subject completely **(6)** _____. Their children will be **(7)** _____ to leave their friends but they think a house with a swimming pool could be very **(8)** _____.

UNIT 5

REPORTED SPEECH

Function
We use **reported speech** to repeat what someone said without using their exact words.

Form
Reported speech doesn't use quotation marks (' ').
When we use a verb in the past tense to introduce reported speech, for example, *said* or *told*, we change the tense in the reported speech.
In reported speech, we change other words the person said, for example, pronouns and time and place expressions.

Direct speech		Reported speech
present simple 'I don't know any good jokes.'	→	**past simple** He said that he didn't know any good jokes.
present continuous 'I'm designing the company logo.'	→	**past continuous** Nathan told me that he was designing the company logo.
past simple 'We lived abroad for a few years.'	→	**past perfect** She said they had lived abroad for a few years.
present perfect simple 'I haven't seen the new promotional material.'	→	**past perfect** He said he hadn't seen the new promotional material.
be going to 'I'm going to get a loan from the bank.'	→	**was going to** She said she was going to get a loan from the bank.
will 'We will get a last-minute holiday.'	→	**would** I told him we would get a last-minute holiday.
pronouns I, we, me, us, my, our, mine, ours	→	he, she, it, they, him, his, her, them, their, hers, theirs
time expressions today tomorrow yesterday next week now last week last Sunday	→	that day the next day the day before the following week then the week before the Sunday before
place expressions here	→	there

1 Complete the reported sentences with the correct pronoun and time/place expression.

1 'I'm going to the park tomorrow.'
She said _____ was going to the park _____.

2 'My sister was practising badminton here yesterday.'
He said _____ sister was practising badminton _____ _____.

3 'Mark, I can help you with your homework today.'
Maria told Mark that she could help _____ with _____ homework _____.

4 'Trisha and Martin went to the cinema last Saturday.'
He told me _____ had gone to the cinema _____.

5 'Danielle, you will start a new class next week.'
He told _____ she would start a new class _____.

6 'We've just eaten our lunch here.'
They said _____ had just eaten _____ lunch _____.

2 Rewrite these sentences as reported speech.

1 'I shop online every week.'   He said _____.
2 'Lisa, we'll drive you to the supermarket.'   They said _____.
3 'I didn't see you and Kate last night at the bar.'   Carina said _____.
4 'We're not going on holiday this year.'   David and Maya said _____.
5 'Sam's been excited about her date tonight.'   Sam's sister told me _____.
6 'I can give you some advice about your business.'   He said _____.

REPORTED QUESTIONS

Function

We use reported questions to report what someone asked without using exactly the same words.

Form

We can report questions using *asked / wanted to know*. We use *if/whether* to report a *yes/no* question.
We have to change the tense in reported questions in the same way as reported speech.

	Direct questions	Reported questions
Yes/No questions	*Are you going out later?*	*Matt asked me if I was going out later.*
	Do you like classical music?	*She wanted to know whether he liked classical music.*
Information questions	*What time is it?*	*He wanted to know what time it was.*
	Where did you meet her?	*Joe asked where I met her.*

1 Write the original direct question.

1 The instructor wanted to know if we spoke any foreign languages.
'Do you speak any foreign languages?'
2 She asked me where I lived. _____
3 He asked me if I could design a website for his cleaning company. _____
4 Rosie wanted to know if I would write the report. _____
5 They asked us what the main news story was that day. _____
6 The manager asked who had gone to the meeting. _____

2 Write the reported question.

1 'Are you going to get your phone line repaired?'   He asked _____.
2 'Does Cara plan to look for another job?'   They asked me _____.
3 'Where will we advertise the new service?'   Scott wanted to know _____.
4 'Have you thought about writing a blog?'   Mum asked me _____.
5 'Why did Paul and Sofia leave early last night?'   My wife wanted to know _____.
6 'What are you doing?'   Alex asked him _____.

THIRD CONDITIONAL

Function

We use the **third conditional** to talk about unreal situations in the past.
We can use *could* or *might/may* instead of *would* in the result clause to talk about results that were possible in the past.

Form

If-clause	Result clause	Examples
If + past perfect	would, could, might/may + have + past participle	*If you had got up earlier, you wouldn't have missed the train.* *I would have studied history if I had gone to university.* *If he had studied history, he might have become a teacher.*
We use a comma when the *if*-clause is at the beginning of the sentence.		*If I had found a job near my home, I wouldn't have moved to London.* *I wouldn't have moved to London if I had found a job near my home.*

1 Match 1–6 with a–f to make correct sentences.

1 I would have applied for the job if I
2 If I hadn't lived in Spain, I
3 David could have saved more money if he
4 If the company had invested in better technology, it
5 If Becky had gone to bed earlier last night, she
6 I would have been able to come to the party if you

a) would have felt less tired today.
b) had told me about it last week.
c) hadn't bought that new car.
d) may not have learnt the language.
e) had known about it.
f) might not have gone bankrupt.

2 Complete the sentences with *might/would* and the verbs in brackets.

1 I'm not sure, but if I _____ (wait) for the sale, I _____ (pay) less for this sofa.
2 The story _____ (have) a happier ending if the main character _____ (not kill) his wife in the last chapter.
3 If Lilia _____ (take) the car today she _____ (arrive) much more quickly.
4 You never know, but they _____ (get) a table if they _____ (make) a reservation last night.
5 If I _____ (brought) my car I definitely _____ (give) you a lift home.
6 If it _____ (not rain) we _____ (go) for a walk.

HOPE AND *WISH*

Function

We use *hope* to refer to things that are possible in the present and future.
We use *wish* and *if only* to refer to things that are impossible in the present.
We use *wish + would/wouldn't* to express dissatisfaction with a situation in the present.

Form

Past	Present	Future
hope + past simple *I hope you had a nice time at the party last night.*	hope + present simple *I hope I pass the exam.*	hope + will *I hope I'll have enough money to buy a new car.*
	hope + present continuous *I hope you're having a great time.*	
	wish + past simple *I wish I had a better idea.*	
	if only + past simple *If only you were here.*	
	wish + would *I wish he would stop that noise.*	

1 Choose the correct option to complete the sentences.

1 I hope you enjoy / enjoyed your holiday. When did you get back?
2 If only it were warmer / is warm right now. We could eat outside.
3 We wish he washed / would wash the dishes after dinner.
4 I hope / wish Helen's having a great birthday.
5 Marina hopes she will see / saw you at her party next Saturday.
6 Hannah wishes she lived / would live by the beach.

2 Rewrite the sentences using the word(s) in brackets.

1 He always arrives late and I don't like that.
  (wish + wouldn't) _____
2 I don't have much time and I want to spend more time with you.
  (wish) _____
3 It's a pity you don't know how to play chess.
  (if only) _____
4 I would like to pass my driving test tomorrow.
  (hope) _____

UNIT 7

MODALS OF DEDUCTION: *MUST, CAN'T, MIGHT/MAY/COULD*

Form	Function	Examples
Subject + modal + base form	**can't** We use *can't* to say that it's impossible that something is true.	*That woman can't be Jessica. She's blonde and Jessica has dark hair.*
	must We use *must* to say that we are sure that something is true.	*It must be after 8pm. Look! It's dark outside.*
	might/could/may We use *might/could/may* to say that something is possibly true.	*There might be a storm later. The sky is very dark.*

1 Choose the correct option to complete the sentences. Sometimes both options are possible.

1 Michael could / might be in a meeting. He hasn't been answering his phone.
2 It can / must be a good film. It has five stars in the review.
3 You can't / must be hungry. You've just eaten an enormous meal.
4 It can't / might be very late. The shops are still open.
5 Sally revised all night last night. She can't / must be really tired today.
6 Dan told me Julie was finishing work early today. She may / could be home now.

2 Complete the conversation with *might, could, may, must* or *can't*.

Nick: When's the meeting?
Marion: It (1) _____ be today. I'll just check my diary. I'm not exactly sure.
Nick: It (2) _____ be today. The manager is away and two colleagues are on holiday. Surely it
           (3) _____ be held next week when everyone gets back.
Marion: Really? Next week is a training week from Monday to Thursday.
Nick: Oh, OK. It (4) _____ be on Friday then, but I'm not sure.
Marion: Look! It (5) _____ be on Friday. The meeting room is reserved for our team then.

QUESTION TAGS

Function

We use question tags to check information we are not sure about or to confirm information that we are almost certain about.

Form

	Affirmative main verb, negative question tag	Negative main verb, affirmative question tag
main verb *be*	You're Claudia, aren't you?	They aren't studying in the UK, are they?
simple tenses	Rob likes Italian food, doesn't he?	You didn't lose your mobile phone, did you?
modals	Julie should call more often, shouldn't she?	That can't be right, can it?
Present perfect	You've just told him, haven't you?	He hasn't been here before, has he?
Past continuous	He was texting his ex-girlfriend again, wasn't he?	Francesca wasn't applying for another job, was she?
	have got uses *have* in question tags	Paul hasn't got an interview today, has he?

1 Tick the questions that are correct. Rewrite the incorrect question tags.

1 ☐ He should go to the doctor, shouldn't he? _____
2 ☐ You remember the name of Steve's girlfriend, don't you? _____
3 ☐ Doctors say there are links between cancer and diet, do they? _____
4 ☐ You've got two brothers, don't you? _____
5 ☐ Joshua can't be at work at this time, can he? _____
6 ☐ Sarah sat an exam last week, did she? _____
7 ☐ Ashley's parents are visiting tonight, isn't she? _____
8 ☐ You've promised to help your sister, have you? _____

2 Complete the question tags.

1 Jack can drive, _____?
2 They don't offer much choice, _____?
3 Ruby and Ethan will be able to get here without a map, _____?
4 This jacket isn't well made, _____?
5 You didn't invite her _____?
6 You're worrying about the interview tomorrow, _____?
7 You told him my secret, _____?
8 It can't be Sandra. She's got red hair, _____?

UNIT 8

RELATIVE CLAUSES

Function

We use relative clauses to give more information about a person, thing, time or place.

Form

Relative pronoun	Examples
who	I thanked the person who found my wallet this morning on the Underground.
when	The best time to call him is when he finishes his meeting at 10.30am.
where	The Blue Lounge was the place where I used to meet my friends.
which/that	I think it was a trip to Paris that made me want to learn French.

1 Complete the sentences with *which/that*, *who*, *when* or *where*.

1 A web designer is a person _____ can make your website look more professional.
2 It's a technique _____ helps you learn more effectively.
3 A good time to do brain training is _____ you feel relaxed.
4 It was my brother _____ used to take us swimming every Sunday.
5 We got married at the place _____ we first met.
6 I'm going to choose a course _____ I'm really interested in.

2 Rewrite the sentences using relative clauses.

1 My best holiday was in Paris. I met my girlfriend there.
   My best holiday was in Paris _____.
2 There's a man who fixes my car. His name is Luke.
   Luke is the man _____.
3 There's a Polish bakery in my village. It sells black bread.
   In my village there's _____.
4 That's the waiter. He spilt coffee on my new skirt.
   That's the waiter _____.
5 We were on Brighton beach. I lost my car keys there.
   Brighton beach is the place _____.

VERB + GERUND/INFINITIVE

Form

	Examples	Other verbs
verb + gerund	Isobel usually avoids driving in the city centre. I finished reading that novel.	admit, avoid, deny, dislike, finish
verb + infinitive	Did you manage to find the song on the internet? We offered to make some coffee for them.	agree, help, invite, manage, offer, plan, promise, refuse, seem
verb + gerund/ infinitive	I like going out. I like to go out now and again.	hate, like, love, prefer

1 Choose the correct option to complete the sentences. Sometimes both options are possible.

1 I dislike / avoid reading novels. I much prefer films.
2 Laura has offered / promised to help me paint the house next weekend.
3 We've agreed / admitted to sign the contract.
4 Help / Finish writing the email. Then we can have dinner.
5 I don't know how Eva plans / manages to do so much. She works full time and has four kids.
6 Jim refuses / seems to be quite annoyed today. I wonder what's upset him?

2 Complete the sentences with the correct form of the verb in brackets.

1 He prefers _____ (go) on holiday to the countryside.
2 I don't think they'll admit _____ (cheat) in the exam.
3 Jennifer's cold is getting worse but she refuses _____ (see) the doctor.
4 I usually avoid _____ (ask) people about their age and salary.
5 Can I help you _____ (choose) a mobile phone package?
6 Politicians have denied _____ (lie) about their expense accounts.

UNIT 9

INFINITIVE CLAUSES WITH IMPERSONAL *IT*

Form

It's (not)	adjective	infinitive clause
It's	important	to eat properly.
	good	to get fit.
	better	to speak to a professional.
	essential	to get some sleep.

Function

We use *it's* (*not*) + adjective + infinitive clause when we want to use the adjective to describe an action or situation.
This means the same as using the gerund as a subject.
It's important to eat properly. = *Eating properly is important.*

1 Match the problems 1–6 with the solutions a–f.

1 I haven't got any interviews yet.
2 I've been putting on a lot of weight recently.
3 I'm not sure what I want to study.
4 What skills do I need to be an engineer?
5 Ouch! I've got a small cut.
6 I pulled a muscle this morning.

a) It's better not to move it too much.
b) It's not good to use the car so much. Try to walk more!
c) It's important to consider what career you want later.
d) It's better to put a plaster on it.
e) It's essential to have a qualification in maths.
f) It's difficult to get a job at the moment, don't give up!

2 Complete the responses with an infinitive clause. Use a verb and an adjective from the box.

| better | important | essential | common | good | difficult | rest | feel | call | wake up | apologise | practise |

1 I think I've broken my leg.
It's _____ an ambulance.
2 I've been really depressed since my divorce.
It's _____ like that.
3 I've hurt my wrist.
It's _____ it for a few days.

4 I practise a lot of English grammar.
Remember it's _____ speaking, too.
5 I said something unkind about my colleague and he heard me.
It's _____ sooner rather than later.
6 I overslept this morning again and arrived late.
It's _____ so early.

WISH AND IF ONLY FOR REGRETS

Form

Subject + *wish* + past perfect	*I wish I had learnt to play a musical instrument when I was younger.*
	I wish I had been more adventurous.
If only + subject + past perfect	*If only I had changed careers years ago.*

Function

We use *wish / if only* + past perfect to talk about things we would like to change about the past.

1 Which of these sentences refer to things we would like to change now or in the future and which to things we would like to change about the past? Write *N/F* (now/future) or *P* (past).

1 Francine wishes she'd kept in touch with her old school friends. _____
2 If only he would stop talking while I'm driving. _____
3 Francine wishes she could help you. _____
4 I wish I hadn't argued with my friend. _____
5 If only you'd worn a warm coat. _____
6 Jacob wishes he had some headache tablets in his bag. _____
7 I wish I hadn't had a cold on the day of my exam. _____
8 If only they didn't live so far away. _____

2 Complete the sentences so they mean the same as the first sentence.

1 Chris didn't eat a healthy diet. Now he's overweight.
Chris wishes *he'd eaten a healthy diet.*
2 You lifted a heavy suitcase yesterday. Today your back hurts.
If only _____.
3 I didn't enjoy my career as a doctor. I wanted to be an actor.
If only _____.
4 Frank didn't finish his IT course at college. Now he needs IT for his job.
If only _____.
5 I got a tattoo of 'Anna' on my arm. Then I broke up with her two years ago.
I wish _____.

NON-DEFINING RELATIVE CLAUSES

Function

A **non-defining relative clause** gives us extra information about a noun.

We already know which person or thing we are referring to.

The relative clause could be removed from the sentence without affecting the basic meaning.

Form

Non-defining relative clauses:	
• are separated from the rest of the sentence by commas. • can only come after the noun they refer to.	*The Ashmolean museum, which is the oldest museum in the UK, was built in 1678.*
• can only use *who* to refer to people, and *which* to refer to places and things. • can sometimes use *where* to refer to places.	*Daniel Radcliffe, who played Harry Potter, now acts in the theatre.* *The college, which specialises in languages, is near Bristol.* *York, where my parents live, is a very beautiful place.*

1 Complete the sentences with *who, which* or *where.*

1 The internet service, _____ is available between 9am and 10pm, is free of charge.

2 These trousers, _____ I bought yesterday, are much too long.

3 The receptionist, _____ is Italian, recommended a good pizzeria near the hotel.

4 Stroud, _____ my daughter goes to school, is holding a summer festival next week.

5 That Canadian actor, _____ stars in the new mini-series, is really funny.

6 The play, _____ was written by a Scottish author, is being made into a film.

2 Write sentences with non-defining relative clauses using the information given.

1 The Theatre Royal is one of the oldest theatres in London. It's on Drury Lane.

2 Mark went to the same school as me. He directed the film.

3 The gym has a special membership fee. I used to go to this gym after work.

4 The music venue in town has been refurbished. International artists perform there.

5 The film's visual effects were unbelievable. They won a special award.

6 The actress played the main part. She died last year.

DEFINING RELATIVE CLAUSES

Form

Defining relative clauses:	
do not need commas to separate them from the rest of the sentence.	*The film which/that we saw last week was directed by Martin Scorsese.*
come after the noun they refer to.	*The director who/that won the award wasn't at the ceremony.*
can use *which/that* to refer to things. can use *who/that* to refer to people. can use *where* to refer to places.	*We stayed in the place where we had our honeymoon.*
Subject and object relative clauses	
A noun can either be the subject or the object of a defining relative clause.	*The actress who wore the exquisite dress at the end of the film is a model.* **(subject)**
When the noun is the object of the relative clause, the relative pronoun can be left out.	*The dress (that/which) the actress wore at the end of the film is exquisite.* **(object)**

Function

A **defining relative clause** gives us extra information about a noun. It could not be removed from the sentence without affecting the basic meaning.

1 Read these sentences. <u>Underline</u> the defining relative clause and write X next to the sentences where the relative pronoun can be left out.

1   The song which plays at the end of the film has been a big hit this summer. ☐
2   Look! He's the actor who I was telling you about. ☐
3   The company that sold me the car has gone bankrupt. ☐
4   The Australian dancer who got the part is unknown in her home country. ☐
5   I recognised the famous landmarks which the director used in several scenes. ☐
6   Do you remember the woman who promised to invite us to the party? ☐

2 Rewrite the sentences using defining relative clauses. If the relative pronoun can be left out, write it in brackets.

1   An area of the brain provides information about the senses. It's called the cerebral cortex.
    The area of the brain _____.
2   I've been watching a film. I think it might be Danish.
    I think the film _____.
3   I booked a room for us in Dublin Bay. It's in a small cottage.
    The room _____.
4   Thomas spoke to a woman yesterday. She can give us information about the show.
    The woman _____.
5   An artist designed the scenery for a West End play. She was in a magazine article last week.
    The artist _____.

UNIT 11

SHOULD/SHOULDN'T HAVE

Function
We use the perfect modal *should/shouldn't have* to criticise or express regret about things that people did or didn't do in the past.

Form

should have + past participle	I/he/she/we/you/they should have gone to the doctor.
shouldn't have + past participle	I/he/she/we/you/they shouldn't have been rude to the shop assistant.

1 Tick the correct sentences. Circle the mistakes in the incorrect sentences.

1   ☐ She should had informed the police about the crime immediately.
2   ☐ They shouldn't have cheat in the exam.
3   ☐ I shouldn't have to parked illegally on the pavement.
4   ☐ You should to have paid for those songs you downloaded illegally.
5   ☐ I should have told the security guard that I saw someone looking in the windows.

2 Complete the conversation with *should/shouldn't have* and a verb from the box.

Oliver: Guess what happened last week! I was walking back to my car at night and I saw two men spraying graffiti on a building and smashing the windows.

Mark: That area is really dangerous at night. You can leave your car there during the day but you (1) _____ it there at night. Have you told the police what you saw?

Oliver: Not yet. I've been so busy this week.

Mark: Well you (2) _____ it immediately. The police need to know. Did you see what the men were wearing?

Oliver: Yes, but now I can't remember. I think one of them was wearing a blue coat, or was it red?

Mark: You (3) _____ a description. What time was it?

Oliver: Late, I think. It was dark. But I don't remember the exact time.

Mark: You (4) _____ your watch. Maybe other people were around at the same time and they saw the men?

Oliver: I'm not sure how the men got in through the gate to the building. The security guard (5) _____ his post.

check
report
write down
park
leave

WAS/WERE GOING TO AND WAS/WERE SUPPOSED TO

Function

We use *going to* in the past to talk about plans and intentions that didn't happen.

We use *supposed to* in the past to talk about things we were expected to do but didn't do.

Form

was/were going to + base form	*They weren't going to come but they changed their minds.*
was/were supposed to + base form	*You were supposed to copy Valerie in on all the emails.*

1 Choose the correct option to complete the sentences.

1 I said I was going / supposed to write to her but I didn't have time.
2 The web designer was going / supposed to add links to the web page. We reminded him several times.
3 Did you say you were going / supposed to run in the park later? I might come with you.
4 I was going / supposed to book a holiday but then John broke his leg.
5 Helen was going / supposed to prepare a marketing report for the meeting tomorrow.
6 We were going / supposed to be moving house today but there was a problem with the contract.

2 Complete the sentences with *was/were (not) going to* or *was/were (not) supposed to*.

1 I didn't think Martin _____ stay for long but then he started talking about his holidays.
2 You _____ remove the bandages until next week. The doctor told you.
3 Well I _____ do anything much – just relax and watch the TV.
4 We _____ get engaged until next year but Andy suddenly proposed on holiday.
5 The cost _____ include everything, food and accommodation.
6 It _____ snow today but it has and so our flight might be cancelled.

UNIT 12

SO, SUCH, TOO, ENOUGH

Form	Function	Examples
so + adjective / adverb	We use *so* with nouns to mean *very, really* or *extremely*.	*The weather is so hot today.*
such + adjective + noun	We use *such* with adjectives and adverbs to mean *very, really* or *extremely*.	*He's such an interesting character.*
so/such … that …	We use a *that* clause after *so* and *such* to show results or consequences.	*The film was so interesting that I watched it twice.*
too + adjective / adverb	We use *too* with adjectives and adverbs to say that there is more of something than we need or want.	*You're speaking too fast. Can you speak more slowly, please?*
not + adjective / adverb + enough	We use *not … enough* with adjectives and adverbs to say that there is less of something than we need or want.	*It's not quiet enough to study in here.*
too + adjective to … / (not) … enough … to …	We use an infinitive clause after *too* and *(not) … enough* to show results or consequences.	*There isn't enough time to see the show.* *The bed was too big to fit in the room.*

1 Choose the correct option to complete the sentences.

1 It's such / so a warm day today.
2 The report was so / such detailed that it took me three days to read.
3 This room is enough / too bright. Please could you close the blinds?

4 She's much too / so busy to help you today.
5 The venue was so / too crowded that I couldn't find a seat.
6 That actress is too talented / not talented enough to play a leading role.

2 Rewrite the sentences using the words in brackets.

1 The music in this restaurant is very noisy. I can't hear anyone.
   (so ... that) _____.
2 This job is extremely stressful.
   (so) _____.
3 The film we went to see has a really amazing original score.
   (such) _____.
4 Anna found a part-time job really quickly. She can go on holiday now.
   (so ... that) _____.
5 Jeremy is very considerate. He would never borrow something without asking.
   (too ... to) _____.

SEPARABLE AND INSEPARABLE PHRASAL VERBS

Form

With separable phrasal verbs, you can put a noun between the verb and the particle.
With inseparable phrasal verbs, you can't.
With separable phrasal verbs, we always separate the verb and the particle when the
object is a pronoun (*you, it, them*, etc).

		Example
Separable phrasal verbs	verb + particle + noun	*I don't have to write down the information.*
		I don't have to write the information down.
	verb + noun/pronoun + particle	*I don't have to write it down.*
		~~*I don't have to write down it.*~~ X
Inseparable phrasal verbs	verb + particle (+ preposition) + noun/pronoun	*I didn't get on with my colleagues.*

1 Underline the sentences which are incorrect and correct them.

1 a) We should have looked the matter into.
   b) We should have looked into it.
   _____

2 a) Please fill in the forms.
   b) Please fill in them.
   _____

3 a) I'll hand the report in at the end of the day.
   b) I'll hand in the report at the end of the day.
   _____

4 a) I didn't pick the phone up when it rang.
   b) I didn't pick up it when it rang.
   _____

5 a) Did you call Karen back?
   b) Did you call back her?
   _____

6 a) You're always running into Jake in the bank.
   b) You're always running into him in the bank.
   _____

2 Rewrite the sentences using the correct form of a phrasal verb from the box.

| get on with   catch up on   turn off   copy in   hear of |

1 I have a good relationship with my colleagues.
   I _____ my colleagues.
2 Please can you include her when you send emails?
   Please can you _____ when you send emails?
3 Do you know this online company which sells gifts?
   Have you _____ this online company which sells gifts?
4 I've been doing the work I didn't do last week when I was ill.
   I've been _____ the work I didn't do last week when I was ill.
5 Please make sure your phones don't ring in the meeting.
   Please _____ in the meeting.

Audioscript

1.04   M = Man, J = Joe

M: That was a great dive, Joe! You're an excellent diver!

J: Thanks. It took me a long time to start competing at this level, believe me. I was stuck at an intermediate level for ages!

M: Why was that? I'm asking because that's my problem at the moment. I'm a good diver, and I win a lot of competitions at my level, but I'm definitely not an advanced-level diver. I feel as if I'm not making any progress.

J: Well, that's quite normal. It isn't very difficult to get to an intermediate level in a sport, but it's really difficult to get to an advanced level. The first, and I think, the most important thing, is that you really have to want to get to the top level. It's all in the mind – you have to push yourself really hard. It's easy to feel secure at the intermediate level and just stay within your comfort zone.

M: Yes, that's true.

J: The second thing is, you have to take risks. You have to try a lot of new techniques and make a lot of mistakes before you know what works. You lose a lot of competitions while you're learning, but you can't progress if you don't try new things.

M: Hmm, I suppose that's true, but I really hate losing!

J: Then you'll never be an advanced diver. One way to measure your progress is to lose competitions. When you finally beat a diver you've always lost to, then you know you've made real progress.

M: That makes sense. I haven't beaten Josh Morgan yet, but maybe I will one day!

J: Of course you will. Finally, you must be consistent. You have to practise a lot.

M: That's part of my problem, too. I haven't had much time to practise recently.

J: Yeah, it's hard, but try to practise a bit more if you can.

M: I don't know. I'm feeling a bit discouraged at the moment. Maybe I should take some time off and not dive at all for a while.

J: No, don't do that. You've already made a lot of progress, and you're a good diver. Just do your best and don't give up!

M: OK, that's good advice. Thanks, Joe.

1.09

1 Um … let's see, was I six or seven when that happened?
   I can't really remember.
2 You never do anything I ask you! You never used to be this lazy!
3 Oh, look at those cakes! I used to love those!
4 Oh, Mum! How many more of these old pictures do we have to look at?
5 Uh, hello … um, could I speak to Sarah, please? It's James. I'm, um, an old friend of hers … from school …
6 Oh, this is a picture of my first dog. It was awful when he died.

1.10

Conversation one

A: Welcome to *Real People*, and thanks to our studio audience! Today we're asking people in the audience to share their earliest childhood memories. OK, the man in the front row, in the blue shirt. Sir, can you tell us your earliest childhood memory?

B: Me? Oh, I … uh, I don't know … I think it was … maybe when my sister was born. I was about three and a half. I vaguely remember her coming home from hospital … I'm not sure ….

A: A memory from the age of three and a half! Does anyone have a memory from a younger age?

Conversation two

C: Oh, John, this exhibition is amazing! Look at all these toys from the 80s! I remember all of these things! Look, there's a Pac-Man computer game! Oh, and do you remember the Teenage Mutant Ninja Turtles? They were so popular with little kids!

D: Oh, yeah, I remember all of these things. It's a brilliant exhibition.

Conversation three

A: Let's look at these old cars! My parents used to have a Riley like this, but in blue! This is such a great car! It would be so cool to have one now!

B: Um … OK. Then can we go and get something to eat?

A: OK. Oh, look at that! It's a 1966 Hillman Minx! Isn't it great?

B: It just looks like an old car to me. Have you seen enough cars now? I'm hungry, Mark.

Conversation four

C: What's wrong?

D: Oh, these cakes smell just like the ones my grandmother used to make. They made me remember her. I used to help her make these cakes when I visited her at weekends. I really miss my grandma.

1.12   T = Tom, M = Michael

T: Oh, wow, look at that old Jaguar! That is so cool!

M: Now that brings back one of my favourite childhood memories!

T: What do you mean? That car is from the sixties. You weren't even born then.

M: No, of course not, but my grandpa used to have a car like that.

T: Really? Wow.

M: Yeah, he got it when I was about 13. He said he hadn't been able to buy a sports car when he was young, so he was going to buy one when he was old! I think the one he bought was a 1967 model.

T: Did he drive it?

M: Of course, and he used to take me for rides in it. He had always wanted an E-Type soft-top, so that's what he got. It was so much fun to ride around in it with the top down. I had never ridden in a soft-top before. I thought it was really great when we went out in that car!

1.14

Tired of shopping online? Want a personal touch? Then come to Bigmart Superstore. Our friendly shop assistants will help you choose the products that are right for you. You can try on all our clothes and test all our electronic products before you buy. Now, you can't do that on a website, can you? You can also take your purchases straight home with you. No need to wait for delivery! And when you've finished shopping, why not relax at our in-store café? I wonder if you've ever tried to get a coffee from a website? Bigmart Superstore – the friendly, personal way to shop!

1.19   K = Kieran, C = Customer

Conversation one

K: Good morning, NetPhone. My name is Kieran. How can I help you?

C: Hello. Yes. I'm calling to make a complaint.

K: I'm sorry to hear that. What's the problem?

C: Well, I bought a mobile phone from your company a few days ago.

K: OK?

C: The problem is that the part that the charger connects to is broken. I don't know how it happened, but I'm sure it wasn't my fault. I tried to connect the cable to the phone to charge it, but I couldn't connect it. When I looked at the phone, I saw that a little piece was broken.

K: OK, so what's happened is that a part on the phone is broken, but the charger isn't broken. Is that right?

C: Exactly, yes. I don't think I did anything to break it. I didn't try to force the cable in or anything. I'm sure it was broken when I bought it.

K: Oh, I'm very sorry about that. Don't worry. We'll replace the phone for you. Can you tell me what model it is?

C: Yes, it's the Studio Sound 3.

K: OK. I'm going to transfer you to one of my colleagues in Customer Services so you can get a replacement. Thank you for calling, and I apologise for the problem.

C: Thanks for your help.

Conversation two

T = Tina, C = Customer

T: Simpson's. Hold please. OK, hello?

C: Uh, hi. Is this Simpson's Electronics?

T: Yeah.

C: OK. Uh … I'd like to make a complaint.

T: Can you hold for a second? OK. So, what's the complaint about?

C: It's my new laptop. I only bought it about 10 days ago and it doesn't work.

T: What's wrong with it?

C: Well, I don't know what's wrong with it. It just won't turn on. What do you think the problem could be?

T: I have no idea. You need to speak to technical support.

C: Oh, well … how do I do that?

T: You need to call 01847 5556721.

C: OK … So there's no way you can just connect me to technical support?

T: Yeah, OK, I'll transfer the call. Hold on.

1.23

Conversation one

A: I'd just like to say that your salespeople are very polite and well informed. I'll definitely shop here again. In fact, is there a place for customer comments on your website? People always complain, but they almost never say anything when the service is good.

B: Thank you, Sir. It's always nice to receive positive feedback, and yes, you can make comments on our website. Just go to the 'Contact us' section. Thanks for taking the time to do that.

A: Perfect! I'll do that.

Conversation two

C: I'm sorry, but I'm not very happy with the service I've had here. The shop assistants were rude and they couldn't answer any of my questions. One of them was actually texting on her phone while I was asking her for some information!

D: I'm very sorry to hear that, Madam. Would you like to speak to the manager? I'm sure he would appreciate your comments.

Conversation three

E: So what should I do? Should I have them repair it or just get them to replace it? If I ask for a replacement, it may take a long time to get here. What do you think, Juliet?

F: Oh, I don't know. It's up to you. Either way is fine, I think.

Conversation four

G: This vacuum cleaner isn't very well made. Look! This part keeps falling off. I think we should get them to replace it. Do you know where the receipt is?

H: What? Oh … er … I don't know … in the desk somewhere … maybe …

G: Come on, Chris, help me look for it. I really want to get this thing replaced. It's so annoying!

H: I can't look for it at the moment. I'm really busy. Can't it wait until tomorrow?

Conversation five

I: Oh! I don't believe it! This printer is so badly made! I had it repaired only last week and it's broken … again!

J: Really? How annoying. Maybe you should buy a new, better quality one. I understand how frustrating it is when things don't work when you really need them.

I: Yes, it is. I just hate this thing!

UNIT 5 Through the grapevine

1.30

1 Hi, Lindsey, it's Jemma. Guess what? I've got some good news! Remember I told you that Jack was going to take me out for dinner on Friday? Well, … Can you guess what my news is? Call me as soon as you hear this message!

2 Rob, are you there? Can you please answer the phone? I've heard you lost your job today! I don't care if you've been sacked. I still love you! Kevin told me that you were really upset. Please call me. I'm concerned about you, and I just want to know if you're OK.

3 Hi, Dad … um … it's me, Leo. Uh, … I'm wondering if I can I ask you, um, a little favour. I've got, er, a bit of a problem with a credit card. So, well, um, I really need your help, Dad. OK, so … Bye.

4 Oh, hi, Mark, John here. Just phoning to let you know that I talked to Catherine. I asked permission to give in that report on Monday instead of Friday, and she said we could give it to her on Monday morning, so that's OK. Let's meet up later today to work on it. Could you phone me later?

1.31   R = Reporter, M = Mrs Hill

R: Pauline Hill, first of all, thank you for talking to me.

M: You're welcome.

R: Mrs Hill, there have been some recent stories in the news about your husband's shopping habits. Is it true that he has more than 400 designer suits?

M: Do you really think my husband's clothes are relevant to my job as Minister for Education? Is that what you call news?

R: I've got a report here that says your husband spent about thirty thousand pounds last year on clothes. That is a very luxurious lifestyle, don't you agree?

M: It's true that my husband and I are very comfortable financially. But I don't think it's anyone's business how we spend our money. Are you saying that it's wrong to be successful?

R: No, I'm not, but do you feel that your husband's lifestyle is giving the public a negative image of you?

M: No, I don't think there is a negative image of me at all. The public admires successful people.

R: Mrs Hill, there is a rumour, and it is only a rumour, that your husband is a shopaholic; that he is a shopping addict.

M: My husband is a shopaholic? That is just not true! The media tells lies all the time, and everyone knows that.

R: Do you think your husband's lifestyle will affect your chances of keeping your job after the election?

M: No, of course not. I'm going to continue to work to improve education in this country.

R: Mrs Pauline Hill, thank you for your time.

M: Thank you.

UNIT 6 Decisions, decisions

1.34   M = Michael, A = Angela, J = Julia

M: So we made the decision to move to London, and here we are! It was a difficult decision, but I think it was the right thing to do. Our life in a quiet village in Wales was great, but there are more job opportunities here. If we had stayed in Wales, I wouldn't have advanced so quickly in my career, and Angela wouldn't have found a job in a big hospital. We miss our friends and family of course, but I'm sure we'll make new friends soon and it's not so far – we can always go back to Wales to visit.

A: Michael is right about our careers, of course, but still, a big move like this is difficult. To be honest, I would have been perfectly happy if we hadn't moved. I was happy working at our local hospital, and I had a lot more time to be with Julia. I think I would have been happier if we had moved to Cardiff, or another city in Wales. London is a bit difficult after so many years in a small village! Well, we'll just have to wait and see what happens, I guess.

J: My mum doesn't think London is a good place for a teenager, and she's worried that I'll get into trouble. I don't agree with her! It's actually great living in London because I'm interested in dance, and I wouldn't have been able to do advanced dancing classes if we had stayed in our little village at home. Of course, I miss my friends a lot, but it's exciting to live in a city!

1.35

1 I'm very worried about the environment. I wish people cared about it more. We can't just wait and see what happens. We're destroying the Earth! I wish the United Nations would put pressure on all countries to do more to end climate change. I just hope it won't be too late when we finally do something.

2 I wish the economic situation were better. I hope I get a job after university, but there are fewer jobs these days. I also wish I had chosen to study business instead of history. If I had a business degree, I would probably have a better chance of getting a job. My parents warned me about that, but I didn't listen because I really didn't want to study business!

3 I wish people wouldn't drive around talking on mobile phones all the time. Even if you use a hands-free device, you're still distracted when you're talking on the phone. Lots of accidents happen because of mobile phones. Even though it's against the law, people still do it. The police should be stricter.

4 I wish people would take better care of our city. I wish they wouldn't drop litter on the pavement and graffiti the buildings. It looks awful! Don't people want to live in a clean, attractive city? I hope the campaigns to get people to clean up the city will work!

UNIT 7 Think again!

2.02

Good morning. The topic of today's lecture is super-intelligence – the level of intelligence that produces child prodigies. Child prodigies generally have very high IQs, but they tend to show great talent in one specific area like maths, science or music. Most of these children show their talent before the age of 13, and some are recognised as prodigies as young as age four or five.

Let's talk about some modern-day examples. First, there's Alma Deutscher from the UK. She started playing the violin when she was three years old, and she began composing music at the age of five. In 2012, at the age of seven, she composed a short opera!

Also in the arts is the Australian painter Aelita Andre. This little girl began painting at the age of nine months! She had her first solo exhibition in New York when she was just four years old, and she sold all of the paintings in the exhibition.

In science, we have Tanishq Abraham, who lives in the USA. Tanishq was writing articles on astronomy for NASA's website at the age of seven. Soon after that, he started university, and he is currently studying particle physics and astronomy.

You're probably all thinking that it must be wonderful to be a child prodigy, but in fact, it can be quite difficult. Firstly, some child prodigies can have difficult social lives. Secondly, highly intelligent children can be under great pressure from their parents and teachers to be successful at a very early age. OK, any questions so far?

UNIT 8 Stories we tell

2.07

A Oh, no! This was the classic office mistake! We had just had a long meeting with our boss, and I didn't agree with a lot of what he wanted us to do. My good friend Jake was in the meeting, too, and after the meeting, he sent me an email. The email was just basically a summary of what our manager had asked us to do, but I was in a really bad mood, so I wrote back to Jake and said, 'Can you believe this? Most of what he wants us to do is rubbish!' Right after I sent the email, I realised that Jake had copied in our manager. I also realised that I had hit 'Reply to all', so of course, my boss got the email, too! He never said anything, but of course, I was mortified that I had done that!

B Look at this hair! I mean, it's SO bad! My advice, ladies, is never cut your own hair! Here's what happened. I decided that I would change my hairstyle – go for short hair. I found an article in a magazine – Easy do-it-yourself haircuts. It's so expensive to get your hair cut at a salon, so I bought some good scissors, studied the technique they described in the article and I was ready! It took me about two hours to cut my hair because I constantly had to stop and look back at the instructions. When I finished, the front part around my face looked pretty good, but when I used a mirror to look at the back and sides, I almost died! I thought I had followed the instructions exactly, but my hair looked like I had just cut off big pieces with a knife! The next time I want a haircut, I'll definitely pay a professional to do it!

C It was really embarrassing, actually. There's this girl in my class, Kelly, and I've always kind of liked her. Well, I decided to ask her out, you know, to see if she wanted to go to the cinema or something. So, I saw her in the hall at uni and I thought, 'Here's my big chance.' I walked up to her, trying to be so cool. Just as I was about to say 'Hi', I tripped over a bag and fell on the floor! That's how I broke my leg. Well, everyone laughed, of course, and I felt like an idiot.

2.08

My most embarrassing moment was the time when my friend Craig invited me to a party. Ah, it was awful! What happened was, Craig was having a party to celebrate moving into a new house, and I invited a girl, Karen, who I knew at university. We had talked a little bit before and after lectures, but I didn't know her very well. Anyway, she said yes, and on the night of the party, I picked her up at the university hall of residence where she lived. Craig had just moved the week before, and I hadn't been to his new house yet, so the first thing that happened was that I got lost and drove around for nearly an hour! When we finally got there, the house seemed really quiet, but we knocked on the door and waited. There was no one there! I phoned Craig on his mobile phone, and he started laughing. I'd got the wrong day. Can you believe it? The party was the next day! I was so embarrassed! Karen couldn't go the next night, or at least that's what she said! I went to the party alone, and I never asked Karen out again.

2.12

This is the story of how Rabbit got his long ears. A long time ago, when Rabbit was first on this earth, he had very short ears. One day he was bored, so he decided to play a trick on all the other animals. He said to Beaver, 'Did you know that the sun is not going to rise again?' Of course, Beaver told Squirrel, and Squirrel told Chipmunk, and Chipmunk told Skunk, and so on. Soon all the animals knew the story, and they were very worried. They said, 'If the sun is not going to shine anymore, it will be dark and cold like winter. We have to start preparing now!'

2.13

Bear loved to eat meat, but he was so worried that he began to eat blueberries and other fruit so he could get very fat. Squirrel started gathering all the nuts he could find. Everyone who had heard the story was busy getting ready for the sun not to shine again. Of course, Rabbit hid in the bushes and laughed and laughed as he watched all the other animals running around. Then a man called Kluskap came along. Normally the animals were very glad to see Kluskap but today, no one greeted him. Kluskap asked Bear, 'How are you?' Bear said, 'I don't have time to talk to you!' Kluskap kept walking, but the animals wouldn't talk to him. Kluskap went back to Bear. 'What's going on? You're not talking to me. Something must be wrong!' Kluskap said. 'Haven't you heard?' Bear said. 'The sun is not going to shine anymore – we have to get ready for winter now!' Kluskap listened, and then he said, 'The one who told you that story is lying. It's not true.'

2.14

Kluskap called a meeting with all the animals. When they were all there, he said, 'Who told you, Bear?' Bear said, 'Skunk told me.' And Skunk said, 'Well, Chipmunk told me.' Everyone said who they had heard the story from, all the way down to Beaver. Beaver said, 'It was Rabbit who told me.' Rabbit heard this, and he was really scared, so he hid in

the bushes. Kluskap knew then that Rabbit had started the story because he was the only one who was not at the meeting. 'He must be hiding,' Beaver said. Kluskap looked in the bushes. He found Rabbit, he grabbed him by the ears and lifted him up. As Kluskap lifted Rabbit, Rabbit's ears started to stretch and get longer and longer! And that is how Rabbit got his long ears.

2.15   L = Lily, M = Mark

L: The most awful thing happened to me the other day!

M: Really? What?

L: Well, I went shopping at that big new shopping centre that's near college. There's a six-storey car park, and there were millions of cars in it, so it was hard to find a parking space. You know, it was Saturday, and everybody was there.

M: Yeah, yeah, so what happened?

L: I'm getting there! So I parked my car and went inside the shopping centre. I shopped and looked around for about two hours, and then I went out to the car park. I went to the place where I had parked my car, and guess what – my car had gone and there was another car parked in the space!

M: Oh, no! What did you do?

L: Well, I thought I had got the wrong space, so I walked up and down rows and rows of cars, but my car definitely wasn't there.

M: So then what did you do?

L: I called the police to report that someone had stolen my car! They arrived in about 10 minutes, and they took all the information. They told me to report it to my insurance company and then they left.

M: That's terrible! So how did you get home?

L: Well, here's the really terrible part. I went down to the first level of the car park to get a taxi home, and guess what I saw?

M: I don't know. What?

L: My car! Right in the space where I had left it!

M: Really? So your car hadn't been stolen?

L: No! I had driven up to the second level to look for a space, and I forgot that I had driven back down to level 1 and had found a space there.

M: Wow! That's terrible! So did you call the police back?

L: Yes, of course. The officer that I talked to thought I was completely mad. It was so embarrassing!

UNIT 9   Body talk

2.16

1 head	7 thumb	13 neck
2 ear	8 finger	14 arm
3 jaw	9 ankle	15 elbow
4 shoulder	10 eye	16 leg
5 back	11 nose	17 knee
6 wrist	12 mouth	18 toe

2.17   P = Patient, D = Doctor

P: Hello?

D: Hello. Is that Jade Lincoln? Dr Singh here.

P: Oh, hello, Doctor. Thank you for calling me back.

D: I got a message that you wanted to speak to me. Now, what seems to be the problem? Have you hurt yourself playing tennis again?

P: Ah, you remembered. My ankle's fully recovered now, thanks to you. No, it's not a sprain this time. I've got a terrible migraine. My vision is blurred and it's painful to move my head. I've been lying down in a dark room, but it doesn't seem to help much.

D: I see. Well, we usually find that two painkillers four times a day can help. I can write a prescription for some pills if you like.

P: Thanks, Doctor. Yes, I think that would help. And there's another thing. I don't know if it's connected to the migraines or not, but I've got a really bad fever. I feel hot and then cold all the time. Could it be flu?

D: Yes, it certainly could be. A lot of people are suffering from it at the moment. It's easy to catch it at this time of year. I suggest you stay in bed, rest well and drink plenty of fluids. Do you have someone who could pick up your prescription?

P: Yes, my husband. Thank you, Doctor.

D: That's fine. If you don't feel better tomorrow, call again.

UNIT 10   Stage and screen

2.23

A: I hear you saw a show last weekend. How was it?

B: Oh, it was great! I went with my brother and we both loved it.

A: What kind of show was it?

B: It was a dance show by a modern dance group who were from Japan. They were fantastic! I've never seen anything like it.

A: What was the venue like?

B: It was an old theatre that had a really good atmosphere. It was quite small, but that meant that you could see everything.

A: What about the costumes?

B: They were really colourful and interesting. They changed a lot and every dance looked different.

A: How much were the tickets?

B: Oh, they were quite cheap. And if you go on Thursday afternoon, it's half price.

A: Would you recommend it?

B: Oh, definitely. You like dance, don't you? Well, you'll love this show, then. In fact, I wouldn't mind going again. We could go together.

A: That's a great idea!

2.25

Good morning, everyone. We've already looked at the history of the medium, in particular how certain types of programme developed, but now I'd like us think about the technology itself. What are the interesting developments in TV today? The more we understand that, the more we can think about what's going to happen in the future.

2.26

One of the big developments over the last few years is smart TVs. Although they've only been on sale for a short time, the first patent for a smart TV appeared back in 1994. The main idea behind smart TVs is that they are both televisions and online computers. They can show traditional television shows, but they can also provide entertainment from the internet. This could be interactive services, such as games, or it could be on-demand TV, which allows you to watch a programme at a time you choose.

On-demand services are very popular with viewers, of course. However, advertisers are not enthusiastic for one very simple reason. When you are watching TV on demand, it's very easy to skip the advertisements. No one wants to make an expensive TV advert which viewers just don't watch.

2.27

Another interesting development which you may have seen is 3D TV. This is where you see an image that seems to be more life-like, rather than just a flat picture. The basic technology was developed in the USA, where 3D films were very popular in the 1950s. It took a long time, though, for 3D TVs to appear in the shops. They are becoming more popular, but one problem is that watching 3D films and TV involves wearing glasses. Many people find them uncomfortable. Another problem with 3D TVs is that they can be very expensive. However, I'm sure prices will fall, and experts believe that 3D TVs will become more popular. Now, has anyone seen 3D TVs? Yes, a few of you have. Would someone like to tell us what they thought of it?

UNIT 11   Breaking the rules

2.29   F = Finn, N = Noah

F: Noah, there you are. I've been looking for you.

N: Oh, hello, Finn. What's up? You seem cross.

F: I want to talk to you about what you said to Eva. She's really upset.

N: What's Eva been saying?

F: Why don't you tell me about it in your own words?

N: OK. It was during the chemistry exam. Eva cheated. I saw her getting a book out of her bag and using it in the exam. I don't know what it was exactly, but she was cheating. I didn't tell anyone.

F: So what did Eva say when you talked to her about it?

N: First of all, she said I was lying, which I wasn't, and then she said it was none of my business. I said that cheating is wrong and it's not fair for people like me who work hard. She started to explain but I didn't want to listen to her lying to me. I told her I'd think about what to do.

2.30   F = Finn, N = Noah

F: Well, Eva's very upset. She said she was innocent, but you didn't listen to her and you should have done. She can explain it. You shouldn't have upset her.

N: I didn't listen to her because I knew she was lying. I saw her do it.

F: You should have asked her to show you the book she had in her bag. It wasn't about chemistry. It was her notebook. She was checking something else, something private.

N: Well, it didn't look like that.

F: You shouldn't have just assumed she was cheating. You have to have proof before you make a serious accusation like that. If you were so sure, why didn't you tell an examiner? You should have done that, then Eva could have explained. Now she won't be able to prove she didn't cheat.

N: Well, OK. I'll speak to her. I won't tell anyone else.

2.33 and 2.34
Conversation one

J: What's wrong, Erin?

E: Well, Jack told me that Kate has been spreading gossip about me. We were going to look for a flat together but I've told her I don't want to live with her anymore and now I'm not speaking to her.

J: Frankly, I don't think you've handled this very well, Erin. Did you even discuss the problem with her?

E: No, I didn't. I didn't think I needed to.

J: What if you were wrong? What if Jack misunderstood? You've probably really upset her and you never heard her side of the story.

E: This is ridiculous. I never asked for your opinion! Whose side are you on anyway?!

Conversation two

J: What's wrong, Erin?

E: Well, Jack told me that Kate has been spreading gossip about me. We were going to look for a flat together but I've told her I don't want to live with her anymore and now I'm not speaking to her.

J: Oh dear. I'm not sure that was the best way to handle this.

E: What do you mean? Why not?

J: Well, did you try talking to Kate about it?

E: No, I didn't.

J: Hmm, well, maybe you should have got her side of the story. I just think it's possible that Jack misunderstood and gave you the wrong idea.

E: Hmm, maybe you're right. I guess I should talk to her.

UNIT 12   Just the job!

2.35
OK. Let's get started, shall we? Today I want to talk about the idea that 'no one should ever work'. This theory was only really taken seriously when an American lawyer called Bob Black wrote an essay called *The Abolition of Work* in 1985. In it, he argues that all human life is spent making, buying and selling products, and that if we really want to be 'free', we have to break this cycle. Black compares workers to prisoners, who have no control over their working lives. The boss says when the worker has to arrive at work, when they can go home, how much work they have to do and how fast they have to do it. And the boss has the right to make the worker unemployed. Black also claims that any 'free' time workers have isn't really free time at all. His argument is that it's only called 'free time' because it doesn't cost the boss anything, and that for most people, 'free' time is usually spent getting ready for work, going to work, coming home from work, and recovering from the stress of working!

2.36
In Black's opinion, work is the biggest killer in the world. Between 14,000 and 25,000 workers are killed at work every year in the USA, for example, and 20 to 25 million people are injured every year. He argues that these statistics don't show the tens of millions of people who have their lives shortened by work. As you might imagine, Black's argument was heavily criticised by other academics and thinkers. Many argued that, although his ideas were interesting, they were too romantic to work in practice. Neala Schleuning wrote in 1995 that humans have no choice and MUST work. Her main argument is that because we need to eat, cook, care for children and keep warm, we have to work. In fact, in order to survive, work is essential. Anyone who argues against work, she suggests, has a very simple view of the world. So, with that in mind, let's now look at current thinking on the topic, which I'm sure you'll agree is …

2.37   O = Oliver, D = Daniel

O: My ideal job would be one where I work with other people. I find it boring to work on my own at my desk for hours. Earning a high salary isn't really important to me, although of course it needs to be high enough to live comfortably. The key thing for me would be relationships with people, and I'd like to help people when they're in trouble. I find it very satisfying when I can listen to people's problems and work out ways to help them. I think my ideal job would probably include that. I also like speaking in public, so I'd welcome the chance to do that.

D: My ideal job would be one where I never get bored. The thing I'm looking for is adventure. I don't mean a lot of action and excitement. It doesn't have to be travel or new places, but I couldn't work in an office. I would find it so quiet that I would go mad!

It would be good to be outside, really, and work with animals. I'd also like to work with members of the public, you know, talk to people about my work and explain to them what I do. I think part of me would love to be a teacher and part of me would love to be a vet!

2.40

A: So, tell me about yourself, Mr Green.

B: Erm. Well, I live in Swindon, and I'm married with two children. I like playing golf and travelling. Oh, and I'm 29 years old.

A: OK. What did you do in your last job?

B: A little of everything. You know, the usual things people do in an office! Filled out forms. Dealt with customers over the phone. That kind of thing.

A: And what do you think are your strengths and weaknesses?

B: I'm not really sure. You should ask my wife. She may have something to say about that!

A: OK. Erm. Can you tell me why you want to work for us?

B: Well, the salary is good and I'm bored with the job I do now, so it would be a good career move for me.

A: If we offered you the job, when could you start?

B: I'm not sure. I'm going on holiday for four weeks next Monday. Any time after that.

A: And finally, Mr Green, have you got any questions?

B: No, I don't think so.

A: OK. Well, thank you very much for coming. We'll be in touch …

2.41

A: So, tell me about yourself, Ms Martin.

B: Well, I'm originally from Glasgow, in Scotland, and I'm married with a daughter. I'm 27 years old and I have a degree from Sheffield University.

A: OK. What did you do in your last job?

B; I've been working as a legal secretary in a law firm for the last six years. My main roles were dealing with clients, preparing reports and organising legal files.

A: And what do you think are your strengths and weaknesses?

B: Well, I think I'm very good at listening to people's problems and offering them good advice. So, I'm quite good at problem solving. And I enjoy working as part of a team and I think I have good communication skills. I can be a bit shy with people I don't know, but I'm trying to improve my confidence.

A: OK. And can you tell me why you want to work for us?

B: Well, I really enjoyed my job as a secretary, but I didn't want to work in an office anymore. Becoming a community police officer would give me the chance to see the law from the other side. And it also means that I get to meet and deal with the public. Working in London has always been my dream, too.

A: If we offered you the job, when could you start?

B: I'd need to give two weeks' notice, but I could start immediately after that.

A: And finally, Ms Martin, have you got any questions?

B: Yes, I have actually. How many people do you employ here?

A: Well, at the moment there are probably about three hundred or so …

Irregular verbs

Infinitive	Past simple	Past participle
be	was/were	been
become	became	become
begin	began	begun
break	broke	broken
bring	brought	brought
build	built	built
buy	bought	bought
catch	caught	caught
choose	chose	chosen
come	came	come
cost	cost	cost
cut	cut	cut
do	did	done
draw	drew	drawn
drink	drank	drunk
drive	drove	driven
eat	ate	eaten
fall	fell	fallen
feed	fed	fed
feel	felt	felt
find	found	found
fly	flew	flown
get	got	got
give	gave	given
go	went	gone
grow	grew	grown
hang	hung	hung
have	had	had
hear	heard	heard
hit	hit	hit
hold	held	held
hurt	hurt	hurt
keep	kept	kept
know	knew	known
learn	learnt	learnt
leave	left	left
let	let	let
lose	lost	lost
make	made	made
meet	met	met
pay	paid	paid
put	put	put
read	read	read
ride	rode	ridden
ring	rang	rung
rise	rose	risen
run	ran	run
say	said	said
see	saw	seen
sell	sold	sold
send	sent	sent
set	set	set
sing	sang	sung
sit	sat	sat
speak	spoke	spoken
stand	stood	stood
stick	stuck	stuck
take	took	taken
teach	taught	taught
tell	told	told
think	thought	thought
throw	threw	thrown
understand	understood	understood
wake	woke	woken
wear	wore	worn
win	won	won
write	wrote	written

Pronunciation symbols

Vowels

ɪ	did
e	bed, neck
æ	bad, hand
ɒ	box
ʌ	but, mother
ʊ	book, good
ə	banana, computer
iː	feed
ɑː	father
ɔː	tall
uː	boot, food, student
ɜː	shirt, birthday
eɪ	date, table
aɪ	cry, eye
ɔɪ	boy
əʊ	comb, post
aʊ	about, how
ʊə	tour
eə	their
ɪə	here, near

Consonants

p	park, happy
b	back, hobby
t	tea
d	die
k	came, kitchen, quarter
g	game, go
f	face, photographer
v	vegetable
θ	thing, maths
ð	then, that
s	city, summer
z	please, goes
ʃ	she, shop
ʒ	leisure
h	hot, who
tʃ	chicken, watch
dʒ	jacket, orange
m	men
n	sun, know
ŋ	sung, singer
w	week, white
r	rain, writer
l	light, long
j	yes, use, music

Grammar review answer key

1
1 was typing, appeared
2 were you doing, heard
3 weren't paying attention, didn't see
4 was running, dropped
5 rang, was sitting

2
1 to have
2 would like
3 eat out
4 not to buy
5 work

3
1 yourself
2 herself
3 themselves
4 ourselves
5 myself

4
1 Where – e
2 Could – d
3 Would – c
4 Should – a
5 Will – b

5
1 The broadband at my office is **faster** than at home.
2 The New Year celebration is **the** most important event in the Chinese calendar.
3 Spain is as popular **as** France for British tourists.
4 That was the **worst** film I've ever seen.
5 Hull isn't as beautiful **as** York.
6 You must listen **more** carefully next time.

6
1 Millions of songs are downloaded every day.
2 Bastille Day is celebrated by the French on the 14th July (by the French).
3 The first X-ray wasn't taken until 1895.
4 German, Italian and French are spoken in Switzerland.
5 *Emma* and *Sense and Sensibility* were written by Jane Austen.

7
1 ever
2 long
3 since
4 never
5 been

8
1 should
2 have to
3 must
4 don't have to
5 ought

9
1 too loud
2 not spicy enough
3 too greasy
4 big enough
5 not warm enough

10
1 much
2 bit
3 fewer
4 isn't
5 many

11
1 starts
2 I will meet
3 I'll
4 We're travelling
5 does the bus leave

12
1 correct
2 If dad had more time, he'd decorate the house.
3 correct
4 They'd buy a bigger house if they didn't live in the city.
5 correct

13
1 eating
2 speaking
3 doing
4 Shopping
5 making

14
1 might
2 won't
3 will
4 will
5 might

Language wrap-up answer key

1 Vocabulary

A 1 take
2 do
3 do
4 made
5 make
6 take
7 doing
8 making
9 take

B 1 measure our progress
2 progress
3 push yourself
4 comfort zone
5 take risks
6 give up

2 Grammar

A 1 Have you already seen this film?
2 They have just moved to a new house.
3 He hasn't eaten his dinner yet.
4 My friends have just left.
5 Have you just arrived?
6 She's already found a new job.

B 1 have been
2 have met
3 have been studying
4 haven't had
5 have spent
6 have been looking
7 haven't found
8 have applied
9 haven't heard

1 Vocabulary

A 1 popular
2 troublemaker
3 rebel
4 joker
5 geeky
6 academic
7 sporty
8 party animal

B 1 makes
2 remember
3 think
4 reminds
5 brings back
6 memorise
7 remind

2 Grammar

1 use to
2 was
3 had wanted
4 came
5 gave
6 Had, had
7 hadn't
8 used to
9 use to
10 grew
11 have had
12 was
13 used to
14 had, got
15 became

1 Vocabulary

1 the wrong colour, exchange
2 work, replace
3 fit, a larger size
4 broken, fix it (get it repaired)
5 missing, order
6 the wrong one, match
7 too small
8 turn on, get it repaired

2 Grammar

A 1 X, the
2 the
3 the, X
4 the
5 the, the
6 the

B 1 how much this is
2 if/whether the price includes delivery
3 if/whether adverts affect how you shop
4 which adverts you find interesting
5 how adverts persuade people
6 if/whether this advert is right for our audience

1 Vocabulary

A 1 design
2 launch (set up)
3 plan (create)
4 register
5 create
6 set up (launch)
7 research
8 advertise

B 1 helpful
2 poorly made
3 professional
4 poor quality
5 rude
6 high quality
7 well informed

2 Grammar

1 checked
2 to look
3 annoying
4 frustrating
5 to fix
6 surprised
7 interesting
8 disappointed
9 worrying
10 to do
11 amazing
12 annoyed
13 to fill
14 confusing
15 to phone

1 Vocabulary

1 ask
2 speech
3 ask
4 telling
5 say
6 explain
7 Talk
8 tell
9 tell
10 asking
11 saying
12 argue
13 chat
14 discuss
15 Say

2 Grammar

1 if/whether he was going to Lisa's party
2 he didn't know
3 his cousins were coming to visit that weekend
4 where David's cousins lived
5 they had just come back from Thailand
6 if/whether they had lived in Thailand
7 if/whether Jenny wanted to meet them
8 they would be at home on Sunday
9 she couldn't come on Sunday
10 maybe he could take them to Lisa's party
11 she would ask Lisa if it was OK
12 if/whether he wanted her to pick them/him and his cousins up
13 that would be perfect
14 thought it was a good plan
15 she was going to call Lisa that night

1 Vocabulary

1 make up
2 advantages
3 make
4 take
5 consequences
6 advice
7 warn
8 see
9 promise
10 weigh up
11 keep
12 trust
13 close
14 gather
15 consider

2 Grammar

A 1 had taken
2 would have been
3 would have done
4 had thought
5 have taken
6 have gone
7 have spent
8 hadn't left

B 1 Pete wishes he had more free time.
2 I hope it is/will be sunny tomorrow.
3 I hope you're having a good time.
4 I wish you were here.
5 I hope you enjoyed the concert last night.
6 If only you lived near me.
7 I wish she would phone me.

1 Vocabulary

1 powerful
2 useful
3 develop
4 learn
5 find
6 explored
7 hopeless
8 challenge
9 solve
10 careful
11 fearless
12 fearful
13 painful
14 powerless
15 painful

2 Grammar

A 1 must
2 might/may/could
3 can't
4 can't
5 might/may/could
6 can't
7 must

B 1 can they
2 isn't she
3 won't you
4 did we
5 has she
6 should we
7 do you
8 does she

1 Vocabulary

A 1 got lost
2 got the wrong day
3 clicked on 'Reply to all'
4 arrived late
5 said the wrong thing
6 forgot someone's name
7 sent a text to the wrong person

B 1 childish
2 entertaining
3 unbelievable
4 imaginative
5 thought-provoking
6 gripping
7 pointless
8 moving

2 Grammar

1 when
2 spending
3 to get
4 that/which
5 to find
6 who/that
7 to help
8 who/that
9 to have
10 taking
11 moving/ to move
12 who/that
13 where
14 that/which
15 to let

1 Vocabulary

1 have food poisoning
2 cut your finger
3 have a sore throat
4 have hay fever
5 break your leg
6 injure your back
7 burn yourself
8 have the flu
9 have an ear infection
10 sprain your ankle
11 have a migraine
12 have a chest infection
13 hurt your shoulder
14 pull a muscle
15 have a cold

2 Grammar

1. to want
2. to get
3. had told
4. to think
5. hadn't been
6. had thought
7. to do
8. had had
9. to imagine
10. to describe
11. had taken
12. to forget
13. to be
14. had understood
15. not to think

UNIT 10

1 Vocabulary

1. costumes
2. lighting
3. director
4. score
5. animated
6. row
7. screenplay
8. venue
9. admission charge
10. special effects
11. orchestra
12. leading actor
13. audience
14. scenery
15. supporting actor

2 Grammar

A
1. This book, which is my favourite, was my uncle's.
2. My sister, who is 21, is at university.
3. *Starry Night*, which is very famous, was painted by Van Gogh.
4. St Paul's Cathedral, which was designed by Christopher Wren, was finished in 1675.
5. My grandmother, who lives in Greece, was born in 1940.
6. This room, which is at the back of the house, is my office.
7. The vase, which was expensive, was stolen last week.

B
1. who/that
2. (that)/(which)
3. that/which
4. who/that
5. (who)/(that)
6. that/which
7. that/which
8. which

UNIT 11

1 Vocabulary

A a 6 b 4 c 8 d 5
  e 3 f 2 g 7 h 1

B
1. spread gossip
2. be considerate
3. hurt (her) feelings
4. cheat
5. break a promise
6. do (me) a favour
7. think twice

2 Grammar

A
1. should have been
2. shouldn't have made
3. shouldn't have gone
4. should have walked
5. should have gone, shouldn't have slept
6. should have bought
7. shouldn't have eaten

B
1. We were supposed to leave at nine, but we didn't.
2. Ollie was going to have a party, but he was ill.
3. I wasn't going to go to the party, but I did.
4. I was supposed to go shopping yesterday, but I finished work late.
5. They were going to move to the USA, but they didn't.
6. You weren't supposed to tell Julia about the surprise.
7. The weather forecast said it was going to rain today.

UNIT 12

1 Vocabulary

A
1. been unemployed
2. write a good CV
3. applying for a job
4. working for a company
5. get a part-time job
6. earning a good salary
7. get on with your colleagues

B
1. fill in
2. pick up
3. call back
4. fall behind
5. catch up
6. copy in
7. look into
8. join in

2 Grammar

A
1. such a good
2. detailed enough
3. too long
4. so difficult
5. such a brilliant
6. so nice
7. big enough

B
1. turn it off
2. call him back
3. ✓
4. write it down
5. ✓
6. ✓
7. getting on with patients
8. run into Mary

Grammar reference answer key

UNIT 1

1
1. correct
2. But a company has just called me about an interview.
3. Have you researched the company yet?
4. correct
5. correct
6. but I haven't got a bag yet.
7. It hasn't been used yet.

2
1. just
2. already
3. yet
4. yet
5. just
6. yet

1
1. 've been waiting
2. 've been calling
3. Have you been revising
4. haven't
5. 've been trying
6. hasn't been working

2
1. has been thinking
2. haven't had time
3. have been seeing
4. haven't watched
5. 've been jogging
6. has it been raining

UNIT 2

1
1. She used to have …
2. correct
3. Did Rachel and Eva use to play …
4. Did they use to have a dog?
5. correct
6. correct
7. It didn't use to snow …
8. correct

2
1. used to play
2. didn't use to drink
3. Did you use to go out
4. didn't use to eat
5. did you use to work
6. used to speak

1
1. hadn't eaten
2. hadn't saved
3. had become
4. Had they visited
5. had (already) seen
6. had left

2
1. knew/had read
2. had started/arrived
3. was/hadn't rained
4. told/hadn't had
5. didn't know/had organised
6. remembered/had given

UNIT 3

1
1. The
2. X
3. The/the
4. The/X
5. X/the
6. The

2
1. X
2. X
3. the
4. X
5. X
6. the
7. the
8. X
9. X
10. X
11. The
12. The
13. X
14. X
15. the

1
1. Do you know how much the camera costs?
2. Do you think you could order me a new mobile phone?
3. Could you tell me where the nearest ATM is?
4. Do you have any idea when it will arrive?
5. Can you tell me whether you accept credit cards?
6. I wonder why she didn't apply for the job?

2
1. when the laptop will be ready
2. what time the bank closed
3. if/whether this tablet is available in black
4. if/whether you sell this model online
5. where I can/could get my car fixed
6. why the shop is closed on Saturdays

UNIT 4

1
1. get/have, delivered
2. getting/having, cut
3. get/have, repaired
4. got/had, installed
5. have/get done
6. have/get, manicured

2
1. get/have
2. him/Jack
3. have
4. have/get
5. get
6. cut

1
1. surprising
2. motivated
3. depressing
4. dissatisfied
5. annoying
6. tiring

2
1. complicated
2. boring
3. exhausted
4. frustrated
5. interested
6. fascinating
7. disappointed
8. exciting

UNIT 5

1
1. she, the following/next day
2. his, there, the day before
3. him, his, that day
4. they, the Saturday before
5. her, the following week
6. they, their, there

2
1. he shopped online every week
2. they would drive her to the supermarket
3. she hadn't seen us the night before at the bar
4. they weren't going on holiday that year
5. she/Sam had been excited about her date that night
6. he could give me some advice about my business.

1
1 'Do you speak any foreign languages?'
2 'Where do you live?'
3 'Could you design a website for my cleaning company?'
4 'Will/Would you write the report?'
5 'What's the main news story today?'
6 'Who went to the meeting?'

2
1 if/whether I was going to get my phone line repaired
2 if/whether Cara planned to look for another job
3 where we would advertise the new service
4 if/whether I had thought about writing a blog
5 why Paul and Sofia had left early the night before
6 what he was doing

UNIT 6

1
| 1 | e | 3 | c | 5 | a |
| 2 | d | 4 | f | 6 | b |

2
1 had waited, might have paid
2 would/might have had, hadn't killed
3 had taken, would have arrived
4 might have got, had made
5 had brought, would have given
6 hadn't rained, might/would have gone

1
1 enjoyed
2 were warmer
3 would wash
4 hope
5 will see
6 lived

2
1 I wish he wouldn't (always) arrive late.
2 I wish I had more time (to spend) with you.
3 If only you knew how to play chess.
4 I hope I/I'll pass my driving test tomorrow.

UNIT 7

1
1	could/ might	4	can't
2	must	5	must
3	can't	6	may/ could

2
1 might/could/may
2 can't
3 must
4 might/could/may
5 must

1
1 correct
2 correct
3 don't they
4 haven't you
5 correct
6 didn't she
7 aren't they
8 haven't you

2
1 can't he
2 do they
3 won't they
4 is it
5 did you
6 aren't you
7 didn't you
8 hasn't she

UNIT 8

1
1	who	4	who
2	which/ that	5	where
3	when	6	which/ that

2
1 where I met my girlfriend
2 who fixes my car
3 a Polish bakery which/that sells black bread
4 who spilt coffee on my new skirt
5 where I lost my car keys

1
1 both correct
2 both correct
3 agreed
4 Finish
5 both correct
6 seems

2
1 going/to go
2 cheating
3 to see
4 asking
5 (to) choose
6 lying

UNIT 9

1
1	f	4	e
2	b	5	d
3	c	6	a

2
1 essential to call
2 common to feel
3 better/important to rest
4 good/important to practise
5 better/good to apologise
6 difficult to wake up

1
1	P	5	P
2	N/F	6	N/F
3	N/F	7	P
4	P	8	N/F

2
2 you hadn't lifted a heavy suitcase (yesterday)
3 I had been/become an actor
4 Frank/he had finished his IT course (at college)
5 I hadn't got a tattoo of 'Anna' on my arm

UNIT 10

1
1	which	4	where
2	which	5	who
3	who	6	which

2
1 The Theatre Royal, which is one of the oldest theatres in London, is on Drury Lane.
The Theatre Royal, which is on Drury Lane, is one of the oldest theatres in London.
2 Mark, who went to the same school as me, directed the film.
Mark, who directed the film, went to the same school as me.
3 The gym, where I used to go after work, has a special membership fee.
The gym, which I used to go to after work, has a special membership fee.
4 The music venue in town, where international artists perform, has been refurbished.
5 The film's visual effects, which were unbelievable, won a special award.
The film's visual effects, which won a special award, were unbelievable.
6 The actress, who played the main part, died last year.

1
1 The song which plays at the end of the film
2 the actor (who) I was telling you about X
3 The company that sold me the car
4 The Australian dancer who got the part
5 the famous landmarks (which) the director used X
6 the woman who promised to invite us to the party

2
1 which/that provides information about the senses is called the cerebral cortex
2 (that/which) I've been watching might be Danish
3 (that/which) I booked for us in Dublin Bay is in a small cottage
4 who/that Thomas spoke to yesterday can give us information about the show
5 who/that designed the scenery for a West End play was in a magazine article last week

UNIT 11

1
1 She should **have** informed the police about the crime immediately.
2 The shouldn't have **cheated** in the exam.
3 I shouldn't **have parked** illegally on the pavement.
4 You **should have paid** for those songs you downloaded illegally.
5 correct

2
1 shouldn't have parked
2 should have reported
3 should have written down
4 should have checked
5 shouldn't have left

1
1 going
2 supposed
3 going
4 going
5 supposed
6 supposed

2
1 was going to
2 weren't supposed to
3 wasn't going to
4 weren't going to
5 was supposed to
6 wasn't supposed to

UNIT 12

1
1	such	5	so
2	so	6	not
3	too		talented
4	too		enough

2
1 The music in this restaurant is so noisy that I can't hear anyone.
2 This job is so stressful.
3 The film we went to see has such an amazing original score.
4 Anna found a part-time job so quickly that she can go on holiday now.
5 Jeremy is too considerate to borrow something without asking.

1
1a We should have looked into the matter.
2b Please fill them in.
4b I didn't pick it up when it rang.
5b Did you call her back?

2
1 get on with
2 copy her in
3 heard of
4 catching up on
5 turn off your phones / turn your phones off

Macmillan Education
4 Crinan Street
London N1 9XW
A division of Macmillan Publishers Limited

Companies and representatives throughout the world

ISBN 978-0-230-45709-6

Text, design and illustration © Macmillan Publishers Limited 2014
Written by Mickey Rogers, Joanne Taylore-Knowles,
Steve Taylore-Knowles

The authors have asserted their rights to be identified as the authors of
this work in accordance with the Copyright, Designs and Patents Act
1988.

This edition published 2014
First edition published 2010

Designed by emc design limited
Illustrated by Peter Cornwell p 52; Sally Elford pp 24, 81, 94, 99; Niall
Harding (Beehive Illustration) pp 22, 37, 106, 107, 108, 109, 113; Paul
Williams (Sylvie Poggio Artists) pp 88, 89, 96, 97, 129, 130.
Cover design by emc design limited
Cover illustration/photograph by Getty Images/Troels Gravgaard, Getty
Images/ Digital Vision (background)

Picture research by Alison Prior
Cover and unit opener picture research by emc design limited

The authors would like to thank the schools, teachers and students
whose input has been invaluable in preparing this new edition. They
would also like to thank the editorial and design teams at Macmillan for
doing such a great job of organising the material and bringing it to life.

The publishers would like to thank the following educators and
institutions who reviewed materials and provided us with invaluable
insight and feedback for the development of the Open Mind series:

Petra Florianová, Gymnázium, Praha 6, Arabská 14; Inés Frigerio,
Universidad Nacional de Río Cuarto; Alison Greenwood, University of
Bologna, Centro Linguistico di Ateneo; Roumyana Yaneva Ivanova,
The American College of Sofia; Táňa Jančaříková, SOŠ Drtinova
Prague; Mari Carmen Lafuente, Escuela Oficial de Idiomas Hospitalet,
Barcelona; Alice Lockyer, Pompeu Fabra University; Javier Roque
Sandro Majul, Windmill School of English; Paul Neale, Susan Carol
Owens and Beverley Anne Sharp, Cambridge Academy of English;
Audrey Renton, Dubai Men's College, Higher Colleges of Technology,
UAE; Martin Stanley, British Council, Bilbao; Luiza Wójtowicz-Waga,
Warsaw Study Centre; Escuela Oficial de Idiomas de Getxo; Cámara
de Comercio de Bilbao; Universidad Autónoma de Bellaterra; Escuela
Oficial de Idiomas EOI de Barcelona; University of Barcelona; Escuela
Oficial de Idiomas Sant Gervasi.

The authors and publishers would like to thank the following for
permission to reproduce their photographs:

Alamy/AfriPics.com p86(cr), Ale Ventura p117(tl), J W Alker p141(tr),
Ammentorp Photography p103, Ammit p43, Art Directors & Trip p28,
Sergio Azenha p104(background), Bill Bachman pp140, 145(zoo
keeper), Rob Ball p23, Big Cheese Photo LLC p60, Blend Images
pp14, 29, David Burton p117(bl), Catchlight Visual Services p47(r),
Alamy Celebrity p119, Ron Chapple Stock p45(br), James Clarke
p50(r), Collection38 p93(br), Roger Cracknell p127, Cultura Creative
pp70, 100/101, Peter Dazeley p139, Dbimages p15, Dbphotos
p145(farmer), DCP Photo p59, Danita Delimont p82(Stephen Hawking),
Design Pictures Inc pp112(background), 142(l), Dex Images p12,
Dorling Kindersley p86(bl), Paul Doyle p47(l), Patrick Eden p10(tr),
Eightfish p147(r), EPA p140(background), Eye Ubiquitous p135(b), Jon
Feingersh p21(tc), Peter Forsberg p44(background), Ewing Galloway
p82(Marie Curie), Darren Greenwood pp32, 35, Gulf Images p121(t),
Christian Guy p116(background), Dennis Hallinan p80(background),
Danielle Hall p21(bc), Hemis pp9(tl), 74, David Hills p63, Van Hilversum
p24, ILoveimages pp71(l), 143, Imagebroker p131, INDASCO p36,
PCN Photography p91, Ingram Publishing p117(tr), Inmagineasia
p117(br), Juice Images p51, Kakimage p117(cl), Stuart Kelly p73(r),
Maksim Krasnov p50(l), David Laurens p21(br), Lemonade p115,
Library of Congress pp80, 82(Einstein), Geoff Love p68(background),
Bob Masters p92(background), Amrtin Mayer p144, Mykola Mazuryk
p9(bl), Alex Minde p45(tl), Mode Images p109(2), Stuart Monk p33(b),
Keith Morris p73(l), John Morrison p26, David Muscroft p117(cr),
OJO Images Lrd p61, Paris Street p32(background), Photolibrary
Wales p87, Pictorial Press Ltd p82(da Vinci&Helen Keller), Purestock
pp18, 145(computer programmer), Harold von Radebrecht p9(cl),
Radius Images p109(4), Kelly Redinger p21(tl), Mervyn Rees p86(br),
Reimar2 p86(bc), Marc Romanelli pp116, 118(t), Andres Rodriguez
p55, Mark Scott p71(br), Alex Segre p79, Ian Shipley p147(c), Studio
Mode p109(1), Stockbroker pp49(t), 71(r), Peter Titmuss p31, Andrew
Twort p56(background), Visum Foto GmbH p148(t), VStock p146, Rob
Wallis p22, Wavebreak Media p10(br), Jim West p49(b), Yay Media
pp27(b), 71(c); **www.cartoonstock.com** p69(all); **Corbis**/Amelie-
Benoist p141(cl), Eric Audras pp8, 16, Gene Blevins p141(b), Guy Cali
p145(lawyer), Darama p111, Giuglio Gil p9(br), Kate Mitchell p93(bl),
Drew Myers p45(tr), Ocean p141(tl), Radius Images p9(cl), Corey Rich
p21(tr), Haen Sel p135(t), Chaiwat Subprasom p141(cr), Dan Tardif
p93(t), Tetra Images p130(br); **Getty Images** pp27(t), 84, 118(b),
120(b), 124(b), AFP pp13, 122, Tatyana Aleksieva Photography p21(tl),
Peter Dench p67, Digital Vision p62, Food Collection p141(c), Adam
Gault pp128, 130, Peter Glass p72, Manuel Gutjahr p8(background),
Bartosz Hadyniak pp92, 97, Hero Images p145(pilot), Justin Horrocks
pp68, 76, Mlenny Photography p9(tr), NoLimitPictures p109(3), Fergus
O'Brien p20(background), Latin Content p120(t), Betsie van der Meer
p17, Tom Merton p151, Carlos Sanchex Pereyra p128(background),
Andrew Rich pp 56,58, Jochen Sands p124(tl), Ariel Skelley p148(b),
Sylvain Sonnet p33(t), Getty Images/Henrik Sorenson p124(tr), Justin
Sullivan p147(l), Stewart Sutton p95, Getty Images/SW Productions
pp104, 106, Visit Britain p53, VM pp44, 48, David Young-Woolff p134;
Joel Levinson p34; **Rex Features** p123, ABC Everett p132, CBS
Everett p125(l), Rex Features/Moviestore Collection p125(r), Startaks
Images p121(b); **Science Photo Library**/Pasieka p85; **Superstock**/
Burger/Phanie pp20, 25, Steve Vidler p45(bl); **Thinkstock** pp57, 141(r),
39, Demid Borodin p110, iStock p11, Dmitry Margolin p112, Stockbyte
p41, Cathy Yeulet.

The authors and publishers are grateful for permission to reprint the
following copyright material:

TwentyTwenty TV for material about 'Brat Camp' and 'Turnaround
Ranch' 2005 reproduced with permission; Material from article 'Boys
now spending almost as much as girls on their prom outfits', first
appeared on website www.mirror.co.uk 19.06.13, reproduced with
permission.

Printed and bound in Thailand

2018 2017 2016 2015
10 9 8 7 6 5 4 3 2